## Praise for *An American Demon*

Jack Grisham finally, irrevocably, puts to death the slander that the early Los Angeles punk scene was "plastic." The first true literature to come out of our pathetic little punk lives, *An American Demon* is haunting and awakens monsters. But it should come with a warning label: it's a dangerous book. Read Patti Smith's *Just Kids*. Then read this. But only if you have the courage to follow poetry as far as it can go.

> — Paul Roessler, producer, composer, musician

What isn't shocking is that Jack wrote a fantastically depraved, heart wrenching, thoroughly engaging book that you'll want to read in one sitting. What is shocking is that it wasn't written from inside a jail cell at a maximum-security prison.

> — Jim Lindberg, former lead singer of
> Pennywise and author of *Punk Rock Dad*

Jack Grisham is a legend to those in the know. Much of the success of punk rock was built on the blood, sweat, and tears of this surf punk, Southern California mad man. After such a compelling read, it's so nice to see him break on through to the other side. . . . Some weren't so lucky.

> — Mark McGrath, vocalist for Sugar Ray
> and TV personality

The book is unnervingly brilliant, compulsive reading for those of us that are glad it's all over.

— Rat Scabies, grail seeker
and former drummer for The Damned

I've interviewed many a first generation punk, and their common denominator is a touch of madness, a brilliant streak of quasi-insanity layered with ample wit. In his memoir, *An American Demon*, Jack Grisham moves to the head of this dysfunctional class with a chilling tale of what lurks in the heart of men. It's sociopathic art in its rawest form, as wickedly relayed through the eyes of a surfer demon. *An American Demon* is a punk rock parable written by a bedlamite, whose immoral compass is cranked up to 11.

— Heidi Siegmund Cuda, author of *Sublime's Brad Nowell: Crazy Fool, Vans Warped, and Got Your Back*

Jack Grisham is the guy my father and mother tried to keep me away from, the guy girls like me ran away from home for. Depending on which day and who you ask, he is both a demon and an angel . . . and everything in between. Instead of making excuses, while keeping the reader on seat's edge, he celebrates life, knowing he has gloriously escaped death, and perhaps a life worse than death, and lived to tell . . . And still, he's clearly enjoyed, mostly, every step of the way . . . *An American Demon* is in-your-face story telling; brutal and beautiful and wildly humorous, this is a different sort of American tale — one that's relentless and with a heart about its ruthlessness.

— Iris Berry, artist, actor, and author of *Two Blocks East of Vine* and *The Underground Guide to Los Angeles*

_An American Demon_

a memoir by **JACK GRISHAM**

ECW Press

Copyright © Jack Grisham, 2011

Published by ECW Press
2120 Queen Street East, Suite 200, Toronto, Ontario, Canada M4E 1E2
416.694.3348 / info@ecwpress.com

LIBRARY AND ARCHIVES CANADA CATALOGUING IN PUBLICATION

Grisham, Jack, 1961–
An American demon / a memoir by Jack Grisham.

ISBN 978-1-55022-956-1
ALSO ISSUED AS:
978-1-55490-950-6 (EPUB); 978-1-55490-956-8 (PDF)

1. Grisham, Jack, 1961–. 2. Punk rock musicians—United
States—Biography. 3. Punk rock music—United States—History
and criticism. 1. Title.

ML420.G8635A3 2011      782.42166092      C2010-906828-9

Editor for the press: Michael Holmes
Cover design: Ingrid Paulson
Cover art: Tim Smith
Text design: Tania Craan
Author photo: Dani Brubaker
Typesetting: Mary Bowness
Production: Troy Cunningham

Lyrics from "Love Song" (Millar/Burns/Vanian/Ward) © 1979 Anglo-Rock, Inc. (USA and Canada) and Rock Music Company Limited (rest of world) used by permission.

To the best of his ability, the author has recreated experiences, places, people, and organizations from his memories of them. In order to protect the privacy of others he has, in some instances, changed the names of certain people and details of events and places.

Printed in Canada

MIX
Paper from
responsible sources
FSC
www.fsc.org      FSC® C103567

To my Kate—
*half my life without you and half my soul within you*

# CONTENTS

My self-esteem—being at times both unbelievably low and rocket ship high—has delivered me into situations heroic and tragic, evil and angelic. I've been called an animal, a demon, a sociopathic nightmare; yet, in the same town, not miles away, I've been called a genius, an angel, a loving child of God.

To tell you the truth, the demon jacket is a better fit. Those fools running around in angels' clothing are constantly being pulled down and dragged through the mud. I was born evil, and I loved it.

The most successful serial killers are always the boys next door—gentle children of summer, flashing smiles like soft breezes through a park, sharpened knives wrapped in grass-stained Levis. I was akin to these monsters. I was camouflaged and deadly, a viper smiling in the dark.

## The Education of the Damned

To be a truly great demon you've got to be attractive—no one sensible gets taken in by a goon. I was born with summer-blond hair, a soft evening smile, and the sweetly dark taste of defiance slashed across my lips—a scrawny, scuffed up teddy bear with a voice that could string words like lights across a carnival midway. Believable, that's what I was: a perfect distraction for the careless mark.

They never saw me coming.

Some of the evil fucks I later ran with were way too ugly to be of any real use. The cops read them like a beacon flashing on a street corner. But not me—the code of the demon, my code, was to fit in, to move from the inside out, to slide into their world, to lodge myself against their love, and then to attack from beneath the skin.

When people refer to demons, they invariably claim we come from the underworld. God, I hate that cliché. It makes us sound like we're all hanging around in a bondage cavern, trying on leather gear and waiting for tricks. And while I do love the smell of leather and I thoroughly enjoy caves, I tortured people for fun, not profit. The concept of a demon coming from underground is pure shit.

If you want to know where demons truly come from, I'll tell you: we're from right here. We exist in a shadow that lies over your world—a kind of transparency of evil that some demented teacher laid out on an overhead projector. We move around you, through you, in you. We are your fathers, your sisters, your lovers. We are your next-door neighbors. We come and go as we please—although it's a bit harder to leave when we've taken residency in a body. The old Hebrews used to call their angels "Those who stand still," and the name they gave themselves was "Those that walk." If a demon was ever called anything, it was usually prefaced with a very terrified "Oh my God!"

### | | |

I think, before we go any further, I should take a moment to clear things up. This is a memoir, not a biography. If you want facts, I suggest you call the local authorities—they're loaded with trivial information on my human form. If you're looking for a discography, or yet another failed rocker's tale, then grab your laptop and pop my name into your search bar—I've left a trail of electronic dust from here to Mars. I'm not going to give you those things or comfort you with what you think is the truth. This story isn't for you—the voyeur feeding on the destruction of a man. This is a story for those that find themselves too far from home, a traveler's tale of monsters and bad ends. It's a story for those that think there's something golden at the end of the road—when there isn't.

### | | |

I stepped onto your world in the Bay Area of San Francisco in 1961, but I didn't stay there long. I was quickly shuttled down to Long Beach—a working-class town chock-full of blue-collared laborers, retired navy men, hustlers, homosexuals, and squares.

My human father was in the military so they'd moved often. He was a junior officer with, at the time, three other children—two boys and a girl. Biologically speaking, I was the sport: a spiritual mutation that crawled out of hell into humanity.

I remember the way my father smelled in his khaki clothes: sweat, grease, and the lingering stale mint of a menthol cigarette clinging to his hands. Often his breath carried the strong smell of alcohol and desperation. My father was a worker, one of those cats with that crazy "do anything you can to feed your family" ethic—something, to this day, I still can't understand. If I was in his shoes, struggling like he did to pay our bills, you want to know what I would've done? I would've split; I would have headed off to Mexico and left us to fend for ourselves. You know, fuck 'em if they can't take a joke.

I later found out that my father's dad had run out on him and his siblings. Maybe that's what influenced his sense of family duty and honor, but if that's the case, my father took care of us out of resentment, not out of love. It was more like a "fuck you" to his old man, than a "love you" to us. No wonder he was always stressed out.

My mother—bless her shaming heart—was another product of a failed marriage.

One day I checked the statistics on divorce in the 1930s, and I discovered that people were fifteen times more likely to kill themselves than they were to walk out of a fucked-up marriage. What does that say for my parents? Their moms and dads must have been beating the living fuck out of each other if divorce was a better option than death.

"You want to kill yourself, sweetheart?"

"No thank you, dear. I think I'll just knock your fucking teeth out with a frying pan, and then I'll get a divorce."

My mom didn't work, or, at least, she didn't have a paying job. She was a stay-at-home wife; in other words, she was our domestic servant. Her chores were cooking, cleaning, and keeping the children out of the liquor cabinet. My mother was a great candidate for Librium, the first real "Benzo," although she chose to stay drug-free at the time. I think she actually enjoyed being a little whacked out on stress and confusion; to be a "pro" at emotional abuse, you've got to have a background in depression, and she took great pride in her work. If you're going to deliver lines like "I should have killed you when I had the chance," you've got to believe it.

I started fucking with my parents at an early age. You humans are so easy to manipulate; a little taste of someone else's will and you get all bent out of shape. My father and mother started asking me to do things, or not do things, as the case might be, and I disagreed.

"Clean your room."

"No."

"I *said* clean your room."

"No."

"You're going to get hit."

"No."

Both of my parents favored the belt or the Hot Wheels track—to them, modern folks that they were, new age plastic seemed to be the most effective tool when delivering corporal punishment. I'd roll on the floor trying to make my little hands into a thousand ass-protecting gloves as they attempted to beat the will from me. I didn't mind, really. I kind of liked the way that hard-plastic track left two bloody red welts running parallel down my legs. It was the mark of a good thrashing, a badge of honor, tied-to-the-mast pirate business: "Fifty lashes for insubordination and willful disobedience!"

I loved it.

I used to laugh at their vain attempts to discipline me. Oh, don't get me wrong, I'd play their game—begging for forgiveness, swearing that I'd never hurt the dog again or start another fire in the living room—but the minute they walked away, and the bedroom door would shut, I'd stand in my pride, dust the groveling shame from my body . . . and then, it was forgotten. My parents were flies on the windowsill of my world.

I had a marvelous set of green plastic army men that I loved controlling. I especially liked this game after I'd just been pummeled by my parents. I'd set up waves of attackers, infantrymen stretching off into the distance under my dresser. I'd order them to kill: "Take no prisoners, leave no village unburned. If you see an adult, destroy it—and bring me the head." I wasn't angry when I played this game. I was cold, emotionless, and unlike them, I was fair.

One thing my breeders never understood was that they were beating a mannequin, a wooden boy clopping along at their heels, pulled deep inside, disconnected from the pain. I was a spectator of the body they thought was me. They couldn't lay a hand on who I really was. I *wanted* to help them, to yell out during the thrashing, "Go for the soul! Go for the soul!" but I *let* them fail. They wouldn't have understood anyway—physical pain is a joke compared to the damage you can do to a heart.

I remember the first time I gave my old man a taste of what I really was. It was subtle, not over the top (as far as a demon's concerned), just a bit of dark psychological terror on a Tuesday afternoon.

My father came home from work. By this time he'd left the service and had taken a job in the private sector. I think it had something to do with shipping, or the packing of crates. I didn't care, as long as I was getting fed. My parents had recently added another girl to their litter, so whatever my father did to supply my needs was fine—as long as they were getting supplied.

Daddy pulled up in his late model white Lincoln—a man on the go. I was playing in the yard with a cardboard box that I'd lit on fire. I was watching the smoke snake its way delicately into the sky when my father saw me. He jumped from his Lincoln, stomped furiously across the yard, and then he kicked the burning box. It exploded in flames—and our small gray poodle escaped from inside.

My father was horrified—and then he broke.

I just sat there and stared at him—the kind of stare that only the damned can stare, deep black eyes filled with the emptiness of space.

I've never, to this day, seen a man look so defeated. All that my father had put into me—every beating, talking to, and punishment—was lying in a blackened pile on that lawn, and the breeze was scattering it uselessly across the grass. He couldn't say anything.

He just turned his back and walked, head down, solemnly, beaten, into the house.

Oh the joy that flashed through my mind. I wanted to pound my chest, run into the street, and proclaim my win to the gods: "I didn't lay a hand on you, fucker—I did it with a glance, with a flame. I hurt you worse than you could ever hurt me, and I never even touched you. I own this hell that you call home. I own you."

I almost felt bad.

I might have been small, but I soared over their lives—a vicious raptor feathered in Snoopy pajamas and wrapped in a blanket.

### III

On some afternoons, or early in the day if need be, I was dropped off at my grandparents' house. I wasn't quite old enough for school; I was four, maybe five, at the time. I'm not quite sure why I was exiled to the west end of Long Beach seeing as I wasn't always privy to my parents' plans, but that's where they sent me. I preferred where we lived, on the east side, in a semi-nice suburban area by the park.

My grandmother was okay, as humans go, but her second husband, Gramps, was a hard-charging navy man who reeked of Old Spice and scotch. He yelled at me constantly for puttering around in his squared-away bullshit: a garage that looked like Captain Anal had placed each and every tool in direct proximity to the great pyramid, and a garden shack that actually had a shovel wrapped in a fucking raincoat. It was a real drag being there. I had two options: one, to sit on the swing in the backyard and practice wishing people dead—in this case, my gramps—or two, stretch my legs, survey the neighborhood, and enjoy the sunshine. One day, I choose the latter.

Granny was in the kitchen waiting for the evening news. I smiled at her and toddled into the living room. As she slipped on her Playtex dishwashing gloves, I slipped out the front door. I was off. . . .

## AN AMERICAN DEMON

My mother's parents lived in a neighborhood that, to their dismay, was a starting-to-go-black piece of the American dream. I thought it was wonderful. Not the neighborhood, mind you, their dismay. There's nothing like a little negative racial encroachment to get the old folks jitterbugging—kind of funny, considering you were all targets to me. I walked past the "colored" park and the liquor store. I waved as I strolled—the street corner boys giving slight head nods and raised eyebrows to the small white prince leading a one-man parade through the jungle. I took my time, occasionally stopping to visit with my subjects. I loved the way they held those half-wrapped presents of Thunderbird wine loosely in their hands. The soft brown edges of the paper bags barely concealed the cheap logo of the bird—it was 17.5 percent hide-and-seek by volume. And then, as so often happens to a child, I got bored, and in that boredom came a thought: "I wonder what's going on at home; I think I'll go check it out."

We visited my grandparents' place fairly often, and it was a long drive—I'd say maybe eight or ten miles from the 1950s tract home I lived in. I figured I knew the way back. My parents usually fought in the car, or anywhere else, so as a diversion to their bickering, I'd play dead and study the landscape as it went by.

I turned east and headed towards the oil fields on Signal Hill.

The way home sure looked closer in the car, but I didn't care. The journey gave me a chance to study my territory, to stake my claim, if you will. I wanted to walk home, and it never occurred to me that the humans would think I was too young to be unattended.

I walked for hours.

When my grandmother finally caught up to me, I was in the middle of a no man's land of oil derricks and toxic waste. I was on top of a mountain of pride, staring at the kingdoms of the world. She was ghost-white with worry. She held open the car door and I stepped inside; to me, a limousine driven by a peroxide-blond skeleton. I leaned back against the seat. If she'd offered me a cigar and a *Wall Street Journal* I would have respectfully declined and closed my eyes, but Granny had other plans. I thought we'd just continue home, but she whisked me back to the land of Walter Cronkite and Cutty Sark. Her eyes were rimmed with tears, her hands shaking on the wheel.

It was exciting to see the effect my actions had on others. It gave me a tingling in the lower reaches of my stomach when an adult lost his or her cool. And what a wonderful feeling of accomplishment I got when I made those larger than me twist and sway like pathetic little puppets on a string. But this was only a beginning—a fledgling's first tries at enforcing his will.

Goethe said, "A man sees in the world what he carries in his heart." The same holds true for demons. If you look for evil, you will find it.

### III

It wasn't hard to see the disease in you humans. Your pain was like stars in a dark winter sky, and I flittered like a black moth from hurt to hurt. A divorce here, a loss there—two streets over a child died of cancer, and every night on our black and white TV, the dark whispers of the Vietnam war played backdrop music to our dining pleasure.

One day, a real life military Jeep pulled up in front of our next-door neighbor's house. I was thrilled to see my toy soldiers come to life—giants in their pressed, muted green uniforms—as dignified, strong, and handsome. I watched them walk purposefully inside. Then I heard the scream, a mother's terrified cry, followed by a distressed series of low sobbing moans. Our neighbor's only son had been killed—he was a door gunner in a helicopter, taken out by a single shot from a villager's rifle.

### III

I started to feel a pull from down the street. I hadn't heard of anything bad happening there, but the attraction got stronger and stronger. I soon realized that it came from an old couple that lived a few doors up from us—Mr. and Mrs. Krieger.

They were old and gray, small and without sharp form—wrinkled clouds hiding in a light blue house. You rarely saw them outside, unless they were walking to the market; the woman, always pushing a small metal cart, and the man drifting along close behind her.

Some days, I'd sit on my porch and follow them with my eyes as they walked by.

I knocked on their door one afternoon. My small clenched fist demanded entry. I was invited in and they held their lives up for inspection.

They'd been expecting my arrival.

The living room was dark, but not unpleasant—trinkets of their lives sat on dusty shelves and reminded them of times that would not return. I politely gestured to the small kitchen table, and then I sat, my legs a few inches from touching the floor.

Mrs. Krieger offered me a piece of old folk's candy, and as I sucked on the stale peppermint round, Mr. Krieger took off his sweater and sat down. He gave me a sadly tired look, and after meeting his eyes I forced him to follow my gaze to his forearm.

He held his hand over his sleeve and shamefully covered the nakedness of the wound I knew he carried.

Silently, I bade him to roll his shirt back.

Underneath the cloth, in a faded dark ink, were a series of numbers.

"You know what this is?" he asked me.

Although posed as a question, it was more an acknowledgement of what I felt.

"I know it hurts," I told him, "and I know it's what keeps you inside—hiding."

He bowed his head slightly and then he talked about loss.

There were words and places he mentioned that were hard for me to grasp—Kraków, Auschwitz, Birkenau—but it was easy to follow his story. The hurt in his voice was like brail to a blind man.

He and his wife were Jews—Polish Jews that had been relocated and stripped of all they had.

I listened patiently as he talked, but there were times that I had to prod him with a question to keep the stories flowing. I was picking his wound, so to speak, so the rich red blood of his despair would roll out into the kitchen and cover my eager mind with his experience. He spared me no detail—each turn, hit, and terror was slowly exhaled from his lungs in a weary old-world voice. I inhaled everything he had—draining him of the pain.

I'm not sure how long he talked, but he was spent and slumped over the table when he finished. If I hadn't known better, I would have thought him dead, but I could see the hour of his passing in my mind. (It was close, but not yet.)

And then it was time for me to go. If I didn't return home soon, my father would be warming the Hot Wheels track on my ass— tattooing his own brand of identification onto me.

I thanked the Kriegers for the candy and walked away. I never went back. They died shortly thereafter—first him, and then her. For years they had held on to the pain of their existence, the damage done to their minds fading slower than their tattoos ever could.

Sometimes you humans are so easily manipulated. You make a demon's work easy. Picture a domino set of flesh, lives lying so close to each other that they can't help but touch—the dots on their skin, sixes and threes, each number representing a different class or race. Now, if you put your hand on just the right one, warm his ear with mistrust and hate, and then just give a slight,

    small

        push . . .

The force of your weakness is astounding. One million, two million, six million dead: the flesh falls until the energy of that first shove fails, and then the survivors wonder how the fuck it could have happened.

A great demon uses his mouth; his words the palette of a rainbow, his tongue an avatar of fear that can only be satisfied with blood.

## III

The tale Mr. Krieger told was horrific, as you might say, and I appreciated it for the scope of his pain, but I didn't always need such grand destruction to satisfy me. Sometimes lighter fare could be just as fulfilling to my young mind. Krieger's rich Bordeaux was the perfect compliment to a late afternoon meal, but now that evening was upon me, I felt like something a bit less filling. I knew just the drink, or the drunk, as it were, to quench my thirst.

My father's great uncle was an alcoholic, in the true Dean Martin sense of the word. Marty was good looking, in perfect shape, and at seventy-two could drop down and give you fifty one-handed push-ups. The only time you'd ever see Marty sober, though, was when he first woke.

Uncle M would descend upon us late at night, unexpected and, as always, hammered. He'd sit at our kitchen table and dribble out stories in that meandering drunken way; he loved telling me what a weak little fuck I was.

"If I didn't love your dad so much," he'd burble, "I'd take you outside and kick your fucking ass . . ."

Burble, burble, burble.

I doubt he could have done it, but you never know about drunken-old-man strength; sometimes they can surprise you.

It was easy to study him. His crossed drunken eyes roamed wildly around the room as he talked. He was completely unaware that I was listening, learning; carried on the thick stench of his malted breath were the key words, and I was waiting for them to fall. You see, the trick to understanding drunks is this: a drunk will throw out line after line of completely useless verbiage, and then he'll let something slip, a word, an emotionally charged button that begs to be pushed, but you have to be paying attention. In my uncle's case, that word was "Anne," the ex-wife that he'd always loved, but who'd left him for another man: his best friend, Terry.

His burble went something like this: "God damn those fucking assholes coming up here stealing our jobs . . . got the fucking kids pulling shit not knowing what the fuck . . . Anne . . . oh God, Anne, how can I live without her?"

"What'd you say, Uncle? Did you say 'Anne'?" I jumped on it— my small finger getting blister-tipped from pounding on that button.

He stared at me in shock, a man silenced by the lisp of an eight-year-old boy.

"Wasn't Anne your wife? Where's she now? Why didn't she come?"

Bingo. He might have been seventy-two and a master of the one-handed push-up, but I had his ass. I had that drunken mother-fucker pushed against his lonely old rope, and he was ready to hang.

"Did she like it when you drank, Uncle? When you were gone all the time?"

I didn't let up. His eyes supplied the dialogue now, and all I had to do was read the words as they appeared.

"What about your friend Terry? Do you ever see him?"

Uncle M grabbed his things and left. He drove off with a cold tallboy tucked between his legs, and the picture of his wife, fucking another man, tattooed on his soul.

Poor Uncle M—he died all alone. He was propped in front of his TV, a bottle of scotch in his hand, and a solid week of decay on his body, before they found him.

Some children learned how to bake, and others learned how to draw. I learned how to sew—how to pull a memory of pain from the subconscious of a mind, and then stitch it permanently in the present.

111

I had to be careful not to stretch my wings too wide. Quirky was okay, noticeably evil was not. Even so, at the request of my grade school principal, I got invited to attend therapy—a blind date with the counselor of her choice. You've gotta love those school psychologists—probably the most closed-minded pricks you'll ever run into. For someone that studies the mind and its associated behaviors, you'd think they'd be a little more in tune with the absurd and the abnormal, but they never were.

We'd discuss feelings as we played checkers. I tried to let nothing slip—played dumb when it came to matters involving mom and dad.

"Your mother tells me you're having trouble making it to the toilet on time."

"Oh. Did she also tell you she was having an affair?" *Shit. Nice work, Jack. You need to shut your mouth.*

An awkward pause, and then a very concerned face looked up from the checkerboard and directly into my eyes.

"What makes you say that?" the therapist calmly asked.

"I saw it on TV."

"Seeing things on TV" usually worked for this crowd. It was the perfect escape in a sticky situation. My mother might get a slight warning after the session about what I should or should not be watching on my evening programs, but I should be cool.

"Oh," she said.

As suspected, the therapist bought it, and we continued with the game.

It was a mistake mentioning that affair. Not like it was going to hurt me or anything, but I just should have stayed cool. That outburst was a direct result of that "shitty" question, and I needed to get a handle on my emotions—the warrior with the coolest head wins the game. Besides, it wasn't like my mother was a tramp.

My father, as I told you earlier, had gone civilian; however, his work demanded certain travel days from him. It was on these days that my mother was left unattended. It's funny that when one mentions the word "affair," your sick human thoughts travel to steamy, shacked-up-in-hotel trysts. The word itself implies many meanings: public and private, physical and emotional. Fucking someone is a joke, a walk through a sweaty park that gets washed off with a bit of soap and a hot towel. But to give your heart to someone . . . that's another matter entirely; because whether they ever lay a hand on you or not, you've given them ownership of your soul, and it can't be washed off.

Sometimes I'd pick up the other line when my father called—holding my finger on the hook and letting it lift real slow. I was careful to make sure they never heard the click, an announcement of an eavesdropper. I loved the false sense of privacy they got from the phone—my mother and father speaking freely, thinking the children couldn't hear. There were calls that said "I miss you" and "I'll be home soon," but there were others. These were the calls that I waited for, the ones that were threatening and torn from distrust.

"Have you been talking to him?" my father asked.

"No, of course not" was my mother's sadly pathetic reply.

She was lying. I'd picked up a call earlier where the booze-soaked voice of a Johnny Cash–loving motherfucker had just told her how much he missed her, and how much he *also* loved her.

This was funny. I loved her little lying game and my father's mistrust. Kind of like pin the tail on the donkey—my father being the blind pinner and my mother being the object getting poked. You know, it really puts things into perspective when you know what liars your handlers are. The lines "I love you" and "I'd never hurt you," when delivered to a child, take on a wonderfully sarcastic tone when coming from the same mouth that deceitfully told your father, "You know I'm faithful, baby."

Now for the shitting, or the non-shitting, if you will.

I didn't struggle with hitting the toilet on time, because I enjoyed fouling myself, and it was planned. You see, when you're small, you're at the mercy of those around you. Shitting my pants was a defense mechanism—sort of a broken child's way of saying leave me alone.

A human cub is quite possibly the weakest of all newborn animals. They have no protection other than that from those who bred them.

"What about social services? What about the police?" you might say.

Yeah, and a child's hand, two inches wide, is gonna pick up a hard plastic phone, ten inches long, and talk baby gibberish to an overweight alcoholic cop who wants no part of a domestic squabble and an ass-kicked newborn?

Get in the real world.

The minute that baby is taken from the hospital, the parents can do whatever the fuck they want with it, including tossing its little ass down a sewer drain if they see fit. My handlers weren't quite that cruel, but they did get a little loose in their dealings with me—a little heavy on the discipline, if you will. And maybe, just maybe, they weren't always too concerned about who was "playing" with the baby. The only way I had to fight back was to shit myself. And believe me, there is practically nothing more disturbing than a human animal that doesn't have the sense to stay out of its own filth.

I'd run up to Grandma for a hug and she'd wrap her arms around a walking bowel movement in a striped JCPenney tank top. Her olfactory senses might have been on the way out, but the load I was carrying in my britches brought her old sniffer right back to teenage capacity. I was five, six, seven, eight years old, and I'm still running up to granny with a pile of shit in my pants.

And shitting myself did have a few other benefits. Besides the creamy warm feeling one gets from a freshly dropped turd in your undies, and the ultimate in up-close pull-it-in-tight disgust factor, when I shat myself, my parents caught the blame. How's that for an underhanded blow?

"Have you been beating on this boy?" says the counselor. "No?

Then why is he still defecating in his pants? Did you know that that's one of the signs of physical or sexual abuse?"

If I could have raped my own ass and laid it on 'em, I would have, just to watch 'em squirm.

A doctor once asked my mother why I hadn't gotten medical attention for a rather large wound on my knee. The doctor was concerned that there might be neglect or physical abuse going on in the home.

I'd been cross-dressing on Halloween. My bag was bulging at the sides with candy, but I wanted more—I needed more. Halloween's just once a year and you're a fool if you don't come home with a full load. I was running across a lawn—it was quicker than taking the sidewalk—and I tripped. I went down hard and caught the jagged metal head of a sprinkler across my knee. It tore my neon green nylons, and I came up gushing blood all over my sack of treats—blood filling my stockings and running down to my heels. I was sidelined for the duration.

A few days later, I watched the doctor's face as my mother answered his uncomfortable question.

"I-I-I didn't realize it was that deep," she pleaded, as the smiling face of my scalped kneecap peered out at her. "It didn't look like it needed stitches."

Oh fuck, I loved watching her panic knowing that I could confirm or deny said abuse with two large, sad eyes and a tousled hair nod.

*I think, this time, I'll deny.*

After a good frightening, parents are usually quick with a cookie and a reprieve on the beatings, so I went for the iced-raisin and a nap. Besides, I'd spent years breaking in these two and I was a bit too lazy to start beating on another family unit.

All kidding aside, this abuse thing was an issue I had to be very careful about. I was a being not necessarily meant for this world, and problems of adjustment were naturally going to take place. It just so happened that a young demon's unstable developmental issues mimicked those of a child who'd been molested or physically and emotionally abused. I didn't want to be pulled away from this family, but it was awfully hard to hide.

The authorities don't go out of their way to find victims of child abuse, but they are casually on the lookout for them. Most semi-responsible health care providers are armed with a laundry list of telltale signs to help them spot the abused. Let me run a few down for you . . .

> 1. Changes in the child's sleeping patterns
> —nightmares or bad dreams.

First off, I've never slept "soundly." I didn't need the amount of rest you humans needed, so I'd stay up well into the night planning the next day's adventures; there was always important business to be tended to—animals to be captured, gasoline to be procured, and I could not leave those things to chance. And as for nightmares and bad dreams, I was a demon for fuck's sake. My whole existence was a nightmare, whether I was in bed or not. I attracted, by my very nature, the very worst.

At night I'd wander through the house—sleepwalking, reliving other lives, remembering other kills. Sometimes I'd wake to find myself standing atop my bed, pounding on an old wooden ceiling that'd now become the collapsed roof of a crypt—one whose white marble walls were mortared with the screams of those I'd destroyed.

I was surrounded with the moving portraits of the dead and, when awake, the dreams of night followed me wherever I went. Stranger's faces became the faces of pigs and rats—assemblies of the bizarre bleating out alien orders and issuing decrees of insanity. A demon is constantly on the edge of what a psychiatrist might call madness, and all this has nothing to do with abuse or conscience, just as a tornado has nothing to do with hate. It was my nature to be tortured and my upbringing was irrelevant.

And as if the night terrors were not enough to hide, there was one other, perhaps an even more telling, indication of trouble. As a spiritual being, I had the ability to see the hour and the manner of your death. Try to imagine, if you will, what it's like to stand before a counselor or a teacher and watch, in future time-lapse photography, the body disintegrate before you: car wrecks, heart attacks, suicides, and sometimes that living corpse in front of me just took a long . . . slow . . . walk . . . out to the abattoir of old age. I saw them all die, and it took all I had to be still, to be quiet, and to face them without a knowing smile on my face.

Come to think of it, I might have enjoyed that conversation.

"Excuse me? Mr. Jones?"

"Yes, Jack."

"Did you know that you're going to be split in half by a Land Rover?"

"What are you talking about, son?"

"I'm talking about how you're going to die. You're going to be involved in a minor fender-bender, but when you get out of the car to survey the damage, an eighteen-year-old girl is gonna plow into you, and shish kabob your ass with her bumper—probably not a good idea to be texting while driving, huh?"

If I was talking about him winning the lottery—a twenty-four-million-to-one long shot, he'd have no problem with it. It's perfectly acceptable to dream that dream. But if I talked about his death—a one hundred percent certainty of life—his little panties would have gotten all blown out of shape. Its panic sign number two on the hit parade . . .

2. Suicidal gestures, death obsession,
self-destructive behavior, self-mutilation . . .

Okay, so I liked playing dead. Who didn't? I saw other children lying on their backs in the park, their tombstone bodies angled towards the sun, watching clouds, seeing pictures of teetotaling clowns dancing lazily in a forgiving sky. I just chose to play my games inside instead: lying idly on my back, with my eyes closed, a bottle of prescription pills spilled out next to my unclenched hand, envisioning my parents' shocked reaction as they stumbled over the body of a cold, gray child decomposing on their cheap linoleum floor. It wasn't a suicidal gesture when I painted them a picture of despair. I was just testing, giving them a taste of what was sure to come—a helpful omen, if you will.

And self-mutilation, destruction? I *had* to cut myself. It didn't mean I wanted to cash it in, it just meant I needed alterations. This might have been my thousandth time around in human form, but your skin is a motherfucker to get right. When a demon steps into a man it's like trying on a new dress or pants. Sometimes you've got to pull parts in or nip parts off before you get comfortable—it can take years to "settle in," and sometimes, we never get it right. You can always spot demons by the way they treat their bodies. I ran mine into the ground every chance I got: head first through a plate-glass window, leg caught burning beneath an unattended water heater, finger slashed to the bone with a careless hatchet stroke. I loved the wounds—the blood rolling over the skin and slowly waterfalling its way onto the ground, forming silent, dark rose petals of pain that broke up the colors of the dirt.

I *was*, technically, exhibiting practically every behavior on that laundry list of symptoms. And you could throw in depression, anger, low self-esteem, guilt, and withdrawal—but I could explain every one of them if they only gave me a chance. (And if my explanation wouldn't have earned me a bed in the local asylum.)

I wasn't depressed; I was just frustrated that my small stature didn't allow me to stomp the living fuck out of some of these loud-mouthed adults. I wasn't angry—my pulse rarely went above sixty—even when I was setting fire to the neighbor's garage. Low self-esteem? Never. I kept my eyes to the ground so you wouldn't be frightened by the flame. Guilt? Please. Guilty of what, being a successful monster? Pride, maybe; guilt, never. And withdrawal: I couldn't let you too close, because if you found out what I really was you'd burn me at the stake. It wasn't withdrawal; it was preservation of the species.

Come to think of it, I was pretty lucky growing up in the surroundings I did. I mean, what if I'd stepped into a present day *Leave It to Beaver*?

For you kids, *Leave It to Beaver* was probably the biggest piece of fifties science fiction ever created for television: a father that didn't beat the kids or cheat on his wife—he also didn't drink or walk around saying he'd like to ram his car into the cocksucker that lived down the street. There was also a mother who was pretty, well-dressed, emotionally stable, and always quick with a kind word or a "better luck next time boys"; and two sweetly mischievous sons whose worst crime was knocking down old Mrs. Brown's laundry line.

Christ, I could just imagine "me" being dropped into the midst of that shit. I would have stood out like a Hitler impersonator at a Survivors of Auschwitz picnic. Even kind old Mr. Krieger would have been screaming "demon" and running for rope.

It was a blessing—for want of an eviler word—that I was thrown in with a cast of neurotic, alcoholic child-beaters. Yeah, I was tucking in my tail and hiding my horns, so to speak. I had to, but it could have been much, much worse. It was actually a benefit to be bred in that briar patch—I was a very sharp thorn hidden within a patch of dull ones.

## I I I

So far, I've given you a taste of the family influence in my life—not as if they could influence my nature, but as the color of a rock influences the colors of a chameleon, I picked up what I could. A touch of alcoholism here, a dash of neurosis there. . . . "Hey, why don't we sprinkle a bit of sadism on top, and a drizzle of self-loathing along the edges?"

Oh my, I was a sundae of defect—a confection of the sweetest maladies humankind had to offer, the best that you had, and when I was older, these maladies would be the perfect cover for my behavior.

### III

I was struggling a bit. Does that sound funny, almost redundant, after what I've just laid down? Well, it's not what you think. It was no struggle getting beaten on, lied to, and dare I say . . . sodomized. I was struggling with what outfit to wear while they were doing it.

The human sexuality thing has always had me a bit perplexed. To a demon, a body is just a body, and I've been in so many hosts that it's hard to remember them all. Oh, there's been the odd stand out that comes to mind, like the time I inhabited a Portuguese transvestite with a wooden eye and a penchant for getting urinated on while she prayed, or that midget nursery school teacher from Perth—he chopped his mother into bite-size chunks and then finger-painted a mural of the Resurrection using her blood as a medium and her face as the face of Christ. These were both very exciting, very memorable experiences, but every time I jumped in a new body I was forced to deal with a hanging appendage or a fascinating slit between my legs.

I'd look around me, trying to figure out which body went with what outfit, but it was never easy. You humans are so hung up on the paint job, and yet you have a hard time following your own designations. I had a cock, so why couldn't I wear nylons and a skirt? I loved the way my legs looked in a pair of fishnets—little diamonds of tanned flesh popping out through the holes—and the skirt: skirts were wonderfully economic when it came to peeing, or playing with my business.

During my younger sister's third birthday party, I was caught hiding in a closet wearing lipstick and a skirt. I was just trying things on, getting familiar with my surroundings, but oh, if my parents didn't throw a fit—especially my ex-navy father who thought men should definitely not be wearing Cover Girl lip cream and miniskirts. Kinda funny actually, if he knew what was really under that ensemble, he wouldn't have been so worried about the lipstick.

Sometimes I think I fucked up when I stepped into this frame, but I know the reason this body was chosen—big powerful men lend a feeling of comfort and safety to those around them and even if you will, a threat and an element of fear or intimidation. Men are more readily accepted as the prime movers in this society, and if I was going to climb far enough to be a real power for destruction, the body I chose was perfect, but in my heart, wanting to fill the bill of terror that was my nature, I knew that women were the real danger. Shit, I sat courtside two thousand years ago when that bitch Salome asked for John's head. You should have seen her move. I knew demons who weren't that persuasive. Her hips were soft cries for comfort that begged to be touched, and the scent of her that filled that room brought not desire but jealousy upon everyone that beheld her—you were jealous of the men around you, jealous of their eyes roaming over what you knew was yours. You were willing to kill for her. Herod was a fool; he took the wrong head that day. John was harmless. Salome was pure evil.

### III

It was the summer of the unloved, and I was drawing psychedelic posters and selling them to my great-grandmother; a nickel a pop— ten cents for the larger ones. I was learning how to profit from a human's weakness for "cute."

My mother was watching me draw, and I thought I might be able to swing a quarter from her purse, so I drew the word love. I surrounded it with flowers and handed it to her.

She studied it for a moment, and then she smugly said, "Why would *you* draw that? *You* don't know *anything* about love."

I was stunned. Who'd she been talking to? I was just about to jam a crayon into her ocular cavity, when I realized she hadn't been talking to anyone, she was just making a commentary on my teachings to this point. She hadn't fingered me as a demon; she was just taking pride in her work, congratulating herself on a job well done. And she *was* right; I didn't know a thing about love.

A demon has no *natural* ability to understand a concept as ridiculous as "love"—the closest we probably come to it is pride or enjoyment, both of these being conditional mindsets. I, as a child, was being beaten and shamed on a daily basis. And with all the constant fighting and accusations of unfaithfulness flying between my mother and dad, I'd never been shown what it was like to care for someone unconditionally. Maybe my mother *was* showing me love when she held me down in a bathtub—ignoring my screams of pain—and then forced the cold rubber hose of an enema up my ass. That was pretty loving. I mean, I'm pretty sure she greased the nozzle tip before she pushed it in—and then stomped on the bag.

Of course I knew nothing of love; she was just a fool whose statement had fallen closer to the truth than she realized.

I got what I needed from them, and love wasn't it. I needed a cave to develop in. That was supplied. I needed food, I needed clothes, and I needed a place to come from. Other than that, I didn't give a fuck about their love. My education was practically over the first time I tasted blood from the back of my legs—when I reached my hand behind my back and got a hard-on from the open edges of the welts on my ass, and when I heard my father call my mother a whore and accuse her of sleeping with her brother.

On my tenth birthday the nightly flashing screams of terror tore through the broken windows of our house and proclaimed my graduation to the neighbors. I was ready to take my act on the road—into the schools and the playgrounds.

I was ready to share the love.

The walls of the sewer were cold, damp, and hard, although the moisture lent a gray-velvet softness to the cement. I was reminded of "The Cask of Amontillado" as I slid between the safety bars—a barrier meant to keep adults out, but thankfully, thoughtlessly, let small children in.

*Maybe they'll seal the entrance with us down here.*

I was exploring with a few children from the neighborhood. They were nobodies, really: James, an older boy from down the street; Billy and Stuart, James's cousins; and Terry from school. They were pick-up friends, the kind you might hang with when no one else was about. *God, it'd be great to watch them go mad as they starved to death—maybe we'd eat each other, killing the smallest first, and then working our way up. Come to think of it, I should probably knock out James with my flashlight. He's bigger than me, and I don't think I can take him in a fair fight.* Of course, I wouldn't take anyone in a "fair fight." Why risk being beaten? I struck where I saw weakness, and I ran, or feigned obedience, where there was strength.

We followed the course of the sewer as it made its way under the highway and towards the shopping center. The pipe was large enough to stand in, maybe four or five feet high, with a small mossy green stream of dirty water running down the center. The beam from my flashlight lit the passageway before us with brown flaccid light—my fucking father forgot to put new batteries in it when I asked him. There was a large pile of something in the tunnel ahead. I actually caught the smell before I saw the mound. Something was dead. As we came closer to the pile I saw movement—rats, large sewer rats feasting on the carcass of a dead dog. I called out, "Here, puppy! Come here, boy. Good dog."

My companions didn't think I was funny, but I loved it. It was kind of like a "free cat" sign on a piece of road kill.

I took the walking spear that I'd brought from outside, and I jammed it into the bloated stomach of the dog—I was a Roman soldier piercing the body of Christ.

"You're fucking nuts, man," mumbled James the lesser. "That thing is gross, let's get the fuck out of here."

I loved the sewers.

### III

There were kids in my neighborhood who were told not to walk by my house. And they were also told not to eat *anything* I offered. It wasn't completely fair, as far as I was concerned; there might have been an incident or two of younger children getting a dog turd sucker stuffed in their mouths, or a paint thinner milk shake as an after school treat, but I liked my sport a bit more . . . well, exciting . . . as with the torturing of young Jim.

Jim was a small boy, a gentle child from another state, who moved in 'round the block from me. He was blond-haired and anxious, champing at the bit to find a California playmate. And one day he wandered into my yard.

I was sitting on the porch with a slingshot. Earlier, I'd been using it to intimidate the neighbor's dog—a Rottweiler whose teeth looked like they'd love a taste of my ass.

"Whatcha got?" he asked. It was kinda hickish—a "Hey, I'm a victim" question, demanding an action rather than an answer. I wanted to show him, you know, fire a BB into his eye and then say, "Slingshot."

I refrained from shooting my wad prematurely, and instead I held the weapon out for his perusal. The moment he touched it, I knew I had him. You can't hold another man's piece in your hand without setting off some sort of primitive bond.

I slowly reeled him in, gained his confidence, and then shared a bit of my world with him. I showed him 'round the neighborhood.

"Here's where you can steal oranges," I told him, "and over here, underneath this tree, is a great place to hide and throw 'em at cars."

I could tell he was a bit frightened at the prospect of guerrilla warfare, but being younger and new, he wanted to impress. I took it easy on him, sort of like a first date, only letting my hand slide around his psyche part of the way—I wanted him to come back.

I courted him for three weeks before I decided it was time for him to put out.

I used to dig holes in the backyard of my parents' house; they were military-style bunkers that I covered with plywood and dirt. I could lay in them on hot summer days—a piece of old carpet on the floor, a few candles, and a stolen *Playboy* for interior decoration. These bunkers were four-star protection from the outside world—and a quiet place to plan.

I was lying up easy one day, enjoying the cool with my pants undone, creeping on Miss November, when . . .

"Jack!"

Jim was yelling over the fence.

"Hey Jack, you in there?"

At first I was a bit upset over the loss of my "quiet" time, but then I realized that this was just what I wanted. Miss November might have been intriguingly sexy, but Jim was about to get fucked.

I climbed out of the hole—tucking an evil grin into my pants pocket as I exited—and I greeted my "friend."

"I stole a magazine outta my brother's room—November *Playboy*. He'll never miss it."

I was cool, a young James Dean pushing soft-core porn in my blue jeans and my white V-neck T-shirt.

"You should see this chick's tits. You ever see tits, Jim?"

He said he had, but I had a good idea that the last tit he saw was leaking milk.

"You wanna check it out?" I asked. "There's no one home, and if they do come back, they won't see us in there." I pointed to the bunker. Though this was my personal hideout, I was willing to share with a good friend, a close companion . . . a helpless victim.

He got on his stomach, and I watched him squirm into the hole, his lithe young body tenderly rubbing against the edges of the opening.

I waited until I couldn't see his legs . . . and then, furiously, I started jumping on the roof of the bunker. The board was buckling under my weight again and again as I flew into the air, slamming down harder each time. Jim was screaming and frantically trying to escape. *Break, break, break*—I willed the roof to fail.

On my third jump I broke through and felt the bunker collapse beneath me. Jim was trapped near the entrance. The cave-in had pinned him under boards and dirt; the weight of the wood refused his exit.

I watched him struggle for breath—a goldfish plucked from the bowl and dropped on the floor.

There was dirt in his mouth and his eyes. He was crying—clear streams of tears leaving flesh colored tracks down an otherwise filthy face.

He was crying for his mother.

"Get my mom . . . please, get my mom."

I was mute as a tar baby: "standin dere, lookin at 'em and I ain't sayin nuthin."

Jim crawled in, and I'll be fucked if he wasn't going to crawl out.

### | | |

Seeing as I didn't kill young Jim, my "bullying" was written off as the action of a problem child—someone you should probably stay away from. And he did . . . at least for a while.

It was right after Jim's visit that I was asked to take a visit myself: downtown. I wasn't in trouble, but you wouldn't have known that from my mother's reaction. She was pissed that she had to dress, take time out of her day, and spend a morning with her son. We were heading to the Superintendent of Schools' office, and I was to be tested on an IQ issue.

I'd fucked up.

I was supposed to be blending in, playing it slightly smart but for the most part average—you know, just another paste-and-booger-eating brat—but school was a drag. Don't get me wrong, I loved learning—I couldn't suck up knowledge quick enough. I read everything I could get my hands on, and I questioned everyone—that was the problem.

I wanted to know why.

"Why do you think he acted like that? Why did they invade that country instead of sitting on what they had? Why do you think she jumped?" The last question referred to a recent suicide by a distraught teacher.

It was the psychology behind the move that intrigued me; I wanted to know why things worked, not how. When I was a smaller child it was all imitation and mimicry, but if I was going to really hurt you, control you, and enslave you, I needed to know what pathway to your emotions was the clearest to walk down.

And after a while, questions like that get noticed.

The children were sitting around on their lacquered mini-butt wooden chairs, struggling through Dick and Jane primers—easy reading for simple minds: "See Dick run. See Jane walk."

My hand went up.

"Why do you think they added Mike and Penny to the Dick and Jane stories?" I asked. Mike, Penny, and her twin sister, Pam, were the recent "colored" additions to the neighborhood.

"Do you think they *wanted* to include blacks?"

So much for me blending in—my thoughts and mouth needed to be a bit more segregated.

The school board decided I belonged in an academy that could better cater to my educational needs; I decided that, as a child, I'd never overtly show intelligence again.

### III

I was sent to an elementary school in an affluent neighborhood a few miles from my home. It was there that I realized the outfits my handlers had given me were cheap and ill-fitting. My clothing had never seemed out of place before—albeit not always gender acceptable—because most of the kids in my neighborhood dressed like little rats. But now, my older brother's pants—a few sizes too big for me—had suddenly become, in this land of trendsetting kid wear, extremely uncool. I heard children laughing behind my back as I passed, not intentionally loud enough for me to hear—the little cowards would never do that—but loud enough. It didn't bother me. I knew that I could make a Black Christmas come early to those little fucks anytime I wanted: a pinch of ground-up glass in their rhubarb cups or a well-aimed stream of piss into their Batman lunch boxes would be sure to silence their mirth. And I'm not saying that I *didn't* fuck with a meal or two but, for the most part, I wore my clothes as a prince would—with pride and a certain "Yes, I am definitely different than you" flair.

Fuck 'em.

To the new adults (the teachers and the administrators), my ragged wear gave me that Oliver Twist, take-pity-on-me look. I enjoyed their sympathy, and I milked it for all it was worth.

Most of the children I saw at school looked like they'd come from what you'd call "good homes." Theirs were homes full of love and protection—but of course you never really knew what went on behind closed doors. Homes can look very nice from the outside while an emotional slaughterhouse is hiding behind the shades. I sensed pain in a few of them—a child beating here, a death or two there—but the majority were happy. These kids were gay little lambs prancing around the playground, not a care in their worlds.

I wondered how they'd stand up to a good thrashing; if their joyful little legs could still run and jump after a vicious leather belt had played its edges along the creases of their asses. I wondered if a hard slap to the mouth might take the playground from their step, and the smile from their face. I wondered if they knew what it felt like to be hurt. They were weak, untested, and inferior to my being.

I was thinking about going it alone—an exile residing under the rusted iron bars of the jungle gym—and I could have easily remained a force of one, but I knew I'd benefit from having a few allies. Well, maybe an ally is too democratic a word, more like servants, really, puppets or minions—stooges, if you will. I knew I couldn't physically pull all the strings that needed pulling, and if I was going to be a leader later in life, then I needed practice. And there's no better way to start than shepherding lambs.

### I I I

The word "leader" has not appeared in this tale yet, and so, as if introducing a new character, I'll fill you in.

Demons have a social hierarchy just as you humans have, and contrary to new-age belief, most of you *are not* destined for greatness; it takes many blades of grass to make a lawn—the majority of you: filler.

It's the same with us. There are demons that are just mildly annoying. They're usually disguised as the pathetic, selfish loser type—that pain-in-the-ass neighbor that lives next door to you, or the aggressive hobo with no teeth and a dirty window-washing rag clenched in his claw. They may be a real headache—blocking your driveway with their car, or fouling your windows at a red light—but they're never going to be prime-time players in the big game; they're just low-level, unpleasant scum.

And then, just as you have your "great humans," your "selfless humanitarians," your "bringers of light to the world," we've got our best. These demons aren't necessarily above low-level annoyance—because fucking with somebody's day is always a good time—but they're created for a bigger bang. They're easier to look at, intelligent, charismatic, and highly persuasive. These are your politicians, your rockstars, and your high-profile media types. They're basically the evil face cards in The Almighty's game of Celestial War.

I've wondered why you humans think God's so good, especially because he's not against having a little fun at your expense. Believe me, I've seen it. Yes, I know it's frightening, thinking that your benevolent King might be laughing at your misfortune. But come on, sitting in the heavens all day, nothing left to create . . . what's a deity to do with its time?

One day, God got tired of patting himself on the back for a job well done, and He realized that He needed a challenge. Not a challenge He couldn't overcome, mind you, because even God knows losing sucks—but just enough of a push against His will to make it interesting. So, in a moment of boredom, God reached down into the mud and formed a playmate—sort of an alter-God. This creation was an inch shorter, a pound heavier, two degrees less intelligent, and nowhere near as loving or kind. In other words, he created a loser.

And that's where I come in. I play for the opposition; the "Not-quite God."

It's all a game, really, and when God gets tired of playing, He'll end it. Until then, we get to participate, or be participated with.

Have you ever played War? If you haven't, it's a children's game between two players, using a deck of fifty-two playing cards. The opponents deal out the cards face down into two equal piles. Then they start flipping the cards over one at a time in unison. The player who lays down the highest-valued card (the ace being the highest; two being the lowest) on each flip wins the battle and his opponent's card. Now, if both players turn over a card of equal value, it initiates a "war." The opponents begin laying a predetermined number of cards, face down, and then a final card is laid face up.

The player with the highest-value card up wins the war and all the cards involved.

God loves this game, and he plays with cards that live, breathe, love, hate, and die. And, by the way, he's also playing with a stacked deck. He reserved the winningest card for himself so, in the end, all the cards eventually wind up in his pile. No one knows when he intends to play it—he keeps it in his jacket, tucked up under his ratty old sleeve. And your guess is as good as mine, but until then, they just keep hammering it out. On a moment-to-moment basis little battles go on all over the world. One of God's cards comes up against one on my man's cards, and the most persuasive, steadfast, flesh-and-blood living game piece takes it down.

Now, if you had to describe me as a card, you could call me the not-quite God's black ace—a trumping motherfucker, one step below the winning play. I've been pulling in lower numbers since the beginning of time. My man keeps me at his right hand, kinda underneath the table and out of sight, but when he wants to win and needs to cheat to do it . . . *slap!* I get thrown onto the pile. Okay, here's where it gets a bit hinky (as if it wasn't already): the Big Man knows my guy's cheating, and he lets him do it, almost like a big brother that lets his younger brother get in a few punches before he beats the living shit out of him. It's all real nutty and extremely complicated God business, but for this story, you only really have to know about me (and maybe you, if you're so inclined). Do you want to know where you fit in this mess? Well, most of you were created as sixes, sevens, and eights—there are a few twos and threes, but really, you're just mid-level players used to round out the deck, something to add a little thickness to the pile as the cards get flipped.

My job in this game was to relearn your ways, grow into adulthood, step into the position that could do the most damage, and reel a pile of you in. And maybe, just maybe, I might even get to go head-to-head with the Big Man's best flip.

III

I was standing in line for lunch—the first knot in a kite's tail of hungry children. I grabbed my sea-green cafeteria tray; on the menu: chipped beef and toast. I was reaching for my silverware when, behind me, I heard what sounded like fun. One of the little playground lambs was being picked on by a larger boy. The big kid was an amateur, fumbling around with his abuse, going straight to the sexual orientation lines. You know, "Hey faggot," and the like. I didn't care for his style, so I turned around and called his name.

"Hey Billy," I said, casual and friendly.

When he looked my way, I swung the tray and connected.

A beautiful green plastic wave crashed into the bridge of his nose; I could almost taste the blood in my own mouth as his head jerked back and he crumpled to his knees, both hands shamefully covering his beaten face. And then I caught the scent of urine. What do you know, little Billy pisses his britches when he's hurt. I smiled and turned back to the silverware; I was hungry.

You can't always be a shit if you're going to lead. Battles must be fought, smiles delivered, and loyalty earned. I wanted an army of my own, and I wanted them to fear me, but I also needed them to defend me from outsiders.

My musings on leadership were curtailed when the cafeteria cop grabbed my arm, pulled me out of line, and marched me towards the principal's office. I glanced back on my way out the door and smiled—the face of adoration plastered on that saved little lamb was reflected in my eyes. It was heart-warming. I noticed other looks also; there was a heavy scattering of "he's cool" nods from the other girls and boys.

The police were plain-clothes officers and they were trying to scare me. They'd been called in to deal with the "assault." I loved the way they were breathing heavily—the overweight bluntness of authority taking up three-quarters of the room. I was pressed into a corner, supposedly shaking, but more concerned with the loss of chipped beef than my freedom.

"You hurt that boy, son." The fatter of the two cops took the lead. "Why'd you do it, youngster? Did he start it?"

My guess was this fucking cop had never been a prisoner of war. He wasn't getting anything out of me other than a pair of sad eyes and tight lips.

"Do you want to go to jail, son?"

*Yeah, that sounds good—no toys, no friends, no . . . wait, I've seen those jail movies, and they serve quite a lot of chipped beef. . . . I'm still hungry as fuck.*

"I don't know, maybe." I let loose a tear. It vainly took a walk round my cheek until all eyes had seen it, and then it dropped to the floor.

"Nobody likes jail, partner," the fat cop continued. "I was hoping we could just talk this out."

As if on cue, his partner—fatter than the first—leans in, opens his coat, and flashes his piece.

"Maybe a visit to the county lock-up might do him good. He looks like he needs persuading."

"Yeah?" I asked. "And what are you gonna do, shoot me?"

Uh-oh—mouth open, words flowing before I could even get a handle on 'em. Shit, I was the pre-ejaculator of talking back.

My mother was immediately called.

After a three-day suspension, a meeting was held at the school in an unused classroom. I was the guest of honor. They set up a circle of chairs, and I'll be damned if the room didn't take on a *Night and the City* look. Dark hulking shadows drifted around the circle; the black and white tones of their displeasure were strictly film noir.

I was directed to sit somewhat near the middle.

All the players were there: the principal, the teacher, the two fat cops, and even the caf cop—I wondered if she was embarrassed, wearing her uniform (badge and all) when the officers were in their civvies. Nah, that bitch was on a power trip, and I would be surprised if she hadn't polished her badge before rolling in. They were five executioners, and my mother sat directly across from me with what looked like a syringe for lethal injection poking from her cheap vinyl purse.

"All rise." The trial began . . .

The lights dimmed and they each took a turn. Hard telescoping angles of my worst behavior were slashed across the screen. It was titillating.

"He threw a crayon at me while my back was turned . . ."

"I caught him with a pack of cigarettes . . ."

"He put three blind children in a closet and locked the door . . ."

I was loving it. But then, Miss Shiny-Badge, crosswalk defender, took the stand.

"He was hanging out on my corner, disturbing the other children, and when I asked him to leave, he leaned into me real close and said, 'No problem, Grandma, I gotta go take a piss anyway.'"

That was it for my mom. I used language like that all day at home, but something in her better-make-a-good-impression brain told her it was time to act. She stood up, walked across the circle, cocked her arm, and with all her might hand-delivered a knockout blow to my head.

It was like the film just broke. The celluloid strip of my consciousness was whirling and flipping through the air at breakneck speed, and I was out.

When the lights came on, I was sitting on the cold linoleum floor clutching the chrome legs of the chair, and my five executioners had reverted back to their regular semi-compassionate selves. The two plainclothes officers were restraining my mother and the crossing guard was crying. I hoped they weren't being *too* hard on her. I slowly rose from the floor, sauntered my way through a fat-lipped grin, and shrugged my shoulders.

That was the last time that assembly of accusers ever put me on trial.

I think school personnel are trained in much the same way that the government trains bomber pilots. The targets are small, far away, and impersonal. They cruise over the drop-zone; the sky, blue and clear. They sight their target and let 'em fly. The flashes are brilliant from above, and there are no crying little faces staring down the barrel of your gun as you blow the eyes out of their heads. My executioners had just gotten an up-close look at their target getting the fuck blown out of him, and they did not dig it one bit. From then on, it was back to the old bombing runs, and when I fucked up at school they'd just make a phone call, or send a letter home from twenty thousand feet. What may or may not have happened after the phone clicked or the letter was opened was really none of their business.

### I I I

The companions I chose were troubled or abused. Not all of them *physically* touched, but somewhere down the line their young lives had been disturbed by an aberration of healthy human behavior. Some of these were latch-key kids, children that came from single-parent houses, or houses where both parents worked during the day.

This was a pretty freaky subculture, a kind of demented Land of Oz trip—twelve-year-old munchkins sitting around naked, smoking cigarettes with their girlfriends, while pennants and photos of them from Little League decorate their walls. The only things missing were the beer bellies and the bald spots.

"My dad's a fucking idiot. He's keeping his smokes in the trunk of our car. Stupid fucker. I got my mom's keys."

Laughs all around and another long drag off the cancer stick.

As I told you, my wheels rolled on the edges of madness, as it were; so you could imagine my discomfort watching this go down. It just didn't seem right—drifty and dreamlike.

*Did that boy just talk about getting sucked off while holding a Matchbox car?*

I found myself stumbling, trying to stay anchored as a woman-child talked to me about shaving a heart-shaped design in her pubic hair, and how she didn't think she needed the pill just yet. For a demon that fought to feign normalcy, wandering into a clan of make-believe adults was painful. I was pretending to be a child, and these were children pretending to be grown-ups.

I remember the night *she* called. Marvin Gaye played in the background as she whispered over the phone.

"My mother has to go to L.A. tomorrow. She's gotta see her lawyer at two. Do you want to ditch school? We could 'do it'?"

I'd heard the voice before, those dark seducing tones recalled veils and blood—a preteen version of Salome. I'd do whatever she asked, but I had to play cool.

"Yeah." Nonchalant and acting experienced, I threw back, "I gotta go to first period so I don't show up absent. But I can split after bell and walk over."

I was terrified.

It was October when she called, and although southern California is robbed of the changing colors of the leaves, the displays in the supermarkets reflected the fall festival. Faces of the dead lined cold metal shelves—a mummy placed two spots over from the latest sugarcoated breakfast cereal. I stood in the aisle and looked for the alter ego I'd wear come Halloween night, but it wasn't there. My mother stood next to me, impatiently grabbing flimsy cardboard boxes with crackling plastic windows—mass-produced urns holding the shells of the dead.

"Here's a cowboy," she said hopefully. "Why don't you be a cowboy?"

I shook her off. I liked the gun, but cowboys weren't scaring anyone.

"How 'bout a Frankenstein, or a robot?" She was pleading a bit now.

I was digging where she was coming from, the whole out-of-control created-by-man trip, but I wanted true terror. I nodded towards the women's stockings. I knew what was frightening, and it wasn't a man.

Life after life, I'd seen the influence women wielded—and not all of it benevolent. There was something about a mother figure going bad that really called to me. Throughout history women were always portrayed as that caring nurturer, offering loving strength, standing with a hand on her man's arm—guiding, comforting, supporting. When a woman stepped onto the stage of corruption it sent a chill down the spine. And the fear that she created was a blanket of safety ripped from beneath you—an umbilical cord used to choke the last breath from your throat.

I wanted to be near one, so I ditched school and walked to her house.

She was dirty; her fingernails unclean and the house unkempt. She lived with her mother who, as close as I could figure, was getting a divorce from her third husband—a man who had been showing a bit too much interest in her young daughter, more than once, and without a condom.

We sat on the couch for a bit. Her breath smelled like cigarettes and Cheerios. She was wearing a pair of pajama pants, blue, with a white almost see-through T-shirt that failed in concealing her training bra. I was fascinated.

She moved next to me and put her head against my shoulder, her left hand resting on my thigh.

"We should hurry," she said. "My mom could be home soon."

She stood, pulling my arm as she did, and I rose behind her, and followed her down a short hallway. The door to her room had been taken off its hinges to discourage her privacy. She'd hung some wooden beads across the entrance though, a small border between herself and intruders.

I was pulled onto her bed, which, by the way, was unmade and a haven for dirty clothes. She pulled her pajama pants down and lay there—eyes closed, legs straight and also closed.

"Take off your clothes, and get on top."

I did as she asked. Completely naked and exposed, I laid on her. "Do it."

I tried to enter her but I couldn't. I was pushing down, thinking it should just connect somehow . . . but nothing.

"Come on," she pleaded, and then her tone changed. "Don't you know what you're doing? I thought you'd done this."

I *didn't* know what I was doing, and I'd never tried to do *this* to someone else.

You might be surprised—a supposed demon that couldn't act as an incubus to a young human—but that's where you're mistaken. In my mind she was mine. I imagined my face on the sweating, condom-free body of her mother's ex. As him, I held her legs up as she cried—forcing myself on her while her mother was lying, head covered by a pillow, in the next room. The images of her rape inflicted themselves on me. I tried . . .

I was unable to transfer thought to body—being still young in human form—and I was ashamed. I couldn't penetrate her.

She started laughing.

"I thought you knew how to fuck," she taunted. "Trip fucked me; he knew what *he was* doing. Are you a fag? You're a faggot, aren't you?"

I knew her words weren't really for me; they were for him. She couldn't talk back to her mother's ex—and I know she didn't find what he did to her funny. She felt power in belittling me, however, and it felt good to absorb her verbal attacks. I swallowed his medicine and enjoyed its taste.

I stood and grabbed my clothes. I was in no hurry; I let her laugh as I dressed. When my shirt was finally buttoned, I simply turned and walked away.

I knew it'd be all over school the next day—Jack couldn't fuck—but I had a plan. I'd start by telling the boys how bad she smelled, and the girls how afraid I was to catch something. "You know she's a whore, don't you?"

I'd make her pay for my incompetence.

Crisp autumn days wrapped themselves around the smell of dying leaves and gray afternoons. I was lonely, and I used my will to attract a visitor. I never knew who was going to come when I played this game, but someone always showed. I walked into our living room and settled down to wait.

*Houdini* was on the television—not the man, the movie starring Tony Curtis and Janet Leigh. I loved the colors in the film, the green-blue of her eyes and the soft sandy-gold of the ropes against Houdini's skin—ropes they used to restrain him.

My father had a rope like that. I remember seeing it in the garage. It was stored above the paint cabinet. I walked out there, and it was just as I thought—a sandy-gold piece of rough hemp rope wrapped in a coil on a high shelf. I took it down and brought it into the house. I tried my hand at tying a knot, and although rough, the cord was supple enough to easily bend and fashion as I wished. It was perfect for tying; I could use it to make good solid knots that didn't slip as you pulled against them. A piece of rope that even Houdini might struggle with, a real tool to use on a helpless young . . .

Someone was knocking on the door—a light hand against the wood.

I'd summoned a visitor.

He or she wasn't large. I could see the silhouette through the entryway glass—a surprise guest.

It was young Jim.

I thought he'd never return, yet here he was—a bit skittish maybe, but perhaps he could be coaxed inside. I was thrilled to hear his standard hello.

"Whatcha doing?"

He should have just said, "Please kill me."

"I'm watching a real cool movie 'bout Houdini," I answered. "Do you know who Houdini is?" I tossed the bait in his direction.

"Yeah, magician or sumpthin', huh?"

He'd grabbed the bait, but it wasn't in his mouth just yet. I pulled lightly back on the line—just a touch of resistance. I asked if he'd like to come in and watch the film with me. He waited a moment before he answered—possibly running a few various dark scenarios through his mind.

"Is your mother home?" he tentatively asked.

A very reasonable question, considering our previous dealings, but I knew I had him. You should never converse with a demon . . . ever.

"Yeah, she's upstairs," I replied, "but I could probably get her to come down and make us some cookies . . . Do you like cookies?"

I was waiting for his answer, but it didn't matter; whatever kind he liked, I'd have 'em.

I held open the door.

"Come on in."

My mother was upstairs, alright, passed out. And there was no way she was getting up to make anything, let alone cookies.

Jim sat on our old couch. He appeared settled, but I could tell that he was poised to run, waiting for an attack that was sure to come. But with each moment that passed, he quieted, became secure in his position, and his taut young muscles slowly relaxed. I watched him, studying the tension around his mouth, waiting for him to let go. I was the perfect host—encouraging my guest to get comfortable and enjoy the film. I offered him a store-bought treat of chocolate chip cookies—out of an unopened bag—and when the white had left his knuckles, I suggested a game.

"Do you really think Houdini got out of those ropes?" I referred to the movie. "I'm gonna try it." I reached for the sandy-gold hemp.

"Let's use this. . . . You first, or me?"

Jim didn't like the idea of me tying him first, so after I chided him for his "pussiness," I offered my wrists. He tied my hands and feet—secure, grand knots, and then I rolled around on the carpet, struggling to get free. I was laughing and enjoying my bonds—assuring him there was nothing to fear, and then I politely asked him to untie me, so he could take a turn.

I had Jim hold his hands behind his back so I could secure them, and when I'd finished that, I tied them to his legs. He was hog-tied—a helpless little calf lying on the floor. I sat back and watched him for a second. He struggled playfully against the cord, laughing and enjoying *his* bonds. And then I watched him go still. He looked up and into my eyes. My pupils slowly grew—spreading across the greens of my irises until the deep black holes had swallowed them completely. In that instant he knew he'd fucked up. I quickly stood, grabbed him by his legs, and dragged him across the carpet to the sliding glass window leading to the backyard.

The old dirt bunkers, which he most feared, were gone; in their place was a swimming pool my father had commissioned through a bonus check. My old man claimed "therapy" to the IRS when he added a small Jacuzzi to the mix, but I was claiming a watery grave for Jim.

"You better start untying, fucker." I was encouraging him to succeed as I dragged him towards the edge. He started screaming for help, but nobody was going to come over to *this* house and answer the cries of a young boy—at least they'd never done it before.

I rolled him into the deep end and he floated for a moment—gasping and sputtering the freshly chlorinated water from his mouth—before he began to sink.

*Fucking* Titanic, *man—raising up on one end like that.*

His eyes grew larger and larger as the breath left his lungs and his head dipped below the surface.

I watched him sink.

I was pretty sure he was done for, when I was pushed out of the way. A plastic-braceletted arm reached in and grabbed a handful of victim hair. Jim was pulled from the pool and saved by my mother.

### | | |

I got my first visit that evening. I awoke from a fitful sleep—paralyzed, unable to move. On my chest sat an imp: blue of color, short, squatting almost toad-like—if a toad could mate with a man. It was holding me down. The only things I could move were my eyes, and with them, I stole quick, furtive glances around the room. The imp was dressed in silk; he sported a checkered shirt and pants. A necklace of what looked like large sharp teeth encircled its fat neck. He was strong—at least, I think it was a he. If not, his tail was hard and poked me in the stomach. The imp's hands were like a celestial vice, pinning me to the bed. The not-quite God demanded communication; the silk wearing imp was the muscle to make sure I listened.

Its mouth opened, and the steam of a cool night exorcised the words from its throat. The voice was old, and if darkness had a sound it would have feared these tones. It was the voice of the not-quite God.

"You've gotta knock this shit off, man. You get yourself locked up and my plans are going to be fucked. You don't want to fuck up *my* plans, do you?"

I wasn't ready for this. I thought I'd been doing a good job—what with all the torturing and stuff. I almost killed Jim, which should count for something, shouldn't it?

"I DON'T NEED YOU LOCKED UP," he angrily replied.

I'd forgotten that a thought was just as good, or as bad, as a word when you were talking to the powers that be. And besides, that fucking imp on my chest stunk. You'd think being God-like and all that this fucker might have retained a nicer looking mouthpiece . . .

"I SAID LISTEN TO ME." Hot, shitty breath and venomous spittle spray-painted a blanket across my face.

"You could have killed that little piece of shit, and then what? There are things I can get you out of, and there are things I can not. Killing as an accident can be dealt with; killing for fun—just because you were fucking bored—renders you useless; and when *you* become useless, *I'll* let *Him* have you."

He was referring to the "Other Man," the Just-A-Bit-Better-Than-Him God. I wasn't exactly sure what this other boss would do to me, but the pictures I caught in my mind weren't good. As for "getting me out of things," an accidental killing couldn't derail my political career, but a straight-up murder would surely disqualify me from anything other than jailhouse ambassador.

I was quiet.

"We've got another problem," He, or actually it, continued. "And you better listen up. You're gonna start running into booze and drugs, and I need you to go easy on that shit. I'm not telling you to be square—because square gets noticed—but I am telling you to watch your fucking ass. This ain't one sip off your pop's Coors anymore. I'm worried about you going over, and I won't have it."

I knew what he was referring to because we'd all been warned before; booze for a demon is dangerous, but not in the way you might think. There was no danger of my soul being destroyed—at the time I had none; the real worry was in the opposite.

I was without emotion, a detached visitor, if you will. That sentimental void was the perfect tool for a demon; it gave me the ability to not care. I could stand, gleaming over you pieces of human trash as you boo-hooed and begged for your poor miserable lives, and I'd feel nothing. I might as well have been doing my laundry. But when you add booze or the equivalent thereof—meaning weed, pills, cocaine, or any other substance that affects you humans from the neck up—well then, we've got a problem. Alcohol adds emotion to the emotionless—and soul to the soulless.

Booze is a synthetic taste of God, created by man to satisfy a closeness that wasn't there when *he*, the man, was created. God, in His infinite wisdom (and need for acknowledgement), left a spiritual hole in man that only God could fill. This way, man would have to search out his Creator to feel whole, and then thank Him for being created.

Shit, that was a mouthful of words just to say that booze makes you feel all cuddly and warm inside.

Earlier I told you that a demon couldn't understand the concept of love, and yet, I've used the word quite a few times in this tale. For example: *I loved seeing them squirm, I loved watching him cry*, etc. The reason I used the word love was to get the story to flow, make it easier to read, and understand. Could you imagine if I said, "I got an unbelievable sense of satisfaction each time I was successful in inflicting pain on someone"? Tiresome reading, to be sure.

When a human feels "love," what they're actually experiencing is a feeling of connection—to the spirit that flows through all creation. They look at the object of their affection and they see themselves echoed within the soul of another, and it is in this echo that they experience what it is to know God.

I was connected to nothing.

You humans, with all your frailty, failures, and feelings, were successful in one thing—although I'm sure "He" was behind it—and that was your ability to make, bottle, and distribute the only products on this earth that could corrupt the incorruptible. Your drugs and your booze affect demonkind much the same way as they affect you, only they affect us with stronger and with greater results. There are actually cases of demons being turned towards God after they'd been ingesting booze or drugs for prolonged periods. I wasn't going to be one of these. I was happy being me. I didn't want to be connected to anyone, or anything. I thoroughly enjoyed my job.

The imp slid up my chest and grabbed my face with its hands; lifeless yet breathing, foul beyond description, it squeezed my cheeks and pulled the terror of its lips close to mine.

My mother's voice trickled from its mouth, "You be a good boy, Jackie." It was cackling. "You stay out of trouble for Mama, okay?"

I sat up sweating and straight.

The damp, rotten wood of the school bungalow mimicked the scent of mushrooms as it sheltered us from the prying eyes of the neighbors. It was night, and we were concealed, cornered between the steps and the building they led in to.

We were sitting on the blacktop— backs against the wind—myself and a few of the neighborhood thugs. We were at the elementary school I'd

## A Moment of Weakness

attended; it was a block from my house, and it was a great place for no good. One of the boys had a joint that he'd stolen from his father. He held the tightly wrapped weed in his mouth as his hands struck the match and then cupped the flame—lifting it slowly to the joint. I watched his eyes close as he inhaled, held in the smoke, and then gave a slightly hacking exhale, releasing the burnt sagebrush scent of the marijuana over us.

I was worried for a second—thinking the pungent stench might get caught in the fake fur of my jacket collar—but then again, I didn't give a fuck—if this shit was as dangerous as the not-quite said, it'd be worth an ass whipping.

The joint came my way and I took my turn. I'd never smoked dope before, but I'd been watching the other boys' actions as the smoke went around, and I was ready. I kept my lips light on it—a gentle kiss. I slowly inhaled and waited for the flash of euphoria that was sure to come . . . I waited . . . I exhaled, and I waited . . . nothing. This was a joke, and not worth my night.

I wasn't gonna have any problem laying back on this, but quite the opposite; it was actually gonna be a chore—having to get loaded just to blend in. If all the other shit that the not-quite worried about was as unsatisfying, well then he wasted a visit. I was actually a little pissed that I had to suffer the breath of that imp for nothing.

"Where the hell have you been?" My father started shouting the minute I opened the front door—it was ten o'clock on a school night, and I'd just returned.

"I was with James and those guys at the school, *Daad*." I stressed the word, elongating it, smart-assing just to show him who the boss was. It didn't quite get the response I was looking for. He was out of his chair and on me like the locusts on Egypt.

"That's the last time you talk back to me."

It was then that I noticed something hanging from his hands. He'd been waiting. My father was clutching the rope that I'd used to tie Jim, and it looked like he meant business. I thought they'd thrown that thing out after the Houdini-pool incident, but I guessed they'd kept it around just in case.

I made a run for it, but when I slipped on the kitchen floor he had me. I went down and I'll be fucked if my old man didn't have that hemp wrapped around my legs before I hit the ground. He was playing the part of the "you're not going to get anything by me" audience volunteer, and I was about to play Houdini for real. I don't remember "steer roper" being in my dad's repertoire of shit-jobs, but that motherfucker was a tying fool. He had me wrapped up and subdued in seconds—although he couldn't rope the smile off my face.

'You think that's gonna do it, huh?" I taunted. "Do you think that's gonna keep me in your fucked-up house?"

"It's not gonna keep you here forever," he confirmed, "but I'll know where you're at tonight, that's for sure."

He was out of breath as he dragged me down the hall and dumped me on the floor of my room—lights off, door closed, but my pride still intact.

## AN AMERICAN DEMON

I'm sure glad I paid close attention to that Houdini flick, because even though I knew it was bullshit, it did encourage me to learn something about escapes. The real Houdini wrote a book about rope removals, and I read some of it in a library pamphlet: "Swell the muscles, expand the chest, slightly hunch the shoulders, and hold the arm a little away from the sides . . ."

I don't think Houdini intended the lesson for children being tied up by their parents, but it sure helped. I'd have to thank him next time I ran into him.

The purpose of expanding and hunching is to create "wiggle" room. When your captors tie a rope around you, you need to stay patient, relax, and expand—creating space or a larger mass to tie. Once they think you're securely bound, you can release the expansion and the ropes naturally slacken. When my father pulled me down I held my legs apart slightly, and I did the same with my hands and my arms. He was a powerful man so there wasn't that much wiggle room, but it was enough. My father tied up a much larger boy than the one he dumped in my room; I'd relaxed, hunched, and expanded—all the while feigning panic.

I started wriggling, and I hate to say it—at the risk of sounding creepy—but I was digging the feel of those ropes. The rough edges dragging down the surface of my skin was almost sexual as I struggled against them. I liked being tied up. I felt a knot give, and I freed my arm. Once that arm was out, it was only a few moments before the rest of the rope had fallen from my body—almost regrettably—and I got to my feet. I wasn't gonna hang around for a re-tie in case my father returned, so I stuffed a few things in a pillowcase and headed out the window.

I went back to the school. My friends were gone, but I knew I'd find shelter there. The janitors were leaving as we were smoking the joint, so I figured, by now, I'd be alone. I threw my stuffed pillowcase on the roof, stood on top of the drinking fountain, and climbed up. It was cold as fuck up there, but wedged between a skylight and a few large pipes, I was at least out of the wind. I was worried about waking up before the kids arrived in the morning—the last thing I needed was some brat ratting out the "guy on the roof"—but my worry was in vain. I barely slept.

The next day I wandered over to a carnival. It was one of those shitty little grocery store set-ups with a rickety Ferris wheel, a Tilt-a-Whirl, and a petting zoo populated by a one-eyed pig and his constituency of retarded goats.

It was perfect.

I love the combined smells of motor oil and cotton candy, popcorn and caramel apples; the feel of sliding my ass over a torn vinyl seat; and the expectation of a ride. The Tilt-a-Whirl—that was my favorite. You couldn't ask for a more frightening summoner of yesterday's beef stew than that monstrosity. I mean, you could practically smell the puke on the seats as you walked by.

The Tilt-a-Whirl chugs along until top speed is reached, and then it screams and groans with each whiplash turn. It's a mechanical monster, clutching kids in its hands as it refuses to go down, even though the police fire shot after shot into its belly. Round and round it swings you—concentric circles of death closing in. The bolts securing your car stretch to the point of snapping, and as you're getting slammed against the hard metal sides of that half-scalloped cage, you picture your capsule flying end-over-end into the parking lot and coming to rest in a blood-filled ditch.

It was too bad I didn't have any money . . . but I could pretend.

I wandered around solo on what the carnival operators were calling "the midway," until I met a carny. He was at least fifty—a tired old border-brother who'd grab work where he could. His face was dirty, but it didn't look like it came from this day's job; it was baked-on filth—the accumulation of a few years of just saying "fuck it." He barely spoke English. I think I'd just found a beard.

At twelve, I couldn't just go wandering about unattended wherever the fuck I wanted to, at least not on a school day. There were truant officers driving around, looking for cats like me. I needed an adult or a handler close by. Come to think of it, the cops probably wouldn't be fooled by a young surfer boy hanging around with a Mexican drifter, but it was worth a shot.

I was stoked on the thought of a "guardian," but hooking up with older creeps could be a real drag. When you're young and broke, you only have one thing to contribute—and you're sitting on it. *Fuck it, if I've got to sell him the thought of "getting it," I will. If he tries anything, I'll deal with him then.*

I stood next to him as he controlled the Hammerhead—a ride so physically damaging that they drew bloody teeth and broken necks on the passenger capsules—and slowly worked my way into his world. I was hoping he'd notice that I was short on cash and my sad face would get me a turn for free, but no luck. He probably figured I didn't want to go on that frightening death trap anyway.

We made weak attempts at conversation but it wasn't that necessary; a deal was struck non-verbally, and after the last rider had drifted away, we walked off together.

We stayed gone for two weeks.

I was a twelve-year-old, living under a highway overpass with an old man. In the daytime, I stole March of Dimes collection tins out of restaurants so we could buy food; at night we kept warm in old blankets. I slept beside him. I wanted him to be able to smell me, the scent of unprotected youth—meat that had fallen off the spit. No one knew where I was, and he was a hawk watching, waiting to descend on me.

I caught a vision of him dying in the desert: he was only a few years older. There was a child lying next to him in the dirt—a boy about my age who he'd raped and strangled. The carny was crying. He held a pistol against his head, and his pants were undone. Funny, he was wearing the same pair of dirty blue jeans that he had on when I met him—I recognized 'em because he'd drawn both our names above the knee.

On our last night together we watched the sun set over the ocean and sat silently under the stars. I cooked our dinner on an open flame—pieces of wood and trash burning in a circle of rocks. It was warm so I took my shirt off and slid my pants low on my hips. I was teasing him. I saw what he was and I wanted to push him towards his fate. I knew he hadn't acted on his lust and anger yet—I could see how troubled he was inside—but he was close, real close. His hands were trembling and a slight sweat had broken out on his forehead. He wanted to reach out, grab me, force me face down into the dirt; he wanted release—but he wasn't gonna get it.

As we sat, face to face across the fire, I caught his gaze and he quailed.

"If you want it, why don't you take it?" I challenged him. He probably had fifty or sixty pounds on me, and I was looking forward to this. It'd been awhile since I'd been beaten, and I missed the sting of a hard punch.

"I don't know what you're talking about, man." He was scared.

"I'm talking about this, fucker." I stood up and put my hand down my pants. "I'm talking about you looking at my shit."

I'd read his mind and he was put to it. I saw him thinking, rolling it over real quick: *Can I take him? Will I get caught? What if I can't do it? What about jail?*

"Hey man, I don't know why you say this. I don't know." The carny chose to puss-out, and it was probably for the better. I could have killed him and gotten away with it.

I kicked the fire into his face—rocks and burning trash showered him.

It was time to go.

"I'm fucking out of here." I grabbed my things. "I hope you fucking burn, Pedro." It wasn't his name, it was an insult thrown back at a lower-class predator.

I climbed up to the highway and stuck my thumb out. I didn't have anywhere else to go, and I was sick of sleeping outdoors, so I headed home.

I heard the carny yelling at me to stop and come back as I climbed inside the first car that pulled over. Pedro probably had no idea why I turned on him—but I do. You see, my hands were shaking as much as his were, and if he could have read my latest thoughts, he would have seen his body lying dead under that bridge, his head caved in by a rock, now bloodied and cradled in my hand. I was getting turned on thinking about killing him, and I was worried about the warning from the not-quite.

The good highway Samaritan, whose car I just jumped in, took me all the way home. He felt sorry for the poor runaway—even kicking in a few bucks when he dropped me off.

I sat on the curb outside my parents' house, until someone inside saw me. It was one of my brothers. I heard him yell, "Jack's back! He's outside on the curb."

He walked over after giving his proclamation announcing the return of the dark prince, and he passed me a message from inside.

"Mom said to leave you out here."

*Good for her*, I thought.

He continued, "She said you'll come in when you feel like it. Whenever you feel like it."

It was nice to be home.


There I was, a twelve-year-old boy who'd been missing for weeks, and no one had been called. No police, no schools: no one. I could have stayed gone and nobody would have cared. I could see it now.

"What happened to your other son?" a curious neighbor would ask. "I thought you had three boys?"

"He went away." Short, and to the point, my mother's answer.

"Good," the neighbor would say. "Probably for the best, huh?"

"Yep."

## III

I was in the garage when I burned my arm—not too bad, but enough to sting and maybe require medical attention, if I so desired. I didn't.

I'd become confused; first, the acrid smell of the burning hair took my attention, and then the tickling of the flame sent a smile across my lips I couldn't ignore. The blister was up before I pulled my arm out.

I loved to watch flames. Fire is a bright, dark world of destruction. A flame is a wave; warmth, with a frosted yellow tip. They're soft, caressing, a see-through orange glow with a center that turns in upon itself as it burns.

Every time I saw an unattended lighter in our house, I took it; silver and brass Zippos—my father's answer to an unlit smoke. He went through about a pack a day—sometimes two if I'd burrowed under his skin deep enough. I guess he thought he could smoke his annoyance out, as if my misbehaving was a tick lodged in his skin.

I poured a line of gas on the floor of our garage that day, a long river of silver that started at one end and wound crazily to the other. It was laid on a surface that a trail of fire wasn't going to hurt— smooth concrete. I flicked the lighter open, and I touched my flame to the lips of the petrol—a Zippo kiss in the dark. The love that was returned was a deep voluminous flash. It painted the garage and rolled over me, causing me to draw back, before I leaned in to inhale the burn. It was over much too soon. I did it again, and again; each time the heat expanded—pushing hot dry pain into my lungs. I was obsessed with the flame. I must have repeated this process four or five times before I decided to take a walk.

The night was cool and breezy. You don't feel so alone on windy evenings. Maybe because you keep adjusting your coat as the breeze tries to lift the edges and peel its skin from you, or maybe it's the touch of the wind itself, laying unseen fingers across your cheeks, pushing your hair back, so the night can get a better look at your face.

It was easy to pick up gas when I was a kid. You walked up to the local service station, handed the attendant a dollar in change while muttering expletives about your tyrant father and his antique mower. It was simple; the high school drop-out chump at the counter gave you a "watch your mouth kid" and directed you to pump number one.

I brought the small gas can with me. I didn't want to be too conspicuous. A young boy, walking late at night with a sloshing can of excitement at his hip is a sure attention-getter to the concerned neighbor. What was I going to say if I got stopped? I sure as fuck wasn't mowing lawns this late, and I definitely wasn't old enough to legally drive, so a casual "Hey kid, where you going with that gas can?" could be a real problem.

I didn't see the neighborhood watch on my short walk to the school. Maybe the wind was on my side, holding the shutters and the doors steadily closed as I lurked by. The elementary school was built at the same time as the homes that surrounded it, and they shared the same poor design—single story glass-and-stucco buildings, mostly. But on the south end of the school's playground there were six wooden bungalows in a row—two lines of three, arranged like tombs for a pharaoh. I walked towards one of the oldest structures, and I touched my hand to its wooden side. I felt the siding give a little, recoiling, afraid of my touch. It knew it was going to be burned, and it couldn't run away. I drew my fingers horizontally, letting my hand drag across its sagging chest: a caress—a last, slow caress before the orange glow of the flame pulled it inside and swallowed its skeleton whole.

I poured the gas into a broken section on the siding. I was a gentle lover—I wasn't so brutish as to splash its grand flank with my fuel. I then wiped the residue of the accelerant from the edges of the crack and stuffed a few handfuls of dead pine needles into the hole. I packed it as tight as I could, and then I lit the outside and turned away. I made sure the flame was moving, but I also had to split. I didn't want my shadow to be burnt Hiroshima-style onto the side of the building—an ash fingerprint for the police to collect.

I walked a few blocks away, then sat on a low cement fence. I waited. I was thinking my makeshift fuse might have failed, when I noticed my eyes hurting. They were itching—watering. And then, I caught the smell: burning wood and the homework of thirty little fuckers who wouldn't be sitting in their chairs tomorrow. They should thank me.

There was a whole string of fires that year: schools, hardware stores, toy corrals, and the grocery. I think some of the kids thought I wore gasoline as cologne.

It wasn't so much the burn I enjoyed—although, like I said, I do love the flame—it was the aftershock. You humans sit safe in your homes—most of you asleep—walking through your days in a dreamlike . . .

No, I can't even call it dreamlike, because the majority of you aren't dreaming of anything. You get up, shower, eat breakfast, go to work, come home, eat dinner, go to bed—and you repeat. On the weekends you might do some things differently, but then the weekends repeat—five days of one pattern, two days of another. You are born asleep; you go to school, get a job, and marry while you're asleep, and then one day you die in your sleep. It's sad really; not for me, mind you, because you're the target—a shooting gallery duck that's easy to hit as you move back and forth along your track. *Ding*, a flashing light and the ringing of a bell when I connect. But for you, it's sad. You were created to experience, to live, to explore; you are the "walkers," and the majority of you are just cowards. You know, sometimes I think I'm working for the other side when I hurt you, because some of you, after a good bit of evil mischief on my part, get your cages so fucking rattled that you go running to God for comfort. You finally wake up, and then you start crying . . .

"God, please help me."

After a big burn I liked to walk around the scene of the enlightenment, looking into the minds of those affected. I was a kid, and some of these were big jobs; no one thought I had anything to do with it. If I was lucky, sometimes the proprietors would be on hand—front row critics to my latest desecration.

A fat woman in an expensive coat was crying, "It was all we had."

God, I loved that "all we had" line. It was usually followed by a very shocked, "Who would do such a thing?"

I almost started clapping. I love the predictability of the injured. "What kind of monster would do this?"

It was me, lady. Look over here. I did it. That's right, the boy with the heart-melting grin and the sea-green eyes just woke your fat ass up. I did it. And I'm glad you fucking hurt. I love what I just did to you.

I slowed down on the flame jobs after I caught myself on fire. I didn't quit, because nobody who enjoys the burn can ever truly walk away, but I was getting sloppy, and sloppy isn't proper. Besides, being a human torch was only good in comics.

On the night I caught fire, I'd filled up a five-gallon can of gas, and I walked over to the parking lot behind the high school. There was a concrete drainage ditch that ran parallel to the back lot. It was a place for the older kids to smoke and get high without the roving eyes of a teacher coming to rest on them. In the street, between the ditch and the lot, was a manhole. It was ripe. New York–style steam drifted out of the small holes in the lid of that pipe. It wasn't because it was cold—it never gets steam-cold here—it was because the green stench of human filth was climbing out of that fucker and exposing itself in the street. It had its pants off, and it unabashedly showed its wares. It literally smelled like somebody had been defecating right on top of the lid, and wiping their ass on the concrete. The lid, an old, hundred-pound rusty metal button, was perfect for what I intended. I stood over the hole and started pouring. I dumped the better part of five gallons of gas down the small openings in that manhole cover, and then I poured the rest of the fuel in the street.

You might be wondering why I'd pour gas down a manhole, but if you'd ever made a cannon, you'd understand. When the cement tube of a manhole is filled with gas and its only exit, when the gas ignites, is a couple of small holes in the manhole cover, the result is exhilarating. The pressure behind the lid gets so great, so fast, that it causes an explosion that can lift a hundred-pound iron cover into the air like a cannonball and toss it high into the night.

I sat back before I lit it. I wasn't in a hurry. That gas wasn't going anywhere. I pulled out one of my father's Kools—menthol—and I struck a match.

The gas was pooled around my feet. I didn't notice—I was imagining the damage I was going to cause when that lid went spiraling into space, and not being fire safe I reached down with the lit match and touched it to the gas. It was slow motion and beautiful until it exploded.

Thousand-candle sunlight hit the air around me, and I was engulfed in the flame. Burning gas was everywhere.

Inside the flame was silence—my ears muffled by a very dull, deafening roar. And the realization that I had to move quickly swept in after the shock. I ran a few yards and then I went down, rolling over the grass and the dirt. In the background, I heard the manhole cover hit the ground and roll like an oversized quarter falling from a giant's pocket. I got up and blindly stumbled down into the ditch. It was luck that got me through the small hole in the fence, which separated the channel from the street. I'd smothered the flame, but I was still smoldering; the fake fur collar of my Sears jacket was melted—the polyester exhaled burnt rubber. I fell down the embankment and then I jumped into the shallow stream of the drainage ditch to finish the extinguishing job. I went face-down in the dirty water and almost inhaled the cold stream to put out the fire in my lungs. It was a quick dip. I could hear shouting and a voice calling for the police. I didn't think the "I was just walking by with this gas can and the street blew up" reply was going to get me anywhere, so I took off, running down the channel. My eyebrows were gone, as were my eyelashes, and a good portion of my hair. I was laughing as I ran; on my face and hands was the beginning of a very nasty burn. Behind me, a billowing black cloud of smoke rose over the city street and drifted up into the night.

I like the term "fire bug." I heard it one day while watching TV. A newscaster said that the southern California area had been plagued by a "fire bug." That was cute. I liked annoying people—getting under their skin, purifying them through fire, or muddying up their lives with gossip and lies.

## I I I

Some older kid was pissed at me. He'd been calling my parents' house—threatening me, hanging up if anyone else answered. I knew I was going to have to deal with him, and I knew how. A weapon would have to be fashioned—he was older and bigger than I was. I figured that if I hit him hard enough in the head, the rest would be easy.

I took an old piece of thick rubber hose into the garage and put it in the vice. I then took a hacksaw and cut the hose into a foot-long section. It was fairly stiff when you cut it down—not as rubbery as you might think. I went into the backyard and started looking for rocks. I needed something that could be stuck in the end of the hose, almost like a hardball, with a point on it that would give me a solid end for crushing his skull. I found just the piece—a smooth speckled-gray stone that was perfect for my needs. After stuffing the small end of the stone into the hose, I took some black electrical tape and started wrapping. I candy-caned my way down, mummifying the rubber hose and the rock. When I was done, it looked like a very threatening King Tut doll: death, wrapped in black.

I wasn't a tough kid—meaning, I didn't walk around looking for fights or randomly attacking people. On the contrary, with children my own age, I rarely had a problem. I was more concerned with the adults in my world, and because I showed no weakness towards them, the other children took that defiance as a display of strength, and at times it was frightening to them. People who are willing to stand up to, or attack, authority figures have always been looked at as dangerous . . .

"If Jack's willing to tell a cop to fuck off, what would he do to us?"

Defiance actually becomes a tool of terror when used towards those who we are taught to respect.

The problem I was having with this kid—the older boy who was after me—was born strictly of my unwillingness to keep my mouth shut. I was "talking shit" about him to a girl he liked, and she told him. It was pretty funny: not the shit talking or the threats from him, but that I thought *she* could be trusted. I don't know what the fuck I was thinking. Sometimes, I mistake scents for actual verbal communication. Her perfume was telling me how sweet and trusting she was, spelling out "I love you, baby" with each whiff I got; her voice, however, was saying something entirely different . . . and not to me.

After I got my weapon ready, I gave him a call.

"Hey, it's me. I heard you were looking for me." *Gee, what am I, a fucking brain surgeon? Of course he's looking for me; he's been calling my house for three fucking days.*

His reply was as expected. "Tracy said you were talking shit."

Tracy was the perfume-wearing informant, and "talking shit" was basically an all-encompassing phrase that meant "fuck you." You didn't need to get all diplomatic when dealing with this crap; the less said the better.

I challenged him, "You want to meet me at the church?"

And no, we weren't heading over there to get with the priest and iron this shit out. Churches are a great place to have a fight.

Strictly from a directorial perspective, you can get a great cinematic look at a church: a couple of tousled-haired youths squaring off in their white T-shirts and blue jeans, a stained glass window, and a rose garden. Maybe a pile of books knocked over on the concrete with a ribbon tied around them. Throw in a pig-tailed, freckle-faced girl as a prize, and you've got a tear-jerking scene.

"Yeah," he answered, "three o'clock."

That was it. He knew the church; it was where all the major battles were fought, it was our "Mount of the Congregation," or Armageddon, to you dramatic bible thumpers.

I wore a long-sleeved Pendleton. It was warm, but I needed the sleeves to conceal the weapon—you can't go rolling up to a fight with a club in your hand. Even in kid land there are rules . . . besides, I wanted to see how wide his eyes got when I pulled out the club and whacked him with it.

When I got to the church his metallic green Schwinn was parked in the bushes near the priest's office. It was a stingray with a banana seat, and a short sissy bar—*motherfucker, his vehicle was cooler than mine*. I'd peddled over on my piece-of-shit brown Huffy. Oh well, maybe I'll take his bicycle as a war prize. I'll ride it to school on Monday with a chunk of his hair tied to the back fender. I ghost-rode my bike into the trash cans—a scare tactic, nosily announcing my arrival, and letting him know that I cared nothing for my possessions. He was waiting.

We gave each other a quick head nod—sort of a "what's up" between two gladiators—and then we started to circle.

It was then that it hit me. I got a glimpse of his home life at his present age—which wasn't good—and a glimpse of him later, as a man, struggling with alcoholism. I felt uncomfortable, unable to hit him. I was confused.

"Come on, fucker," he said. "Let's fucking do this."

I was lost—my plan of cracking his skull seemed foreign, unrealistic.

"What are you waiting for?" He was egging me on.

The weapon that I'd made slid from my sleeve and settled comfortably in my hand. I didn't consciously will that—it was instinct, and yet, my thoughts weren't in line with my actions. He saw the club.

"What the fuck is that?" He was frantic in his question. "Is that a fucking club?"

I didn't know. I didn't know what he was talking about. I was watching myself stand there, poised to attack, and yet not moving. He reached over and pulled the club from my hand—no resistance on my part; sleeping almost, but with eyes open, an observer.

I didn't know what just happened. It was like a hiccup in my day—a few moments in time where I was unhinged from the machine that was my body.

I watched him walk away. I'm not sure why he didn't pound me for my poor sportsmanship and my failure to act; maybe he was as confused as I was, turning my club over in his hand, admiring the craftsmanship that went into the creation of the weapon that had been intended to shorten his existence. He left me standing there.

I picked up my bicycle and started to walk it home. There was nothing wrong with it, I could have ridden, but I didn't feel as if I deserved it. They didn't hold parades for losers and the confused. Why should I ride? I started to cry.

What the fuck? I had no emotions. The only time I cried was to trick you into thinking I was hurt, or to get me off the hook on a deal gone bad—this was bullshit. I sat down on the grass, laying my bike beside me, and the moment I got settled, a crow landed on my handle bars and stared at me.

It was him: the not-quite God.

I put my head down. I was ashamed, and I didn't want to hear it from him. But I also didn't want to stay weak. I thought it would be best to speak first. Prove that I still had something, some backbone.

"I don't know what the fuck happened back there." I started bold. "I went in, wanting to crush his fucking skull, and then I went blank. Maybe I'm sick."

Surprisingly his answer back was soft, almost fatherly—I didn't think he had it in him.

I was right—he *didn't* have it in him.

It was the real deal: the Man.

"You didn't want to hurt him. He's a boy coming from a troubled home much like your home. He has feelings, he cares for others, and you can also care for others."

His voice was slow and warm like an old blanket, and if my tones were hypnotic, then his were Demerol entering a vein; God, the creator of worlds, visiting *me*. I felt myself going under, opening my mind to the ministration of his words.

"You can stop," He said. "You can go back, offer that boy a hand of friendship. You don't have to continue down this path. You can walk away. You can come with me now. I'll take you."

I stood up; ready to follow, and then I saw Him, *just a fucking crow*.

It was like being slammed in the face with a cast-iron skillet—my head jerking from side to side, then bobble-dolling itself to rest. I woke up.

"You come to me as some piece-of-shit bird and you think I'm buying?" The hold he had on me was broken.

"I was sick. I was fucking sick or I would have bashed his head in."

I bent down and picked up a rock.

"You don't own me; and if I was you, I'd take off—before you get hit."

The crow smiled and lifted into the air. He was fast, but not fast enough. I fired a beautifully aimed shot that knocked him out of the sky. He fell to the ground, only a bird now—but one that was about to be sorry that he lent his body as a host.

I wasn't surprised at the Man's visit, and don't you be surprised at the way I treated him. That clown was bad news. I'm asking you, who makes a game and then fucks with all the players, not even giving them a fair shot? Earth was supposedly my man's arena; the not-quite was given control of the flesh and the material world. God was supposed to stay out of it and give us room to operate.

You see, we couldn't do anything to your soul, which belonged to God. Your eternity in Him was guaranteed. But what we could do, and what I have done for centuries, is fuck with the transient. Your time on this earth is but a flash, I know, but I could make it a very long, uncomfortable flash. Under the rules of engagement I could legally do anything I wanted to you, including death if I saw fit. But why would I do that? You die, and you go directly back to

Him; there's no way around it. But if I can make your life so fucking miserable during your time here, that I send you home to Daddy, cursing his name, then I get satisfaction for a job well done, and the Man gets a little pin-prick in his celestial behind from us.

If, and I do mean if, the Man was playing by the rules, He really couldn't touch me, and my threats against Him were like the bravery of a child standing outside the cage of a great bear. I could poke Him with a stick—not too much, mind you, because he has been known to cheat, but I could poke Him a bit and feign bravery. However, what He could do to me, and just did, was fuck with me on matters of the soul. His weapon was the opposite of ours—spirit against flesh. He could tickle the ivories of my callousness and try—through the spirit—to get me to switch sides, and basically thank Him for creating even me. Fat chance.

I might have been upset over my failure to destroy a childhood adversary, but I felt pretty good about going against the Man and holding true. I removed a shoelace from my shoe and I tied it around the neck of that injured crow. I tied the other end to the back of my bicycle seat. There was going to be a parade after all, and it looked like I was going to be pulling a float. I jumped on my bike and proudly pedaled for home, the avatar of God bounced along behind me.

I used my powers of persuasion on the kids at school. No one gave me any grief for bringing a weapon to a fight. If anything, the mere fact that I brought it cemented my reputation as someone to watch out for.

"That boy is out of his fucking mind."

### I I I

It's not easy learning how to grow up. Sure, I was a demon, but we're not infallible—I think that's what makes us demons. We've got a short circuit built into us: we often fail miserably. Some of us don't even survive our transition to human form, and others of my kind fail to make the proper adaptation to your world. It's hard to hold it together. If you've ever been to a country where the writing system is completely foreign to what you know, and you have no translator, and no guide, then you have a micro-understanding of what it's like to be a demon in this world. The language is different; the body is slow and cumbersome; facial expressions, clothing, taste, sounds—all different. You're alone, with no guide to explain. You've got no handbook to what being human's all about, and to tell you the truth, you fuckers are shockingly crazy. It was like God took a whole bunch of live, sparking bits of wire, stuck 'em in a can, shook 'em up, and then spilled their crazy asses all over earth. Free will? More like free for all.

"The school called. The vice principal says that you have three reports that need to be turned in. Have you not been doing your homework?"

It was my mother. I'd just come in from outside and that was my greeting.

"He's full of shit." It wasn't the best reply. As a matter of fact, it was argumentative and hostile, but what did you expect me to say? *You're right, mother dear, I've been spending way too much time smoking and burglarizing houses. I'll get right on it.*

"He said if you don't turn them in tomorrow you're gone. They're kicking you out. They've had enough."

She grabbed me by the arm and expertly led me towards my bedroom—meaning, I had fingernail half-moons dug into the flesh of my forearms, and my head had bounced at least six or seven times off the walls in our hallway. She started screaming. It was time to tune out.

I'd invented a new game that I was eager to try; it was called "Blind Boy." The object was very simple: you just stare into space no matter what happens to you. If you can maintain a completely unaffected visage you get extra points. If you wince while getting punched, slapped, or kicked, you lose points.

I was shoved down into the desk—my legs forced into the space between the chair and the drawers, my ass and the rest of my body rag-dolled into the hard wooden seat. I went limp and blindly stared at her—ten points.

She was screaming louder now, but I was focused on the game. I felt heat from her fury, but no words. She slammed my head down onto the desk and I saw her mouth moving. I think she said, "Start writing," although it could have been "Start writhing," for all I cared. She was wearing a nice shade of lipstick, though—*I wonder if that's the new frosty Cover Girl lip gloss she has upstairs? It looks like it might go well with my . . .* She kicked me.

I started crying but didn't blink—five points. My head lying sideways on the desk made an easy journey for my right eye's tears as they fell on white college ruled paper. The left eye's tears had to work a little harder; they had to roll up and over the bridge of my nose before they traveled down the right cheek. They felt like flies marching single file across my face.

I felt her pry my hand open and then she pressed something hard into my palm, forcefully wrapping my fingers around it. It was a pen, one with a very sharp point. I'm figuring Paper Mate. I wonder if it will still write with a thin layer of torn flesh covering the ballpoint tip—fifteen points.

"WRITE!" I heard her that time, but only because it was accompanied with a slap to the ear. Fuck. Minus ten for flinching.

She left the room. I could hear her storming around our freshly painted avocado green kitchen, matching wooden cabinets angrily slamming and what sounded like very unladylike words being ground down into the cheap linoleum floor—I think a few choice profane comments even made it into the garbage disposal. What was she doing? She was looking for something. Maybe she was going to mop—my father *had* thrown his dinner against the wall a few nights ago, there was probably some dried mashed potatoes along the baseboards.

Whatever she was looking for, she found; and now her footsteps furiously pumped down the hallway. She was coming back. With . . . scissors. For some reason she was looking for scissors. . . .

And then she grabbed me by the hair and yanked my head off the desk. The vertebrae in my neck cracking knuckles into my brain—twenty points.

"Can you see now?" she screamed. "Can you see the paper now?"

She was forcing me to look at the paper, and her hand—scissor accompanied—was flailing wildly, and slicing words through the air.

I was hung, suspended, dangling from her fist; my hair was wrapped around her hand like a spool. Then, she cut me loose by shoving the scissors into my scalp line and slashing my hair at the roots. I wished they were sharper. Those dull blades ripped more than they sliced and great chunks of my hair were torn, not cut, off. I was scalped and dropped back down to the desk; a "Blind Boy" with what was now a very nasty receding hairline, and a score of forty points—a new record.

I walked to school the next morning as if nothing happened. Of course, I had no bangs—looking like one of those fucked old men with hair everywhere on his head but the front. Actually, it was kind of dashing in that snatched-my-head-out-of-a-lion's-mouth sort of way—a thrilling narrow miss.

I stopped at the liquor store to share a Marlboro Red and some Lemonheads with some kid from school.

"What the fuck happened to you?" It wasn't impolite that he asked, being as looks, to a seventh grader, were practically everything.

I leaned against the wall and pushed the ghost of my hair away from my eyes.

"I was scalped, man. My fucking mom lit my hair up for not doing homework." I laughed and took a drag off a cigarette—a deep penetrating pull. It felt great, filling my lungs with the morning air and a cloud of heavy blue-gray smoke.

"Let's go." I didn't need to explain it further—super cool and unaffected; I was the shot-caller.

As we crossed the street to the school, the smoke from my cigarette left a trail of bravado at the stop light.

"Is Sarah having a party tonight?" my companion was asking, but I wasn't telling. I didn't know him that well.

"I'm not sure, man. I haven't talked to her, but if she is, that's gonna be one fucked-up house."

Sarah lived down the street from the junior high school. She was a tall girl with brown hair and slightly crooked eyes that were conveniently hidden behind a pair of cat-eye frames. She wasn't the prettiest thing around, but at fifteen, she was fully developed and very popular—at least with the boys. Sarah was sort of a mascot.

## Just Say Thanks

Her parents were going away for the weekend, and she was pawned off on her aunt—a drugged-out, last chance babysitter who lived a block away. I knew auntie; at least, I'd seen the inside of her house when I burglarized it. She was three years away from a fatal overdose, but for now, she was a guardian that went to bed at a very accommodating seven o'clock.

I met Sarah at her aunt's house, and then we walked over to her parents' place, where I helped her break in. We couldn't very well have the party at Auntie's—although a drugged-out older woman lying in what I'd imagined to be a very naked and very unprotected state did sound like fun. . . . I'd just have to visit her another night.

Sarah's mom and dad used to own a dog—I guess it was Sarah's too, but I never heard her talk about him. The fucking thing got hit by a car the previous summer. Her parents acted like they'd lost a child, and they kept all the doggie supplies in remembrance. They had more pictures hanging of them with that pooch then they had of Sarah—no wonder she sought attention elsewhere. Anyway, her folks should have at least closed up the doggie-door—Fido's entry into the house—but they didn't. Maybe they thought the ghost of that canine was gonna come back and snuggle up with them. Oh, that would be funny, a blood-soaked carcass with two busted legs jumping up on the bed for a cuddle—*sweet*.

Thank the not-quite that their dog was a large one, because I crawled through his door and unlocked the place. We had some time before the other kids showed, so as Sarah flirted with me, I helped her get ready. We took all the booze out of the liquor cabinet and all the beer out of the fridge and stashed it in her parents' room, and locked the door. This might sound strange, but being kids, money for booze was hard to come by, and replacing expensive bottles of liquor that had been tossed back by allowance-lacking preteens was nearly impossible. The last thing Sarah needed was to get popped by her parents for having a party, and for drinking. I made a suggestion that we just say fuck it, drink it all, ransack and rob the house, and then blame it on a burglar, but that suggestion was met with an un-amused eye-roll and immediate disapproval.

The party slowly got rolling—the guests were instructed to jump over the back fence for entry and to keep the noise down. Sarah didn't want kids being seen coming and going from a supposedly vacated house. I was stoked to be there. There were quite a few high schoolers hanging around—boys mostly, attracted by Sarah's attributes—and it was good to be included.

I was sitting on the couch when he came in. A demon, dressed sharp, and traveling with a young girl. He was good looking, tall, tan, maybe eighteen or nineteen years old, and the party bent its attention around him. And yet, he walked directly to the chair next to mine and sat down.

For all that your movies and churches would paint, there really aren't that many demons on this world. I've gone whole lives where I've never seen another child of the dark, but I've lived other times where the concentration of the damned was as stifling as a ghetto. We were placed according to whatever divine will suggested, and in periods of great change or disturbance, we would be thick as flies on the carcass of a cow.

I was shocked, and yet comforted to see him.

The talk was of nothing, really. He was a visitor, spending the weekend with his estranged father. The girl, according to him, was just some cheerleader chick that he met at the liquor store. She sat beside him, and I watched as he slid his hand up her thigh, pushing her short skirt back—she didn't attempt to readjust it.

He leaned over, reached into the girl's large purse, and pulled out a small bottle of whiskey. He saw the shock—almost warning—in my eyes; he smiled and continued to his drink. I saw him take a pull from the bottle. He was cool—he didn't make a big deal of drinking like the other kids did; he could have just been drinking water, for all the trouble it gave him. He took another pull.

I could have been imagining it, but I think he blurred—almost imperceptibly, but just enough for me to notice. It had to be the booze.

He turned towards me.

"Are you drinking yet?"

I looked at his girl and didn't answer. I was trying to be cool, and I felt embarrassed by his question. These kids were older, and I needed to fit in. He just nodded to another drink and continued.

"What about anything else?" he asked. "You been getting high?"

I told him—almost as one conspirator to another—about the weed and the sips off my dad's drinks. He was listening, but I could tell he wasn't too impressed.

"You ever been burned?" he asked.

I wasn't sure where he was going with this, and I was nervous. But I nodded my head yes, and he continued.

"How the fuck did you know flame hurt, until you were burned?"

Okay, I'm not stupid; he wants to give me a little taste of the booze so I know what it feels like, and then I'll be better equipped to deal with it later. I reached for the bottle.

"Are you fucking kidding me?" He whipped the bottle back as if I was gonna snatch it from his hand.

"I know what a young bro like you is worth, and I ain't taking the heat for giving you this." He held the bottle out when he said it, and the worth he was referring to was the power he felt from me as he walked into the room. He knew what I was meant for, and he wasn't gonna stand in anybody's way—especially the not-quite's. He held the bottle up.

"They tell you what it does when you get sucked into this?"

I nodded.

"Yeah," he laughed and didn't believe me. "Sure they did." He took yet another drink and continued, "I've seen demons pulled apart at the seams 'cause they didn't take this serious. Only the strongest of us can sample this and walk away."

Great, I'd run into an egotistical demon. I reached for the bottle. I was planning on one-gulping it, showing him what true strength was, but again he pulled it back.

"Not this, not tonight. I know you ain't ever been fucked up, because I can see it on you. There's a thing that happens to demons, and it ain't good. Sometimes when we stick this in us something kicks in. I met an old demon once, and he called booze the 'great persuader.' He refused to drink it. He said he didn't need anymore persuading than he already had."

I was curious now, but not entirely sold. I knew all about the damage this could do, but what he was talking about seemed different.

"What do you mean persuader?"

"Well," he paused, "now that you're listening. This shit is better than they said. It's like fucking with fate when you drink it. It's like rubbing against the leg of the Man—hanging on Him like a cheap climaxing whore—knowing the not-quite is jealously staring at you from across the room, you keep flirting, and you're a hairline fracture away from getting the beating of your life, and then you step off, and all's forgiven. This is everything he told you not to do and all the excitement you'll ever get for doing it. And the persuader, the persuader is your inability to walk away, to leave the booze alone once it has you; even when you know that one day you will fuck up, and all you were created for will be gone."

He let it sink in for a minute.

"Do you want to try something that's close to this?" He held up the bottle, "Or, do you want her?"

I looked at his girl. He'd pushed her skirt all the way up, and she had nothing underneath. I thought about it, but then I pointed to the bottle. He slid her skirt back down, and then stood and bade me to follow.

He walked into the kitchen.

"We took everything out of here." I told him, "There's nothing here."

I was going to lead him into the bedroom and show him where the shit was, but then he opened a kitchen cabinet and pulled out a can of cooking spray: Pam.

"There has to be a bag around here somewhere." He started opening and closing the cabinet doors. He asked me who lived here so I told him.

"Hey Sarah," he called out, "doesn't your mother make you lunches?"

What the fuck was he doing?

The mascot came in and she pulled a lunch-size brown paper bag out of a drawer and handed it to him. He wrapped his hand around the bag and then he rolled the opening edges back over his fingers—kind of like a collar on a large sweater, or a condom that hadn't been completely unrolled. With the bag in one hand and the cooking spray in the other, I watched as he sprayed the lubricant in the bag and then hurriedly put the bag to his mouth. He started hyperventilating—bellowing the chemical into his lungs. I saw him stagger, and then step back with a smile—eyes closed, head back, swaying on his feet.

It was only a few moments.

He opened his eyes and he smiled at me. He didn't burst into flames or disintegrate. He looked okay, as far as I could tell. Fucking drama queen, I was ready for a grand finale, and he just showed me a sputtering little dud.

He handed me the spray and the bag.

No problem.

Bag in one hand, cooking spray in the other—check. Spray lubricant in bag—check. Place bag quickly over mouth, and start huffing—double check.

I took a succession of deep breaths—in-out, in-out—a deep sea diver sucking on a regulator that wasn't giving enough air. And then . . . it hit me.

I pulled the bag away and kept my eyes open. The walls of the house and the children inside had gotten sucked into the pattern of my breathing. They moved in towards me, and then pulled away— in-out, in-out. Waves of energy: collapsing, expanding, collapsing, expanding—a dirty blue buzz filled my ears.

And then the buzz slowly faded, and the walls and the children became stable again.

This wasn't that non-materialized weed high I was trying to get at the elementary school. This was real and it was exciting. I felt connected to my body. I felt connected to the house and those within it. Wasn't it moving with me as I breathed? Weren't we one in that motion?

I grabbed the bag and I took another hit. Repeating the process exactly as before and yes, yes *I was* connected, the house and the children *did* breathe with me, *I was the house.*

I took another hit.

I was hooked.

Sarah put her hand on me and told me to stop, but I shook her off. I looked for my friend to hand him the bag—give him another shot—but he was gone. I asked where he was, but nobody remembered seeing him. I didn't care, I'd thank him later for the tip, but now . . . I needed another hit.

I got as many pulls as I could, and when it ran out, I headed over to my mother's house and finished off her can. My mind was swimming in a Teflon pool of euphoria, but I wasn't done. I went down the street knocking on doors and asking to borrow the cooking spray. It was ten-thirty at night—you could have fried an egg on my lips, and I was on a Pam run.

My demon friend was right, something definitely had a hold on me and I was rolling with it; I didn't give a fuck if anyone saw me—including the not-quite. I was huffing that shit, on and off for two weeks, even walking around with a greasy bag tucked in the back pocket of my pants. Anyone I ran into was offered a hit. I caught a kid walking to school one morning and I forced him to huff some.

"Suck on this, fucker." I shot spray in the bag and pushed it onto his face. I dropped the can and grabbed the back of his head forcing his face down.

"Breathe. Breathe, or I'll beat the fuck out of you." He struggled but I had him tight, and he was forced to hit it—gasping into the bag. I might have overdone it a bit—seeing as he passed out—but he was breathing when I left him, albeit a little shallow.

It was a fourteen-day run before they stopped me. At least, I think it was a "they." I woke up one morning and I couldn't breathe. I was confused, my thoughts weren't coming clear, and I was suddenly terrified. I knew I'd fucked up. I didn't want to fuck up his plans. I didn't want to be handed over to the Man, so I swore off. I got down on my knees, and I prayed.

I asked the not-quite to help me.

Blasphemy upon all blasphemies, you may cry, but not so. What is prayer if not communication, an earnest entreaty to a God or deity? I prayed to the unseen lord of my belief, and as far as I could tell, my wish was granted—at least it was kind of granted. My God wasn't "quite" as good as the other guy, so I only got a short reprieve, just enough favor to stop huffing Pam for a little while.

It was frightening how quick it took me. I'd heard about obsession in you humans, and I knew it was just a sign of weakness, but in me, a demon above weak, it was like a switch had just been slammed on. Now imagine that that switch had melted into the wall so that nothing you could do would shut it off—I couldn't stop until the power got cut. This was something I was really gonna have to keep an eye on. But you know, I kinda missed the feeling of that bag against my lips . . .

## I I I

I guess I should take a moment to describe myself at this time. At thirteen, I was beautiful. My hair hung below my shoulders in shades of brown, blond, and gold; I had olive skin that resisted the sun's abuse—when it rubbed against me, I received nothing but tan. I wasn't too tall, but you could tell I was about to flare, and I was thin. The body of a demon, unlike an angel, is not soft; it's been hardened by the flames of destruction. I was mistaken for a girl frequently—carrying that image of androgyny that made me attractive to either sex, I was an old creep's dream and a young girl's first crush.

There was a uniform that boys wore at the time. There wasn't any list—nobody came around and gave you a dress code—but you knew what you had to wear to fit in and be cool: a striped Hang Ten T-shirt, blue jeans or dark brown cords, and a pair of Wallaby's or Chuck Taylors—this was standard 1974-issue, and I wore it well. Of course, I also had my jacket, a light brown Sears coat with large plastic buttons and a fake fur collar—which just happened to be a bit melted. . . .

I played my part.

I was hanging around the liquor store seeking spare change and bumming smokes, when they pulled up. I saw *him* first. He was your standard overweight old creep who gave me the up-and-down as he walked in to get some booze. He wasn't going to be long on this planet. I got a glimpse of him lying naked and blue on a bedroom floor as a very attractive blond woman in fifties-style black lingerie was making a crybaby call to the police. On the bed, near her, was a selection of what I took to be various odd sexual apparatuses—fucking old creep.

I came back to the now, and I took an amused look inside the store at the fat man. I could see him naked. When he came out, I was gonna say something about his taste in sexual activities, but then I saw her. It was the blond, the semi-clad phone caller. She was reflected in the liquor store windows as she sat idling in the car.

She was staring at me, and the wickedness that flew through that rolled-up car window was stunning. I was flooded with pictures of depravity, and I'll be fucked if she didn't straight out lick her lips. A flush spread over my young face, and I stared back.

The fat man walked out of the store and pressed a bill into my hand. It was a twenty.

"You look like you could use some money, kid. You ever do any yard work?"

Yeah, that's like asking a blind man if he ever had trouble finding his car keys. *Of course I do yard work. I'm a teenager in a lower-middle class neighborhood—look at the fucking grass stains on my shoes, asshole.* Not only was this guy creepy, he was stupid. If I didn't know they were human, I would have thought these two were a pair of demons out canvassing victims—not that you human fucks aren't above chopping people up and kidnapping kids, but these were just a pair of straight creeps looking for a lunchtime snack of young boy.

Okay, I'll play.

"I mow the lawn at home, sir." I should have sucked on my finger when I said it, or bent over and touched my toes and smiled.

Fuck, I was already working for that twenty, a bad child actor in a D-movie porno. I didn't think this shit actually happened in real life. I liked fucking with this fat prick.

My father had one of those old "doctors' studies" sex books hidden in his bathroom cabinet—I'd found it when I was snooping one day—and it was loaded with a whole bunch of whacked out stories on sexual behavior: gay sex, straight sex, three-way sex, sex with animals. You name it, and the "doctor" had done the research. It was supposedly all on the up-and-up, because it was a collection of case studies, but I don't ever remember my doctor writing "cock-sucker" or "rim job" on my medical chart.

The fat man told me what they were *supposedly* looking for.

"Cindy's got some weeds and bushes that need trimming back at the house."

I'm figuring Cindy's the hot blond. He may as well start the shitty soundtrack right now—boom whacka boom whacka boom boom—*Cindy's bush needs trimming? Okay, I'll do it, mister.*

"You're looking at an hour or two of work," he said, "and two more twenties if you want it."

Sixty bucks for two hours. The going rate for teenage lawn slave was about five bucks an hour, and at my house it was nothing. I was in for sixty. I grabbed my skateboard and followed him to the car.

She wasn't quite what she looked like from far away—not even close. Her face was acne-scarred and the dark circles under her eyes spoke of diet pills and too many cigarettes. If you were going to have a fantasy involving an older blond and a pimp-type husband, you sure as fuck wouldn't have written her into the script—or him for that matter.

She opened the car door and leaned forward. She reached back, grabbed the lever, and pulled the seat up behind her. I squeezed into the rear. The car smelled like dog, and I glanced around for what I thought must be a little Pekinese or some other mini-canine disaster—I hated those little fuckers, they reminded me of my grandma . . .

"What's your name, baby?"

Great. She had teeth to match the circles under her eyes—gray—and it sure as fuck wasn't a little dog I smelled. I started hoping they *really* had yard work for me to do when the fat man got behind the wheel.

Their house wasn't far. It was another one of those fifties-style tract homes like the one my parents lived in. The outside stucco was painted a faded light grayish blue—picture a cloudless sky on a hazy day. We pulled into the driveway, and I noticed the sprinklers were on. *I hope this yard work is in the back, I hate getting wet with my clothes on—fuck that, I just hope there is yard work, and I don't care if I get soaked doing it.*

"You left the fucking sprinklers on, Tony. Great job." Her voice was pure sarcastic snot. If a fingernail could take on a personality and become an old Jewish grandmother, then make it so, and drag it across a chalkboard—classy.

*Jeez, nice lady. Come to think of it, if I have to be fooling around with someone, Tony, or fat man, is actually sounding a bit cleaner than Cindy, the blond.*

"It'll dry. I'm giving the little fucker sixty bucks—he can wait." I followed them inside.

We walked through a back door directly into a living room that looked like it was furnished by a high school junk dealer. The brown paneled walls were plastered with plug-in neon signs advertising beer companies. The TV sat on a large rough wooden spool of some sort, and an old-man's recliner and a black leatherette couch were waiting for something to be turned on. It was a shithole. Where the fuck did they come up with sixty bucks? I *was* digging the floor covering though—dirt-green shag carpeting that ran, as they say, wall-to-wall.

They told me to grab a seat and I went for the recliner—it was probably "his" chair, but I wasn't going to sit on the couch and let one of them sit next to me. Fat man walked into what I'm figuring was the kitchen, and Cindy flopped down on the sofa. She actually didn't look too bad from a distance, and the low light helped her complexion.

"You want something, kid?" Tony was yelling from the kitchen. "We got soda or something else if you want it."

I was figuring the "something else" meant booze, but I wasn't about to get on it after what happened with the cooking spray.

"I'll take a soda, please. In the can if you got it." I was polite, but I knew better than to swallow a pre-opened drink—I'd fucked with enough offered beverages to know better.

He threw me a cold can of Shasta cola and then he walked back in with two mixed drinks—short glasses, brown liquid, and a couple of ice cubes. He handed Cindy a drink, turned the portable stereo on, and then he sat next to her on the couch. The recliner I was sitting in was facing them—a chair, set up more for talking than watching TV.

It was all bullshit at first. Some talk about her ex-husband or something—that explained them having a house—and a few questions about what I did and where I went to school. She'd kicked her sandals off as she'd sat down, and she started rubbing his leg with her foot. She was wearing a halter top made out of terry cloth, and her shorts were of the same blend—I think it was intended to be non-white-trash beachwear, but it'd failed on the non part. Every couple of songs, the fat man got up and fixed new drinks until he was tired of rising and brought what looked like a half-emptied fifth into the living room and sat it on the floor near the couch.

She was getting extremely comfortable and started imitating the application of lotion on her legs and arms. She leaned in and kissed him. He pushed back against her, and I didn't look away as he slid his hand up her leg and covered the crotch of her shorts with his fat fingers.

This was what they wanted. They wanted to put on a show for a young boy, and I'd already been given the money for admission.

I watched as things progressed. He undid her top and removed her shorts before he'd taken anything of his own off. In between kisses and times when her face was buried against him, she glanced at me—dark, passionate glances of invitation—but I didn't move; I just watched.

He wasn't even close to attractive when he mounted her, but I loved seeing her give in, her legs wrapped around his fat hips and her fingers tracing the light scars of old lovers' trails down his hairy back. He was what I now know to be quick at the trigger though, and he was soon spent. He rolled off and lay back on the couch, a moment away from a booze-and-climax-induced sleep.

She didn't make a move to get dressed. She laid there; legs open on the sofa, her hands gently caressing the inside of her thighs with her fingertips. I don't know if the light had gotten better, but her looks had sure changed. Her face was softer, beautiful and smooth. She opened her eyes and then she sat forward and moved off the couch towards me. She knelt at my feet and raised a hand to the buttons of my jeans. She pulled expertly on them and one by one they let go. I lifted my hips and let her pull my pants off. I kept my shirt on.

I was worried that I was gonna fuck this up.

After my earlier failed attempt at having sex, I thought I was incapable of doing it, but I didn't need to do anything here. She climbed onto the chair and sat down on top of me, a bent leg on each side, her naked body coming to rest when I was fully in her.

I tried to push against her but she held me down, my arms practically strapped to the sides of the chair, and her mouth against mine pressed my face against the headrest. Her breath was no longer sour; she tasted like summer and a swim in an ocean. I let myself go. It was better not to struggle, let her take what she wanted. I lasted no longer than he did. My eyes closed at the end, my body unattached.

I looked up and he was awake. He was masturbating as he watched us; his fat, greedy face and leering mouth taking it all in. He stood up when I saw him, and he walked over and started rubbing her back. His stomach hung down, covering his penis, but I could tell he was aroused. He got on his knees and knelt behind her. I could feel his hot breath on the inside of my legs as he leaned in. I froze. She was still holding me down, but she leaned up, and I felt him put his mouth on me. I went dark. I shut off, separated from my body, and counted the seconds before he quit.

Fuck, this was longer than it took him to be done with her—hours, it seemed, but then she turned around and slid down to the floor with him. He penetrated her and that was my way out. I grabbed my pants and quickly dressed—pulled 'em right up over my shoes—and then I split. I didn't care about the rest of the money, I could get it later. I wasn't a boy any longer: I was a creep.

I didn't tell anybody about them, but in the following three months I went back as often as I could. They taught me about lust, and how to use someone to feel good, regardless of how that person felt. The difference between preying on someone sexually and preying on someone to physically abuse them was the issue of time. In the sexual world, abuse—as long as it was accompanied by even short moments of pleasure—could be drawn out for months, even years, if you knew how to handle it properly. You were negotiating the right to abuse through barter. They taught me the give and take of abuse. I had been a child in my ways, selfishly taking and never giving; yes, I'd gotten the instant flash of gratification reserved for the abuser, but my victims usually went running. With a game like this, I could put out just a small bit of "give" and harvest months of "take" before my victims ran away . . . if ever.

It was a Wednesday night. I was at home, and I got a call from Cindy. When I heard her voice I was pissed. I didn't want my parents questioning my relationship with these sick fucks.

"I told you not to call here."

"Tony's dead." She was crying.

It was the scene I saw on that first day, only she wasn't calling the police like I'd envisioned, she was calling me.

"I think he had a fucking heart attack. He was going down on me and then he just lay down and stopped breathing."

I didn't give a fuck about Tony. This was weird. I was a hundred percent on my visions and this was freaking me out. *How the fuck did I get this wrong? How could I have missed this?*

"What should I do? Who should I call? We were doing blow . . ."

I hung up on her and took the phone off the hook. This was

gonna take some thought. I sure hope I didn't fuck up my visions by inhaling all that Pam.

### I I I

I walked up the street to the park. I didn't feel like attending school that day, and I had a favorite spot where I could sit and think. It was a hollow, located within a group of trees—a perfect place for a picnic, but I'd never seen anyone else there.

Sometimes you humans tell ghost stories. You gather at night, or in a dark hallway, sharing tales of the living dead who float over staircases and materialize underneath your beds. It's all in your imagination. The human brain is a machine built for fantasy and lies. Anything you want to see can be conjured by the mind. There aren't any ghosts; you're either here, or you're not. What you see in the dark is nothing to be afraid of; it's what you don't see that will hurt you.

When I sat, or walked, and thought about the ways I could harm you, I left a trail, a splash of energy—like wet footsteps around a pool—and when you came behind me, you couldn't see me there, but you knew the footsteps meant something uncomfortable had walked by. You could feel the backwash of the wave that went before you. The time I spent in that hollow thinking, reviewing my life, had created a pond of uneasiness that had deepened as the days passed. It might have been my refuge, but if a Sunday afternoon family tried to settle there for lunch, their minds would be as open as the picnic basket they brought and their first thought would be that a cloud had covered the sun. But when they glanced up, the sky was still a brilliant sparkling blue. The blanket that was spread— at first, roomy enough for a happy family of four—had suddenly become crowded. Thoughts that were meant to be hidden seemed on the verge of spilling out onto the gingham print. Father, with his mind on that new girl at work—her legs and what they'd look like as her feet were pushing against the ceiling of his car; and mother, wanting to leave, hating him for holding her down and hating the children for their dependence on her love; little Rose wondering what it'd be like if Mr. Rogers, that nice janitor at school, touched her beneath her dress and young Bill, knowing that he'll never be anything like his dad, he isn't good enough, he isn't strong enough, he isn't well hung.

The picnic comes to an early conclusion. Ten, maybe fifteen minutes after arriving, they're ready to go. No food has been touched, no game played. They hurriedly pack their things, and they leave. But as they walk over the crest of the hollow and head back to the car, the day seems warmer, the air brighter; they're suddenly in no hurry to leave. Father puts his arm around the waist of his fair wife; he pulls her close and tenderly kisses her neck. And she, in return, leans against him, and feels grateful for the strong arms of his support. The children, well, they're still fucked; young minds are extremely moldable, and it's been said that my effect can be torturously everlasting.

I sat for a while under those trees, and I thought. It didn't seem strange to me at the time, but looking back now, I realize the lack of self that my visions held. If I was gazing into your future, I could see your death, but as for me, I saw nothing and never thought to look towards my end. The past was tied around my body as a tangled thread is wrapped around a spool—if I tugged at the line, cleared some of the knots, I could recall the faces of thousands of years. But as for my future, it was a frayed end that gave my mind the purchase of only a few days and even then, it wasn't as things would happen to me, it was as things would happen to you at my hand. I was created without hope.

I was shaken from my thoughts by a chemical smell and the sound of footsteps on the grass. Staggering, heavy footsteps, as if someone was under the influence . . .

"Hey Grisham!"

It was Mark from school. He was standing on top of the hill looking down at me. I enjoyed Mark. He was harmless to everyone but himself, but it wasn't in a depressive, suicidal way that Mark attacked his being; he did it with a smile, light-hearted and comfortable in the path of his destruction. You have to enjoy someone who smiles as their ship goes down. Mark liked chemicals: glue, gas, and PCP. His brain was soaked in toxins.

I could smell him as he stood upwind, the unmistakable odor of mint and formaldehyde floating off his clothes.

"You going to Christy's?" he slurred.

Christy was a girl two grades up from us. Neither Mark nor I really knew her but we pretended we did. It may sound crazy—and it took me a while to understand it—but kids always talked about other kids like they knew them, especially if the kids you were talking about were older or way cooler than you. I don't think Mark even knew what Christy looked like. I did. She was pretty much standard-issue as far as cute teens were concerned, but she was stuck up. I saw her in the market one day, pushing a shopping cart for an overweight mom that was pulling the cheap brand of toilet tissue off the shelves. I'd never spoken to Christy before, but I'd never pass up a chance to embarrass.

"Hey Christy, what's going on?" It was like catching Miss Too-Cool taking a dump. Her whole cigarette-smoking, older boy–dating act just got pulled away and all that was left was a little girl two years out of braces and footsie pajamas who was playing maidservant to a fat, ass-wiping mom hag. She limply smiled and hoped that her mother wouldn't beg an introduction. I didn't push it.

"See you around."

I owned her. It was like I walked down that grocery store aisle with a broom and a dustpan. I'd just swept up a whole pile of dirt on that stuck-up little bitch, so any party she had, I'd be welcomed at. Who knows? I might just turn that gossipy little tidbit into a sex slave.

Mark and I walked the few blocks over to Christy's pad and when we got there, it was already rolling.

It might have been a school day, but at twelve p.m. these kids were getting it on. Parties like this were called "nooners," and they usually consisted of whatever booze could be stolen from your parents' house, and any drugs that could be found. The invitees were twenty or thirty incorrigible little fucks that didn't mind walking off school grounds at lunch and didn't worry about what time they got back—if at all; none of these kids cared about school anyways, and nobody drove. There was a greasy tower of bikes being built in the driveway. I could see the vehicles of a few acquaintances. It looked like this was going to be fun.

Christy lived in the "Ranchos"—an early 1960s housing tract built on the other side of the highway from my parents' house. Most of the homes there were set back from the street. High protective fences circled the front yards, and if you were so lucky as to have purchased the deluxe villa, you got a bomb shelter tucked under the garage. These little atomic crypts were really cool—white-walled, thick-cement hideouts from Russian nuclear terror. But if you really thought about it, they were pretty fucking useless—yeah, you might dodge the first strike, but when you ran up to the market to get smokes and a TV dinner you'd be fucked.

Mark and I walked in and gave head nods all around. Christy met my eyes, blushed, and turned away. Like I thought, she was mine to do with as I wished. We sat and talked shit on whoever wasn't there. I stayed away from the booze and drugs—I was still stinging from that last flash, and when I got up to use the bathroom, I detoured into her mother's bedroom.

I closed the door behind me so I'd have plenty of privacy. You might be wondering how I knew this was her mother's room; it wasn't hard. Besides my preternatural ability to smell a score, no matter how small, it was a three-bedroom house. The bathroom door was open—I could see the toilet and a fucked up vinyl shower curtain hanging on a pole, so I crossed that one off my list. Two of the other doors had stickers on them. The room that I took to be Christy's had a rainbow and a pink happy face sticker; the other door had a stop sign and what looked to be a fist hole punched into it. Unless her mother was a total retard, I was betting on the unmarked entryway to be hers. I was right.

Her room was surprisingly clean and well kept—the bed made, and the top of her dresser uncluttered with shit. I went right for the jewelry box. Bingo: a handful of gold necklaces and a man's wedding band. The ring was too large for my finger, but I had no trouble fitting it in my pocket. It was Christy's dad's. There was a picture of him on the nightstand by the bed—a victim of a heart attack and, as I could sense, sorely missed by this family. I caught a glimpse of Christy's fat mom holding his ring and crying. Oh well, I'd save her the trouble of having to do that again. I made quick work of the rest of her jewelry and then opened the bedroom window and crawled out. Going in her room was one thing, coming out into the hallway and getting caught with treasure in my pocket was another.

I walked along the side of the house, and then I went through a gate leading to the driveway. Mark was standing there—dusted. The slang term for PCP is "angel dust" and dust is a motherfucker; it's an anesthetic hallucinogen that at times gives the user a complete psychic separation from his body and an almost superhuman ability to not feel pain. Cops love running into dust users because it's always a fight. Arresting a duster is like loading a wild animal into the car; the cops can club the fuck out of them, and they just keep kicking.

Speaking of cops, look who just pulled up . . .

I wasn't surprised when two of Long Beach's finest rolled onto the driveway, but I was a touch worried. I thought someone might have ratted me out for the burglary, but then I remembered, kids don't usually call the cops on other kids—they just talk shit and try to settle it with a fight at the church.

"What are you boys doing out of class?"

*Christ, these guys gotta get a new script writer.* Don't they realize how tired that shit sounds? Kids would be way more threatened if they just jumped out of the squad car and shouted gibberish. Could you imagine . . .

*"What you—fuck—die monkey—kill city fucker!"*

I know that would do a number on me.

"What's so funny, youngster? Do you think this is funny?"

*Shit, I forgot what's happening. I'm being interrogated.* I put on a sweet face.

"Not at all officer." *That's more like it—meek, concerned, and respectful.*

"I was smiling because I was just telling my friend we shouldn't be here, and right after I said it, you guys showed up and proved my point."

"Good thinking, son. Why don't you two beat feet?"

They should have known better. How could you ride around all day dealing with criminals, and not spot the line of shit that I just gave them? Did I say Long Beach's finest? If I was them, I would have pulled out my gun and started shooting. Anybody as clean as I claimed had to be dangerous.

This whole time Mark was standing there with a dull, glazed look on his face. His mouth was hanging slack, and a string of spit hung down to his shirt collar. He didn't know what the fuck was going on. He was just watching, waiting to spazz out if they grabbed him.

The police headed through the gate and walked up to Christy's.

"The door's open!" I yelled. "Thanks, officers."

I heard them knock, and in they went.

Mark was still standing there, clueless, as I bent down and picked up an ornamental lawn boulder. It was fairly heavy, maybe fifty pounds. Mark watched as I carried it to the front of the police cruiser and lifted it over my head. I made a quick offering up to the sky and then I smashed the fucker through the front window of that car. Glass, and what was left of Mark's brain cells, exploded on impact. I ran. Mark slowly rolled the word "Fuck" off his tongue and just stood there staring at the freshly landscaped hole in the vehicle's windshield.

## AN AMERICAN DEMON

I was around the corner and running back towards the park when the police reemerged. The glass hadn't even settled on their front seat when they saw Mark standing there—caught in the act, so to speak.

They grabbed him. He resisted. They beat the living fuck out of him and arrested his ass for destroying police property, drug use, and stupidity.

He should have known better—you never befriend a demon.

I bent down, grabbed a handful of sand, and squeezed. The pressure of my grip forced the tiny grains out through the gaps in my fist. The compact, slightly moist mass of broken shells that remained, I ground into my forearm until my flesh was raw and bruised.

I closed my eyes and listened to the surf. Its voice was angry and beautiful.

## The Ocean

A large wave makes a sound like an avalanche rolling unimpeded to the shore; the earth a corral of mountains and cities built to keep the storm at bay. I was being swallowed by madness. I wanted to stand in that avalanche but not be held back. I wanted to roll over the earth, cutting and carrying off anything in my path. . . . I wanted to destroy anyone against me.

I took off my clothes and walked naked towards the water. I was holding a bottle, and I let it fall from my grasp before the first wave touched me. There wasn't a note inside. I had no desire to contact anyone on a distant shore. It was empty. I'd sat alone in the dark, pouring the majority of the contents from that container down my throat, and now, as my stomach burned, I wanted to swim.

I'd slept uneasily the night before. Not that that was anything new, but the dreams I had troubled me.

I dreamt of a child. She was standing before me and the face that she wore was a copy of my own; her grayish-green eyes bound in tan flesh, her lips slightly stained with the pale shade of innocent blood. She looked up at me and, with a tender smile, bared her teeth. I offered her my right hand, which she firmly squeezed and then pulled into her mouth. I watched calmly as she bit—a slow guillotine separating skin from bone—and yet, I felt no pain. She ate of my flesh, and as the blood flowed into her throat, she drank in honor of me.

I woke and was surprised to see both hands in place. My right arm was numb from sleeping with it pinned beneath my body, but there was no blood. I walked into the bathroom, and I stared at my face. Her eyes had followed me into the waking world, and I found myself looking through them into the mirror—the only difference was the lack of broken-glass cruelty that mine carried; hers had shown none of these edges. I didn't like these mornings; the ones where it took me hours to come out of a dream. I wouldn't be going to school today. I didn't feel like it. And at fifteen years old I made my own decisions.

I decided to burgle a few houses—I'd stop at one if I scored righteous, but I wasn't lazy, and no one would be home until at least three, so I could probably knock off three or four homes.

Most residential burglaries are not committed by pros, they're committed by kids, or local junkies looking for quick cash. I love these fucking citizens who think well-organized gangs of career criminals were working their neighborhoods. Shit, we were living in the lower middle class; there was never any real money or jewels in these shit-holes, it was chump change. Luckily, I wasn't burglaring to get rich; I was breaking into your house because I liked fucking around with your stuff, and I loved violating your privacy. If I had the time, there wasn't anything I didn't get into.

But the first thing I had to do was find a house. It wasn't hard in my neighborhood. I strolled up street after street, a youth enjoying the sunshine on his way to . . . well . . . wherever.

I was still having trouble shaking the image of that little girl, but I was sure that after I crawled through a window or two, the ghost of that child would vanish quicker than your feelings of security.

I found my first victim.

The woman of the house was getting in the car as I walked by.

She was glancing at what I took to be a grocery or to-do list. I waved as she looked up—my smile and eyes brighter than that midday sun. She lit up and waved back. I'd take one lap around the block, making sure she was gone, and then I'd go in. She passed me in her car as I was rounding the corner, and she threw me a wave. I thought she was going to stop and offer me a ride. Could you imagine?

"Can I drop you somewhere, sweetie?"

"Oh yes, ma'am. Could you take me back to your place? I was going to rip you off while you were gone, but if you'd like to watch, I might have something in my britches . . . just for you." *A young man can only wish.*

When I got back to her house I walked nonchalantly through a side gate and into the backyard. No stopping, no hesitating, I did it like I belonged there. I had the strange feeling that I was being followed, but who, besides me, would be sneaking around that day? I was in—fast. The back door was locked but the window next to it was wide open. My entry took me straight into her bedroom where I peeled off one of her pillowcases to use as a loot sack. The pillowcase was rainbow striped, with a high thread count—*somebody was being nice to themselves.* I could tell right away that she lived alone; there wasn't a touch of man in the place. What the fuck was she doing home on a weekday? I rifled her dresser where I found a passport and a tray for jewelry. The usual crap: necklaces, earrings, a couple of cheap pins, and some sort of locket. Once again, it wasn't value I was really after, it was fear. I wanted her to come home and never feel safe again. No lock that she bought would ever secure this house as long as the figure of an intruder wandered through her mind.

I opened one of her drawers and threw the contents on the bed. Undies—it was her "privates" drawer. Oh, this was fun; I put her panties on my head and pulled them down over my face bandit-style.

I heard a door slam.

I went fugue—a rabbit frozen in the headlights of an oncoming car. Any minute now she'd walk into the bedroom and there I'd be: a statue wearing a control-top panty mask, and holding a very soft but heavily laden pillowcase.

I held.

Nothing—no footsteps, no breathing, no screams; *I must be out of my fucking mind*. There was no one here. She must have left the front door ajar when she left and a breeze pushed it shut. I decided not to stay long, but before I left, I'd check the closet and the kitchen.

There wasn't much in either place, but from the kitchen I took a set of carving knives and a bottle of Cutty Sark—I loved playing with knives, and the whiskey could be traded or used as an aphrodisiac. In the closet I found a Polaroid camera. This lady was actually pretty clean. I was shocked. Normally, in the single gal's homes, I found a "back massager," or some sort of phallic friend, but in here, nothing. I got an idea. Maybe her libido needed stimulating.

I went back towards the bedroom with the camera.

Fuck, I still had that feeling of being watched. It's one thing to be doing something, not knowing someone's watching; it's another, to think someone's watching you, when they definitely are not.

I looked up, and she was sitting on the bed.

It was her, the young girl from my dream.

She said nothing—looking straight through me down the hall, a light blond sentinel, guarding the bedroom of a woman she couldn't possibly know. I don't know why I did it, but I set everything in my hands on the floor but the booze. *That* I clutched—my fingers deathly white around the neck of the bottle—and I backed away. She stood and walked towards me, still looking through me, as she came into the hallway. It was then that I turned and ran. I didn't care who saw me come from that house. I just wanted gone and fast. I was two blocks away before I stopped long enough to take off my sweatshirt and wrap that Cutty Sark up in it. I wasn't gonna trade that booze or give it away—*I* needed it. I remembered what that Pam had done to me—the sense of forgetfulness that the high had bestowed, and I knew this shit would have the same effect. Maybe that's why I wouldn't let it go when I was in that house; maybe I knew I was going to need it to make that little girl go away. I wasn't worried about the booze getting a hold on me; I just wanted her to release her grip.

I walked out to the highway and hitched a ride to the beach. Nobody at my house questioned when I was gone anymore. My parents had given up a long time ago. My father had read a book on how to handle troubled youth, and it was suggested to him that he'd fare better if he held loose on the reins and gave a young maverick his space. *Yeah, that's right, Pops; you handle those reins loose. But it might help if you had 'em in the first place.*

I was spooked. There I was telling you there weren't any ghosts, and here I am catching the first car out of town. I got a lift quick. Young boys and chicks are like found money to some of these drivers, and if you don't mind a groping hand or two, the rides come easy.

It took me three tries to make it to the beach. I should only count two though, because the second driver reached over and went crotch deep on me with his hand, forcing me to bail at a red light, but all in all, it only took me about an hour to get seven miles.

Have you ever had a thought that pushes all other thoughts aside? A selfish thought, a thought that stands in the front of your mind and won't let any other thoughts come forward and have a look out? The vision of that young girl was like a fat man standing in front of a rail at the zoo. I couldn't see past her, and I needed her to move.

I'd been warned about the booze, and I saw firsthand what substances affecting the mind could do to me, but I figured I'd grown since then. I was getting used to being in human form, I'd matured; I was even rounding the corner on the physical puberty of this young body, and I was strong. I'd be careful, I'd concentrate on the thought I wanted removed, and I'd let the alcohol be the solvent that did the job. If I stayed strong, it couldn't possibly have any other effect on me. That young demon I ran into was strong. He was getting loaded and was doing well, at least as far as I could see. If he could do it, so could I. I got dropped off at Main and the highway, and I walked to the far end of the beach where I found a quiet spot to sit. It was almost sundown and the fishermen were climbing off the jetty and heading to their cars; soon, there wouldn't be anyone here but the gulls and the waves. As uncomfortable as I was, I decided to wait; I was a virgin as far as getting drunk was concerned, and I thought it best to treat this with respect—no prying eyes invading our wedding night. Yeah, I'd sipped booze before, but that was foreplay—like clumsy hands roaming over hitchhikers in the front seat of a car. I wanted this to penetrate, to tear the thought of that little girl from my mind, and never let it be replaced.

It was dark when I took my first sip. The sun had died long ago and my only light was diffused from the beachfront houses. There was a rotating green beacon at the end of the jetty, but all that did was deepen the green glass shade of the Cutty bottle as the light swept past. The fifth had already been opened—my burglary victim benefactor must have poured herself a small neat drink. I was glad she wasn't greedy.

I held the bottle to my lips and closed my eyes; it was then that I knew the child sat beside me; her hand resting on my thigh. I held my eyes shut and refused to look at her—my skin crawling with prickling waves, my muscles pulled tight against the skeleton of my body. I drank. She squeezed my thigh as if in warning, pleading almost, *Please, let me stay*, but I refused. Eyes closed, I hurriedly drank again. I could taste it this time; the first sip had been obscured by the wishes of her departure, but now I knew the liquid was sweet and sharp in my throat. I could feel it cascading inside—a butcher's knife of warmth cutting a line past my heart and down to my stomach. I drank again, but this time I gulped deep; I could take more down if I opened wide and poured. I had the taste of charcoal and decayed wood in my mouth, and as the alcohol took effect, her small hand loosened its grip on my leg.

I opened my eyes and looked directly at her. Her once-blond hair and green eyes had begun to blur into the evening—a little watercolored girl that'd been too long in the rain and the cold. She was fading. There was one drink left in the bottle—maybe two if I went slowly—but I didn't need anymore. I was done. I slid my hand up the neck of the Cutty and then partially covered the opening with my thumb. I shook it over her, splashing what was left on her face, this unholy water pooling in her eyes. She was smoke now and being dragged down into the sand by the weight of the booze. I stood up and sprinkled the rest over her, finishing the job that the first splashes started. . . .

And that's where you, and I, began this evening—when I bent down and grabbed a handful of sand. Trying to see if the pressure of my grip would force her image through the gaps in my fist, and when I was sure she wouldn't materialize again, I ground the broken shells into my forearm—a raw and bruised reminder of her image.

The beach sloped into the ocean. The large waves had been washing up and over the berm and then pulling the sand back into the sea; in doing so, they'd created a smooth ramp down to the surf. The first wave I met rushed past me and then, in retreat, grabbed at my legs, seeking to hold. But as I was standing near the top of the berm, its strength was not enough to overcome me, and it left unsatisfied. I walked down, closer, welcoming the ocean's grasp. The next wave was stronger, staggering me. In my drunken state, its attempt to pull me under was successful. My legs were swept from beneath me and I was pulled down the bank and below the surface—my body tumbling with the current. I didn't fight it. Why would I? I was comfortable, relaxed, put at ease by the alcohol, and I felt at home in the ocean. My clothes had been removed earlier, and I was ready for bed. I yawned, and instantly my lungs were filled with bitter sand-infused water. I choked, exhaled, and reached for another breath. The fury of the sea was overpowering, tucking me violently into bed, forcing me to sleep. Again, water pushed its way into my nose and mouth. I tried to welcome it, succumbing to the depths, but my body resisted. I vomited, expelling the whiskey and what looked like blood into a cloud around me. The embryonic fluid of a demon, floating in the stomach of the ocean. I gasped again and went dark.

There's nothing for a demon when we die. You humans rant on and on about your afterlife, your white light tunnel to heaven, but for us, death is just a passport to a new assignment. Picture yourself opening a door into a dark room. You step in, close the door behind you, and that's that. No light, no tunnel, no peace; it's just black. The consciousness of your last life escapes like air, slowly released from your lungs—from death to youth—in a long sweet exhale, and then you open your eyes and you're someone else.

The not-quite wasn't going to let me go. *I knew it.* I was too long in this dark night. I should have opened my eyes already—awakening as a baby in a new place. But instead, I was cold and rolling, back and forth. I was a slave chained to a ship—chained to the world.

The first thing I saw as my eyes opened was the beach. It went somersaulting by as a wave washed me up the berm. I was naked, and my limbs were a beautiful shade of robin's egg blue. It was early morning, the sun hadn't fully resurrected, but it had risen. I was being rolled up, and down, each successive wave pushing me further from the sea. My hair hung wet and matted in my face, a lock of sand and blond needing to be spit from my mouth into the air. I was shaking. I tried to stand and get my bearings, but my legs were numb beneath me. I fell twice before I admitted defeat and crawled my way up the beach. Hours I'd been in that ocean, and now, I lay on my back like an overturned turtle, shielding my face from the morning and fighting the air until I could accept its breath with gratitude. I had to move, I couldn't stay there forever.

I stumbled around until I found my clothes; they were piled as I left them, and I took my time dressing. I was glad my body, or my things, hadn't been found by the morning beach patrol. It would take some explaining, a dead boy getting off the table, and walking away.

"I was sleeping, sir."

"You were blue, son. We had a hard time getting you out of the water. We didn't even bother trying to revive you. Are you sure you're okay?"

"You bet, officer. I'm just gonna sit here until my heart starts beating, then I'll get going."

I wandered over to my friend David's house, where, after a brief exchange of what-the-fuck-happened-to-yous, I was invited to hop in his bathtub and warm myself. It was going to take some time.

I lay back against the cool, chipped-white porcelain of their old tub, and I let the hot water rise against the chill in my body. I was tired, and strange as it may sound, I was kinda ready to cash it in. Walking into the world of death did something strange to me. I felt like a child who ran his finger across a frosted cake—that quick taste of sugar couldn't possibly be enough, and the memory of its sweetness was sure to drive me back. I'd never heard of a demon entering that dark room and then being refused exit into a new life. It made me angry. I don't like working for anyone, and I know I ain't pulling the strings around here, but on a day-to-day basis, I don't want to think about others puppeteering my life. And now, the dream of being a slave chained to this world was all too real. The not-quite was forcing me to stay. Dying on that beach would've been cool— a tragic, hip ending to a warped little high school boy. The headlines read: "Naked Body of Local Teen Surfer Found Drifting on Saturday."

Now, that's a nice way to go out. You've got that whole sensational thing working there—teen, naked, surfer. The only thing missing are two coeds and an alien. If I was reading the morning paper, I'd sure get excited. And besides, I had another, practically sentimental reason for wanting to be found dead on the beach; it was because I've had an attraction to the ocean since I was a child.

I started surfing in the winter of 1969. I was eight years old. My father would drive me to the beach in the family wagon—a beat-up old Chevy that I'm pretty sure came off the assembly line with a hundred thousand miles already on it. It was an embarrassment on wheels. I learned how to smoke in that car. My old man would be chain-puffing cigarettes the whole seven miles to the water with the windows rolled up. Just by sitting and breathing next to him I could practically intake a carton a trip. I was gonna ask him one day— after he'd given me a good beating for stealing a pack of his smokes—was it really my smoking that pissed him off, or was he just too cheap to part with a pack?

Either way, my old man dropping me off worked great for both of us. He got to abandon the pain in his ass for a solid eight hours, and I got to disappear into the sea. It didn't matter if the surf was small and mushy, or overhead and hollow, I was there all day.

The ocean has always been a place for forgetfulness and dreams. I needed breaks just like anyone else—times to let go, disappear, and recharge. If you wanted to be touched but didn't want anyone else to lay a hand on you, then the ocean was your friend. It would hold my body in its arms, and I never faulted it for all the lives it took; quite the contrary, I admired the pain the sea had caused. The waves held the voices of the dead and whispered the unfulfilled promises of coming home.

My first surfboard was a ten-six, dark green tank. That's what the kids called 'em, "tanks." They got that moniker because those boards weighed close to a hundred pounds, and if one of them got loose in the surf, it could easily wipe out a battalion of children as it rushed to shore; if it got really crowded—like on a summer day— I'd let my board go on purpose so I could be alone in the lineup. When I got good at riding it, I hammered some nails through the nose, pointy end out—a spiked battering ram. I hated dragging that fucker across the sand—going down wasn't bad, but the trip back up was a real bitch.

Some days the wind would be fighting with the ocean. The

waves would rise up and then be slashed viciously by the gusts. I'd stand shivering on the shore as the bully breezes tired of their game and then staggered drunkenly over the sand. On these days, I'd watch the ocean from the liquor store across the street—a spectator of nature's hustle. It was too wild to surf. There was an alley outside the market, and I'd slouch against the wall—the saltwater drying in crystals on my skin. I pimped change from tourists and practiced looking like Clint Eastwood as I chewed the end off my smoke. I loved the smell of the beach, and the way the days would take their time going home.

"Are you still breathing?" David had opened the bathroom door and poked his head in. I was breathing and actually feeling about ready to regroup.

"Two fucking hours you been in here. Get out."

I answered him, but getting the words out was tough. "I was fucking freezing. I kept running the hot water but your fucking water heater is a piece of shit. Next time your dad robs a bank why don't you tell him to get a new one?"

"You're a fucking asshole. Get the fuck out. And for your information, my dad just said he'd get us a keg!"

David was in my grade at school. He was fifteen, had a pimple for a face, and was sporting hair that was better designed for a clown—his mop was so unruly that it needed a sedative just to be combed. His brother, Terry, was a year younger and a touch better looking, but neither one of them had ever been laid.

They lived with their mother on the weekdays—and that's how I knew them—but on the weekends and the holidays, they went to their dad's place on the beach—that is, if their dad wasn't in jail. If you paint the picture of a fucked-up bank robber in your head, and you make him just a bit scarier and quite a bit dumber, then that's their old man—late fifties, overweight, with dark hair and an extremely greasy mustache, a scar under his left eye, and he goes by the name "Racer." I don't know how the fuck he got tagged that—probably self-named—because I never saw that fucker doing anything fast except going back to jail.

Their pops was a real creep, and his offer to buy a keg was just his way to perv out on teenage beach bunnies in the privacy of his own home. Oh well, it's the gift that counts and not the thought, right?

We had no trouble stocking Daddy's house with good-looking teens. I could always pull girls—with or without a party—and free booze was, after all, free booze. It didn't take long for the house to fill up, and Daddy got his wish: there was no shortage of cheerleader lightweights and bikini-wearing, two-beer pukers.

Contrary to popular belief, there are only two successful aphrodisiacs in this world. The first is starvation, but sadly we won't be dealing with that today. The second consists of sub categories: drug abuse, addiction, and alcohol experimentation. Bank Robber Daddy was counting on one of these teens getting so fucked up that either he'd start looking good to her, or she'd pass out and he'd drag her into his bedroom. I told you he was creepy.

I appreciated his depravity, but I'd be more inclined to deprive him of a need than I would to watch some young girl get taken advantage of. He wanted it more; his addiction to sexual stimulation was easy to see. I was gonna have fun watching this frustrated fuck try to score.

Beer was never really the drink of choice for these young girls though; the majority of them wanted wine—a cheap fruity wine like Boone's Farm Strawberry Hill. They loved the long neck of the bottle and the way their lips would take on a nice shade of pale pink as they drank. I loved the scent of sweetly sour berry when one of them walked into the room. These girls were debutante winos in miniskirts, pissing their undergarments and puking alcoholic Kool-Aid all over the sofa.

The swell had picked up from the night before—practically doubling in size—and you could hear it thumping on the beach behind the house. I was standing in the side yard thinking about the next morning—and how great the waves would be, when Julie showed up. She was older than anyone there (besides "Racer"), and she definitely didn't belong with these kids. She was wearing some sort of beach wrap that made her look like she'd just gotten out of the shower, and her brown hair was pulled back harshly from her face. I was thinking she was coming to see the pops, but if so, she was there to buy drugs, or he was paying for it—he wasn't pulling that kind of ass. I was wrong on both counts; she'd wandered in from another party down the beach.

I walked up to her and started talking—not much really, just the usual shit. I gave her a smart-assed, "What are *you* doing here?" and a hopeful "Can you buy us booze?" I wasn't drinking, but I wanted to keep the party primed. She thought I was cute—some women like assholes, and she stayed close to me, even putting her hand on my back a few times. I found out that she wasn't that old—twenty-two to be exact, but when you're fifteen, anyone who can buy booze is ancient.

The party had wound down. Pops had failed to score. His attempt to drag a young winette into his room had been thwarted by a group of the young winette's friends—after I'd tipped them off, of course. But Julie was hanging around. We'd started kissing a bit earlier, at first a few quick pecks, but now I was practically lapping the booze off her tongue. She made no pretense at modesty—letting her top slide down and flashing a shameless half-tit at young Terry. She loved it, and I decided to see how far she'd take it.

I walked her over to the couch and we sat down. The only party goers left were the six or seven unlicensed young boys that'd be staying over for an early surf session—at times, David and Terry's house was a weekend crash pad for surfers who couldn't yet drive. She was pretty hammered and the pills that I spotted in her purse probably had something to do with her now slurred speech. She cuddled in and purred against my neck.

"I want you to fuck me."

This was what I was waiting for. I was happy to oblige. I took her into a bedroom, and I licked the wine from her lips. We rolled around on the bed, and she drunkenly got tangled in the covers. After I took her clothes off, I let her know what I wanted.

My experience with females hadn't been good. I found them untrustworthy, abusive, and dangerous. I'm not going to say I disliked them—because there was a definite physical attraction to them—but if the image of a viper had ever fit anyone, it would be her—whoever she was at the time—and I took every chance I had to hurt her, before she got to me.

I knew my friend David had never gotten laid, so when I had Julie begging for it, I told her I'd screw her but she had to do David first. She barely argued.

I called him into the bedroom, and she started kissing him. She pushed him back on the bed and, against his feeble embarrassment, pulled off his pants and climbed on top. David was stoked; he lasted all of thirty seconds, and then she came over to do me, but I told her she had to fuck David's brother too. Again, no hesitation. I called Terry into the room, and he got the same treatment, but he was actually a bit more willing than his brother, and he lasted a very impressive five minutes until he also succumbed.

I had that bitch do the whole party, one right after another, until she was done. It was eight fifteen-year-old boys including David and Terry, and they'd all been virgins. I took her after she finished. She was one step above comatose, sweaty and dirty from the sex. I started calling her names before I entered her and I didn't let up. She was crying so I put my hands to her neck to silence her. She was struggling now, a cobra trying to strike as I wrestled an admission of evil from her.

"You're a fucking slut, aren't you?" She was rolling her head from side to side, mouthing the word no.

"You liked fucking all those guys, didn't you?"

"You're just a fucking piece of shit, huh, baby?"

I felt her body shake beneath me, and she let go as I did. I released her neck and there were fingerprint bruises already starting to form where I held her. She was slowly moving from side to side, a true viper trying to burrow into the blankets after she'd fed. She was smiling, content, and satisfied now. She whispered . . .

"I love you."

You've got to be fucking kidding me. I'd just met her, turned her out, called her names, and practically choked the fucking life out of her, and now, she loves me? If I hadn't been able to see this bitch's death, I would have thought I was fucking one of my own kind. She *was* evil.

As I was walking her out—no number exchanged, no plan to get together again—my "lover" was stopped by the boy's dad. He knew what had gone down, and he wanted his share. She turned on him. This girl who had just fucked nine boys fired verbal on the old man.

"You think I'm gonna let you fuck me, you fat piece of shit? Why don't you go jerk off in your hairpiece, old man."

The boys were laughing, and Bank Robber Daddy just stood there slack-jawed with a rapidly shrinking penis as Julie shook her loaded ass right out the door and down the alley.

When I was of age, I'd sometimes go to strip bars with my friends. They'd be saying, "Check out that ass," or "Look at the tits on that bitch," but not me.

I wanted to see the girls' eyes.

I wanted to see what she was thinking about when she danced.

Some of the girls would be balancing their checkbooks; others would be ashamed and turn their heads. Some of them would be bored, but some girls . . . some girls would look you straight in the eyes and fuck you as they danced. They didn't care who saw them, and they didn't care about you. To them, you were a tool—a money-carrying pig. If they got off when they were using you, fine, and if not, it didn't matter to them, because when you became worthless, you were thrown out like yesterday's garbage. I didn't make Julie do anything she didn't want to do, she fucked the room, and I appreciated the way she used us.

## I I I

The surf had doubled during the night, and I could hardly wait to get back into the water.

In the winter, west swells would bounce off the jetty and thread their way towards the beach—big, rolling peaks that would angrily stand and call the beach homes and the pier to battle.

My place was the South Side.

South Side was a West Coast Pipeline, with cold water, no reef, and raw sewage. The San Gabriel River emptied its ass north of the break, and inland garbage swam down the channel into the lineup. One day I saw a dead cow drifting in the current, its twisted legs galloping futilely towards shore.

The city would bring bulldozers out on the big swells, and they'd construct a great berm of sand to protect the houses along the ocean's edge. Diesel fumes choked the air as the sand got piled roof-high before the boardwalk.

I loved paddling out on days of large surf. The ocean becomes exclusive when it rages. Not just anyone can enter; it takes a willingness to be used, to be played with, and maybe to be overpowered to the point of death.

I was a return visitor, and nothing the sea could do would bow me today.

There was a crowd of spectators perched along the berm and hundreds more crowding the railings of the pier. The lifeguards hadn't yet closed the beach, but they were one large set away from shutting it down.

I got suited up at David's—my standard black Speedo, which was basically as close to nothing as possible; as I said before, the ocean was the only thing I allowed to touch me completely. I would have worn nothing if I could have gotten away with it; I prefer to meet the sea unprotected.

I walked slowly up the berm and made a show of heading out. The surfers that were afraid to enter the water got a good look at what they thought courage was, but it wasn't courage that made me enter—as you know, it was my willingness to be drowned.

A huge wave ran towards the beach and threw itself up and over the berm. Spectators were washed down the city side of the barricade—tumbled with their cameras and their dignity into a dirty holding pool of saltwater that separated the boardwalk from the beach. I was untouched.

I didn't wait for a lull in the surf to paddle out, I ran down the slope into the water, sacrificing myself to the next wave that came. It exploded around me, tossing me into the air and viciously slamming me into the sand, but I came up laughing—loud rolling laughs that mimicked the avalanche of the surf.

I righted my board and stroked into the fury of the ocean. I was spinning wildly, the currents grabbing at my legs and arms, shaking and then releasing me, as a father might do when he wrestles with a son. I scratched and clawed my way through threatening walls of greens and browns until I cleared the sets, and then I sat and listened to the eerie stillness around me.

I was the only one out.

Lest you forget, I love the flesh. I use the material world as a weapon. Your desires, your secrets, and your sensation of touch are all distractions, diverting your focus from God. Quiet meditation is a tool of my adversary—the enemy of a demon. The more excitement the better—more thrills, more noise, and more pain or more pleasure. If it feels, then it should feel more. The beach, on a day like this, slammed the door in the face of God. He would not be looking on as the surf thumped, the boulders on the jetty rolled, and the pier groaned and bent under the weight of the crowd. The sirens on the lifeguard jeeps were wailing against the sky, the flash of the cameras, and the roar of the gallery—the hundreds of onlookers calling out each turn, dip, and crash—would shut God out.

A large set appeared on the horizon. I saw it caress the undercarriage of an offshore oil platform as it moved in. It was the largest I'd seen all day. It started with an explosion at the end of the jetty—

slamming into the beacon that was stationed there, shifting the structure of the rocks—and then it swung wide across the channel and headed right at me.

It was a left, really—a wave that dictated the ride should move away from the rocks, but I wasn't going to let this one call the shots. It was a monster and I stroked into it. When the waves reach the size of this one—maybe an eighteen- or twenty-foot crest—the water that moves up their faces is traveling at an unbelievable speed. A wave is a line of energy moving like a hand beneath a blanket, thrusting the surface forward from underneath. I pushed myself down over the ledge as it began to break—a move almost like dropping off a three-story building onto the ground. I stood on the board and I free-fell about halfway down the wave before my board caught an edge. As I felt it grab, I faded towards the left, but then dug deep and wrenched the board in a hard turn towards the right—facing the wave, and heading into it, instead of away. I caught it off guard. The giant wall hit the shallows and lifted into the sky for one sweet second before it threw itself in the direction of the houses on the beach. It was then that I stepped on the tail of my board and kick-stalled it to get as deep as possible in the tube, posing in a soul arch with my arms out and my head thrown back, surrounded by a great screaming cave of water.

The sound inside a large wave is like the roar of a jet—it whispers around you as you travel through it. A vacuum, trying to hold you in place until the roof of the ocean's house can crush you beneath it. I stood in that pit until the pressure of the wave blew me into the shallows and the cheers of the crowd. I was released, a hero untouched.

The screams from the gallery chased any remnant of God from that beach—the excitement absorbing all calm—and as the lifeguards closed the pier, I paddled out for another.

I had an on-again-off-again girlfriend for a couple of years. In fact, I had a few of them. If you're going to have one girl, you might as well have two, and if you have two, well, then three or four would be better. It was only flesh, anyway, and why should I go without, if I felt the need?

When one of these girls would bring me home, it was like a November breeze just blew through the front door—the young lady's cheeks might have been **About a Girl** flushed with the living bewilderment of young love, but her parents were nothing short of cadaverous as they stood frozen against the living room couch.

I'd extend my hand.

"Good evening, Mr. Jones. It's a real pleasure to meet you."

How polite, an offering of a handshake. And if, perchance, he brought that hand close enough to smell, he would have caught the fragrance of his daughter's perfume—the aroma of her virginity played out across my knuckles.

What made these parents let their children walk with me? I would have been at my throat—a wolf ripping through the soft flesh of a rival. Sometimes, the fathers couldn't even meet my eyes. They were afraid of their weakness, and in these cases, I'd let my hand trail across their daughter's lower back as we left the house—sometimes being as brazen as sliding my hand over her ass.

I met Jenny when I was sixteen. It'd been a relatively calm year for me—calm was the usual—minus a few grand flashes. I was burglaring, lying, cheating, and lighting the odd fire or two, but I was also surfing, and swimming for the school team. I was fast, as you might expect, but I was lazy and refused to put any work into my sport. Why work at something when you were as fast as or faster than the other kids just by showing up? I did just enough to get by.

There were times that I had a few issues with the high school faculty, but usually, it was only after one of them had attempted to exert his or her supposed authority over me. Who the fuck did they think they were kidding? A sweater-vest and tie, coupled with a degree from the local city college, did not a leader make. Did you know one of them even took a swing at me once? He was a great big brute who surprisingly was going to live to a very old age—although his last six months were going to be spent getting beatings from an unbelievably sadistic night nurse at Sunnyvale convalescent home.

It was a rainy day and the streets in front of the school were flooded. I didn't own rain boots, and I wasn't about to get my feet wet, so I walked over the hood of a car that was parked at the curb and I crossed the street—nice and dry. I didn't think twice about it, I just continued on my way up the front steps of the school, where I was roughly grabbed and questioned by this fat beast of a teacher.

"Do you walk on the furniture at home?"

I wasn't sure where he was going with this.

"You some sort of monkey or something?" Obviously this fat fuck didn't teach anthropology. I took a quick look at the ridges along his eyebrows and after noting the sloping forehead and the dragging knuckles, I communicated with him as I saw fit.

"Fuck you, asshole. Get the fuck off me."

Oh no, he didn't like that one bit.

I wasn't as big as I am now—6'4", 220 pounds—and he was a heavyweight gladiator. I'm figuring he must have done some of that tight-wearing wrestling bit that some of those boys do, because he was all about grappling, and he only threw one glancing punch. I couldn't shake him off though, so I reached down and grabbed his cock—no wonder he was pissed off, I almost apologized when I felt that thimble-full of dick in my hand. It didn't hurt him.

He dragged me into the office and threw me onto one of the

wooden benches that lined the waiting area. He gave me an order: "You sit the fuck down."

I gave him a reply: "Fuck you."

He was back on me again. A few angry shakes and then he released me, repeating his order. "I said sit the fuck down!"

He reminded me of a man who couldn't get his order straight at a drive-thru restaurant. So I questioned him. "Did you say you want chicken with those fries, motherfucker?"

I thought I had the best of him for a moment—he was having trouble processing my reply. The chicken thing fucked him up, but he snapped out of it and jumped on me again. It was then that the school secretaries got involved—a gaggle of five or six long-necked spinsters rushing to my aid.

"You leave him alone!" they practically cried in unison.

"He's a child. Get your hands off of him!"

What do you know? Thimble dick, the gorilla, must have had a bit of cuckold in him, because when those ladies barked an order, he got all weak and wimpy. They should have made him clean my ass with his tongue.

It was beautiful, the secretaries and a passerby—that just happened to be the senior girls' class president—all came to my defense. They accused this great brute of viciously attacking me, and I got to go home on stress leave—a day or two of "getting my head together" while the teacher was forced to make a formal apology in the school bulletin.

It was different being out of school because someone else fucked up. I missed the angry faces, and I didn't like people thinking that I needed protection. I would have stayed put if they'd let me, maybe even audited one of the gorilla's classes; I could have sat in the back drawing tiny little phallic images and then held them up during his lecture—a judging system based on penis size—but the principal wanted things to calm down. I preferred not. I decided to have a party—a celebration of the gorilla's humiliation.

My parents were going out to dinner that Friday night, so I made a few phone calls and got the word out.

"Show up at Jack's no earlier than six thirty. Bring friends."

I love a good party.

My parents left for dinner at six, their heads filled with images of prime rib and baked potatoes. They were going to take time for themselves, a leisurely meal with cocktails and a wobbly drive home; little did they know, I'd be serving their dessert that evening.

By six thirty-five, there were two hundred kids in the living room and an amateur band was set up under the stairway launching into a terrifying rendition of Zeppelin's "Kashmir." I was ring-leading, and it was a great success.

I had a reputation as a handsome, troublemaking fuck-up, and if a kid was going to a party, well then, who better than me to be his or her host? Something was bound to happen. It was the party of the year.

Jenny showed up at about seven with a couple of friends. She was cute and real clean in that healthy, Midwestern way. She was from the next city over, and her parents had schooled her in keeping Jesus and her vagina sacred—I was able to turn her on that vagina thing, but getting her to shake off Jesus was impossible—besides, why bother, it was way more exciting for me when my target thought the fucking they just got could send them to hell.

It was nice, running into girls from different neighborhoods—their opinions of me were untainted and unformed for the most part. Often, my first introduction to a local girl would be followed by fifteen minutes of why it was safe to talk to me, and no, I didn't really steal a lot of cars.

She wanted to use the phone. It turns out her parents demanded a check-in call.

*There is nothing sexier than a girl that has to check in.*

I was getting aroused just thinking about this white sheet laid out in front of me—I was going to Jackson Pollock the fuck out of her with the dark mud of depravity. I handed her the phone, and she bent down—sticking her head into the clothes dryer to shield Mommy and Daddy from the noise.

"Yeah, Mom. We went to dinner at Laura's, and now we're in line for the movie."

Hmmm, she might have been clean, but like all women, she was a liar. . . . There's nothing like a woman's willingness to bend the truth.

I decided to let her be for a while; I needed to think over my approach. I was wondering if I should go with the "scared kid whose party got out of control" thing, thinking this might play to her good-girl nature. Or, I could swing with the "I'm popular and you should really dig me because everyone else does" role. It was a toss up. Maybe after I took a lap or two around the house it might come to me.

Things were getting loose that night—a few fights, and every five minutes or so, another beer bottle broke on the kitchen floor. I was probably going to get my ass kicked for this little soirée, but as an unbelievably amazing-looking senior kissed me on the cheek and said, "Great party," I realized it would be worth it.

I decided to run crowd control. There was a traffic jam of coeds at the front door and no one could get in or out of the house—the bodies were stacked so deep that if a fire broke out it would be nearly impossible to escape. I thought about running around to the garage, grabbing a can of gas, and barbecuing half the student body, but I held it together—wishful dreaming. After all, I did need a place to sleep that night. I forced my way up front and leaned in hard. It only took one heavy-set tumbling girl to clear the way. She went down and took half the porch with her. I was laughing at her embarrassing discomfort, and I almost had the door completely shut—only four or five inches to go—when an extremely hairy arm with my father's wristwatch attached to it forced its way through the opening and then made frantic grabbing motions at whoever was the door monitor—me. I alerted the party.

"Get the fuck out! It's my dad!"

It was like an atomic bomb had just been detonated in the living room. Teenage bodies were blown out the doors and the windows—an explosion of running breathless children flash-firing into the street, leaving only your proverbial cloud of dust . . .

Except for me.

I was tethered to my father's hand—a successful grab on his part had snatched me as I was retreating from the front door—and I was now getting the party-throwing life choked out of me. I saw Jenny run by—a look of pity on her angelic face—and in that instant, I had my plan. I was going to go with the "bad boy with a heart of gold who just needs the right woman to straighten him out" thing. I mouthed the words, "Thanks for the inspiration, Dad," before my body—without sufficient air—collapsed on the front entryway.

Jenny should have known better from the start. She could see I was out of control, but I think somewhere deep inside it turned her on. Some women love reforming criminals and saving stray dogs.

Now, some of you might wonder why I'm even bothering to write about this girl, and if not for one thing, she wouldn't have made it into this tale. You already know that I'm selfish, inconsiderate, abusive, and sadistic. It's also in my nature to be warped and yes, even, as you might say, evil. And if you'd like to use the word monster, I wouldn't fault you; after all, I've given you the background. However, even I wouldn't subject you to one more enjoyable story about me causing others pain unless this narrative benefitted. You see, it wasn't in what I did to Jenny that mattered; it was what I did to get her that you need to know about.

Jenny was a Christian—a Lamb of God.

This didn't mean she was any more protected than anyone else, quite the contrary. You can't study the "supposed" good, without having knowledge of the "supposed" bad. These Christians actually make themselves easy prey to me and my kind by their judgment. They place themselves directly below the throne of God, and they open themselves to all sorts of attack. Ignorance is not evil;

evil takes an intent to act against what you think is good. If these Christians think sex is bad and wrong, and yet their bodies cry out for procreation, well then where do you think we hit 'em? That's right; we go straight for the balls.

When man was first created, he had no knowledge of evil. He was simple; a moron, two steps above retarded—a half-moon crescent of a smile hanging underneath a pair of dull brown eyes. He was an animal, basically a cow, lolling in the pasture of his Lord, and it was the not-quite you can thank for that cow's ability to reason.

Shortly after creation, God and the not-quite were out for a stroll through the garden. God was showing my boss his handiwork—sort of a "see how great I am" look around, and they ran into Man. He was squatting naked on the edge of a river, relieving himself in his drinking water.

"So what's this, then?" the not-quite asked God, as he pointed to the animal.

"It's a man," God proudly replied. "He can think for himself."

The not-quite chewed that over for a moment and then he asked, "So what's so good about that, then? All these other animals think for themselves; they seek shelter, they find food, and they breed. What makes this one so special?"

God was stumped. It was like he just realized he designed a car with no motor. My boy had him, but he had to go lightly . . .

"Does he think above mere existence?"

"Oh yes," God replied, "he ponders the stars in the heavens, the earth and its mysteries, the creation of all."

And as He was speaking, God was instilling these attributes into man. Man's eyes were beginning to sparkle, his stupid grin was settling down into a more purposeful line of lip, and my boy moved . . .

"And does he question even you, and does he have the knowledge of good and evil?"

"Of course he does . . ."

God was caught, and man was filled with doubt and knowledge, before God knew what happened. God rounded on the not-quite. He was angry, but He was also a God who wouldn't admit to being wrong.

"Yes," He proudly replied, "I created him with all that. I created him with the ability to see that I was a good God—a God of love, wisdom, and kindness, a God to thank and to respect."

It was then that man noticed his visitors—and his fouled drinking water. He walked up to God and asked him a question.

"Who are you, and what the fuck are you doing in my garden?"

When you're trying to entrap a Christian girl, you have to go to church—that was the give to my get. I had to play the part of a boy ready to conform, a boy seeking forgiveness, a penitent boy crawling on his knees before God.

Okay, so *now* what?

Did you think I was going to burst into flames when I walked inside the church? This isn't some bullshit Hollywood movie about demons that are afraid of holy water. I love the shit; I'd bathe in it if I could, it's actually a bit cleaner than what comes out of the tap. I did everything I needed to get in her pants, including saying, "I love Jesus too," and I wasn't struck down or harmed in any way. The Man doesn't work that way.

Jenny and I would sit in church and as the pastor gave his usual spiel on hell and the Revelation, I'd gently let my hand come to rest on her thigh, I'd ever so slightly turn my fingers inward, and then I'd slowly push my hand up as far as she'd let me, sometimes making it to, and resting it on, her crotch before she pushed it away. Oh, she was principled, that's for sure, even setting a three-month rule on our dating before she let me go "all the way."

I didn't remember Christ adding the three-month no-pussy clause into the Ten Commandments but somehow she thought this was a good standard for non-sluts or Christian teens. I was pissed, she'd already given it up to some other dude, so I didn't understand why it had to be kept nice for me—once a bag of chips was open, the polite thing to do was pass it around before they got stale.

When it came time to seal the deal, she got out candles and incense. She made me say a prayer with her before we took off our clothes, and then she reverently crawled into my bed. I guess she figured that since I'd made it three months, she could give me any part of her I wanted, and I wouldn't think she was loose or dirty. So she did. There wasn't a known position or port-of-entry that didn't get filled, and she did it all in a very respectful, religious way.

In a way, it was she that entrapped me—making me hang around, listening to all that talk of love and redemption. I was digging the flesh, but she was making me pay for it with the Word. She joined an offshoot religious group—small, maybe five or six players—and I was therefore forced to come along. Things got tight. There wasn't any more cruising for pussy during the prayer groups. If my hand was laid on her thigh, it'd better be for healing purposes and nothing else, because there were six pairs of eyes watching my unholy intentions. I was asked to speak in tongues— a language that came to me easily—and I was told to learn scripture, also easily done. They thought they had the beginning of a real convert, and you know what, they were right. Some of that crap was starting to wheedle its way in. I was almost starting to feel bad for what I'd done when I "backslid" and got arrested.

It was a simple vandalism deal. No real crime, as far as I was concerned. A couple of my acquaintances and I purloined a few machetes and we snuck into Disneyland after it was closed to chop up a few rides. I was thinking of taking the head off Snow White— breaking into her bullshit little kiddy-ride and decapitating the dwarf-fucking whore—but we got caught. Disneyland has its own army of underground police and we were radared in and rounded up in the twinkling of a wand. It was an Adventureland army of Gestapo that dragged us off to the Disneyland jail where we were then extradited into the Anaheim city lock-up.

It wasn't the first time I'd been arrested. I'd been picked up on a few minor charges before, but I always got a break. The not-quite had given me an invisible get-out-of-jail-free card. There was always a problem with my arrests—paperwork would get lost, victims would refuse to testify, judges would display unheard of leniency—and I always walked easy.

This time I spent the night in jail, and in the morning I was brought before a judge. I pled guilty—figuring at the most I'd get a twenty-five dollar fine (the cost of admission to the amusement park) and since no chopping had been done, I figured it strictly an issue of entry fee. I was wrong, but I caught a break as usual. He could have given me six months for trespassing plus, but the judge only sentenced me to five days in the county jail.

I wasn't pleased.

The lack of manners in our county facilities is appalling. The detainees might be masters in the skill of getting caught, but not a one of them was well versed in table manners. I refused to eat. It wasn't any big deal, I didn't drag my feet and swear allegiance to some grand political movement, and none of the guards knew any-thing about it; I just wasn't about to eat watery, light yellow imitation eggs while the badly tattooed, sweating pig from God's great earth was sitting across from me, wiping his watery-yellow snot on his county-issued sleeve and burying his face in his trough. Besides, it was only a few days.

Jenny picked me up at the gate.

I could tell something was wrong as soon as I got in the car. Her eyes were puffy, almost bee-stung swollen, and I could tell she'd been crying. I knew it couldn't have anything to do with my bull-shit arrest—how the fuck can you be a good Christian if you haven't done a little backsliding? I mean, after all, Jesus needs something to save you from, doesn't he?

"It was Andy," she sobbed.

*What? Who the fuck is Andy, and what did he do to me?*

"I couldn't help it," she blubbered. "You were gone. I was angry."

"Who the fuck is Andy?" I had no idea what she was talking about.

"Andy. My old boyfriend. I slept with him last night."

I threw a punch before even thinking. It was a bad intentioned right-cross that flew from the passenger side armrest and traveled into the side of her head; the force of the blow slamming her face against the driver's window.

"You fucking bitch."

I was on her. Out of my seat and on top of her—the car veering wildly as she pulled it to the curb. I reached into the center console and grabbed the knife I kept there. I held her throat with one hand as I cocked my arm back, poised with the knife in my hand. The blade quivered and flashed, hung in space for a moment before it dove and caught the momentum it would need to pierce her heart.

Jenny grabbed her purse and swung it in front of her—a flow-ered light-brown leather cross to ward off evil—and the knife hit the thick purse and was reflected into her upper thigh.

I missed.

I looked up into her face and caught the unforgettable mask of terror. Excited, I was ready to stab again. I pulled the knife back and then I saw it. It wasn't just terror that played out across her face; it was resignation, acceptance . . . and desire?

You've got to be fucking kidding me. This bitch thought she deserved what I was doing to her. She thought she deserved to be beaten and stabbed for cheating on me.

I dropped the knife.

Of all the fucked-up things I've done I never once made someone believe they deserved to be punished. That little bit of love that wheedled into me through those prayer groups made one move on my character before I dumped its ass in the street. I almost felt sorry for her. I opened the car door and got out. She was crying, begging me to get back in. I slammed the door and jogged off, cutting down a tight alley so Jenny couldn't follow. I called out to God. I figured he wasn't about to show, but I knew he heard me.

"You're a fucking bitch. You got that little girl so sick she thinks she deserves to be hurt."

I could hear her honking in the background and Jenny calling my name.

"I should go back. Finish her off. Send her to you, huh?"

I slowed to a walk.

"You're no different than me. And it's no wonder, since I have your blood flowing through me. Come to think of it, you and the not-quite have an uncanny resemblance—you're both total fuck-holes."

Jenny had blocked the alley from the other end. I stopped talking as I walked up to her. She was looking for forgiveness, but I had none. I grabbed her body and pushed my mouth against hers, forcing my tongue between her lips. She didn't fight. I lifted her skirt, tore her underwear off, and then entered her as I pushed her back against a dumpster. I could feel the remains of Andy in her as I took her.

I decided to rev up my game against the Man, vowing that any building dedicated to His Holy Honor would now become a target. But unlike Him, I was non-denominational in my attacks; be it a synagogue, a church, or a temple, they would all suffer equally at my hand.

There's a lot of new-age bullshit floating around this world—and most of it is just entrepreneurial nonsense devised by television crazies to part well-heeled wannabe believers from their money. But for a demon, the Law of Attraction really does work. If I needed something, say a tool to bust the window out of a car, all I had to do was picture myself rearranging a nice thick chunk of Detroit glass and—*pow!*—I'd have what I needed. Sometimes it would be a crowbar, or a piece of cement, or an ornamental lawn boulder; whatever I desired would appear.

## Out of the Closet

Things came to me when I wanted them. And now I wanted an army.

I first heard punk rock in 1977, and I was struck. It was a Sunday night, and I was sitting in the car, getting ready to vandalize a church. I had a can of spray paint and an idea. I'd passed by this monstrosity dedicated to You Know Who earlier, and I felt the front entryway needed something a little more inviting.

It was night, but not quite dark enough to make a move—the early evening dog walkers and the cocktail-after-workers hadn't settled in yet, so I was spinning the radio dial, slumped down in the car seat. I was traipsing through the usual bullshit and soft-chord rock; this shit was great if you had a girl in the car—nothing says "I won't tell all my friends I fucked you" like a little Fleetwood Mac. I was almost at the end of the dial, two turns away from the Mexican stations, when I heard it: a simple hard chord, almost like an old Chuck Berry riff—if Chuck were hammered and didn't know how to play. But it wasn't so much the chord that caught me, it was the words—they were angry, forceful, and they were openly claiming what I tried so hard to hide. The DJ that night played songs about anarchy and murder, drug use and burglary; he played songs extolling the deepest desire to kill; and he played songs about the eyes of killers. It was as if someone had held a microphone to my thoughts and played the tape in front of a backing band of cut-throats and body-snatchers. I blushed.

I don't know if you've ever held a secret. Maybe you're a young boy chomping on cock and you don't want your daddy to know; or, maybe, as a young girl, you'd been lusting after your high school gym teacher—the woman with a face like a catcher's mitt and an ass like a blackboard—and you were afraid to tell your girlfriends that boys weren't really your thing, that your little cunny got all tingly and moist when Ms. Jacobs showed you how to hold a racquet. Well, that's how I felt. I'd been wanting to openly hurt you for years. I was feigning being human when, in reality, all I wanted to do was stand on my chair and yell, "Die, motherfucker!" I wanted to make you hurt like you'd never hurt before; I wanted to be your worst memory.

I didn't know what to do. I could sense this music was a turning point—a pathway laid out on a most evil road, but I wasn't sure if I was supposed to take it or not. I didn't have to wonder long.

"Is that the Krylon Flat Black you have in your hand, or are you going with a glossier look tonight?"

It was a voice on the radio commenting on my medium for vandalism. It was the not-quite. I laughed.

"It's neither," I said as I held up the cans. "I thought the priest might like a cherry-red dick on his door and a canary yellow 'Cum Worship' on the bricks."

His laughter was like static, blown through a comb and wax paper.

"Do you like it, Jack?"

"Do I like what?"

"It's for you, you know."

These fucking Gods; they think everybody's an omnifucking-knowitall. I didn't get it. *What is for me? The song? The church? The paint? What the fuck was he talking about?*

He continued. "I want you to come out."

"What?" Incredulous disbelief rolled over me. "You want *me* to cop to being a demon?" I wasn't about to be openly waving the rainbow flag of hell through my neighborhood.

"Not really," he said. "I want you to get involved. You're perfect for this. You've always wanted an army, and this is where you'll find them . . ."

*Anytime this fucker is ready to become clear I'll be listening, but this raving bullshit is . . .*

"I want you to join a band, you fucking idiot! Get followers, get fans, start a fucking band!"

The music abruptly returned, and I thought he'd left, when . . .

"By the way, there's an unlocked door on the back of this church and they just got a new PA; it's a little heavy. You might want somebody to help you lift it."

### III

The trick to building a great force is to first surround oneself with those of like mind—and yet, I knew they couldn't be *too* like. I didn't need six or eight other leaders, but I also didn't want all mindless followers. An officer needed to bring something to the table—mostly strength; but fear, in great measure, was also a quality you could not ignore; and creativity, the ability to please me in ways I wouldn't think to turn (new terrors, new madness)—and yet all the while remain under my command. I pictured myself running with a band of rogues—each with their own strength—slashing and burning, torturing prisoners and ransacking buildings. I couldn't quite see their faces, what with all the smoke and flame, but I knew that when I saw them on the street, their actions would beckon them to me.

I had gym class with this little skater chick named Danni. Danni was a boyish-looking cute—not something you'd pound on a Friday, but definitely middle of the week fare. She'd sit all doe-eyed begging me to tell her tales of robberies and sexual escapades, and I obliged. Picture me preening in the sun as I rolled sneaky business off my tongue. Danni came to me one day and she was excited; she said she'd met someone just like me, and she thought the two of us should meet. I doubted he was "like" me, but I agreed to stop by her house and introduce myself.

I knew him in an instant.

His human parents had called him Todd, but they could have called him "mistake" just as easily. Todd was a big spoiled kid, whose father had supposedly tried to kill him when he was younger, and whose mother had, for years, ingested great heaps of methamphetamine with her coffee—*would you like one spoonful, or two, Susan?* Todd now resided with his grandparents, Bob and Lillian. I was the first of our kind that he'd ever met and, upon first glance, I could see the nervousness in his face. I put him at ease with a few questions, disregarding any of the usual preliminary talk that one uses with a new friend.

"Don't you just love it, Todd, when it's late at night, and you're inside a home, and the occupant wakes up and hears you?"

"Yes, I do."

"And when you're running down the street—your heart trying to beat its way out of your chest—and you hear that unmistakable revving roar of a police cruiser coming hard down on you . . ."

"Yes," he replied, his eyes partly glazed. "Yes, I love it."

"And when you hear the coppers shouting at their partners, and the good Samaritans getting involved, yelling, 'He's in there, he's in there . . .'"

"Yes," he shouted. He was a convert ready to commit. "I fucking live for that shit!"

"Well, then . . ."

## AN AMERICAN DEMON

He saw his likeness as I painted a mental picture of a business of evil, theme-songed by a band that was more a front for destruction than it was a group of musicians.

He was whole-heartedly in.

I didn't know the first thing about being in a band and neither did Todd. When I was younger, I'd pretended to be a singer, but that's all it was—I'd jump on the bed with a fake microphone yelling out what lyrics I could remember from AM pop-rock tunes. It usually ended up with me falling into a dresser or a chair and coming up with a lump on my head and real blood for make-up.

In reality, I couldn't hit a note if I tried.

I was glad the not-quite had come up with punk rock, because I would have been fucked if he'd wanted me to belt out show tunes. That might have been kind of funny though, seeing gangs of Liza Minnelli look-alikes cruising around in rhinestone-covered cars, getting in fist fights with the police. It's a drag I couldn't sing.

I knew we needed instruments—I was pretty sure on that—but the singing thing didn't seem to matter that much. I'd grabbed a couple of punk rock 45s from Zed's, the local punk record shop, and the singers on most of these discs were awful. Some of 'em sounded like they didn't have any teeth and were insanely drunk when they recorded—I later learned that both of these assumptions were pretty much right on.

Danni had an old guitar and an amplifier—a birthday present from her mother—in her room, so we borrowed them with the promise that we'd bring them back. After a few practice sessions, that guitar was worthless. We didn't know how to tune it, so we yanked off all but the top two strings. We'd slide our fingers up and down the neck, stopping when it sounded cool. We didn't show it much respect—when we weren't trying to play it, we hammered nails with it or used it to baseball trash into the neighbor's yard.

I've heard of guys having a "band plan," or an outline for success, but we didn't. The not-quite hadn't given me any real orders other than start a band, so that's what I did. These fucking deities don't really work like that anyway. I think it's 'cause they can see too far into the future, and they're lazy fuckers that don't like giving you all the details. They've seen the outcome, so they take for granted that you see it too. I mean, look at that shit with Moses. God drags this old Hebrew on top of a mountain, hands him a couple of rocks with a few rules scribbled on 'em, and then He says, "Handle it." Yeah, great plan, guy—how 'bout a detailed plan of attack?

"Moses?"

"Yes, Old Great Burning Bush."

"I want you to run these downstairs and show 'em to the guys. Now, Hezekiah isn't going to like it so when he says, 'What the fuck?' I want you to hit him with tablet one—commandments one through five—but get ready to turn around because Enosh is going to try and jump on your back, so you hit him with tablet two—commandments six through ten. And I recommend the lamb for dinner. And the figs? Well, you probably shouldn't fuck with them because . . ."

You know, detailed instructions.

Come to think of it, these deities probably shouldn't be too pissed off when we fuck up; if you don't tell someone exactly what you want, how can you get pissed when we don't comply?

I figured my "involvement" would just be mayhem as usual—maybe stepped up a bit, and seeing as how we were officially a band now, we probably needed to start advertising—come up with some sort of trademark that we could spray paint on walls. I love logos; they're eye-catching, and they convey such powerful messages with one quick glance. I had a couple favorites that I'd used from time to time—I couldn't claim authorship, but the patent wouldn't be enforced.

We were out on a run one evening—not jogging, I hadn't taken to working out; a run was what we called burglaring, or any other nefarious activity that involved sneaking about. We were at the local high school, breaking into the band room to steal instruments. They were shit, but what do you expect? I lived in a state that refused to support live music in the classrooms—we had to take what we could get. I grabbed a saxophone and a stand-up bass, Todd got some bullshit crate full of percussion gear and a marching drum—fucking big kid, I don't know how he thought that a box full of maracas and metal triangles was gonna work in a punk rock band, but that's what he took. We were on the way out when I saw it—a beautiful mural painted on the front wall of the band room, happy children marching with their instruments beneath a rainbow. *How nice.* I stopped Todd and asked him to take a look. Todd was a great artist—most demons are—and we decided that since the school supported wall painting, we'd be generous and spend the rest of our evening adding to their gallery.

I had a case of spray paint at home—in fact, I had a few of them. My father was always hassling me to get a job, so I got a gig at a paint store. The spray paint had been purchased using my hide-shit-in-the-trash-can discount.

We drove over to my parents', picked up the paint, and set to work. We had time; it was only midnight, so I figured we'd have a solid five hours before the earliest janitor would arrive.

I've always been interested in art. It's so expressive, so liberating, and so soothing. I grabbed a can of spray paint, removed the cap, and made a grand flourish with my arm—a vertical stroke filled with intent and purpose. To that stroke I added another, horizontal—a line representative of the edge of night—and to those two, I added four more—two vertical, two horizontal. It was complete. I stood back to appreciate my work. Beautiful . . . a six-foot swastika painted on the front windows of the administration office.

"Grisham!" It was Todd.

"What the fuck are you doing over there?"

*Jesus Christ, some people don't appreciate talent.*

Todd had been busy. The walkways had been decorated like the sidewalks on Hollywood boulevard, but no stars adorned these squares; it was a yellow brick road of swastikas and death heads that meandered through the quad.

We left no empty spaces. Hours we toiled—great clouds of paint dust hanging in the air, filling our lungs and nostrils with the fine granules of that shiny gloss black.

When we were through, and the small twelve-ounce bodies of used spray paint cans lay abandoned on the pavement, I surveyed our work. It was a gallery, an outdoor gallery dedicated to hurt and pain. And the centerpiece, the first thing you saw as you walked onto the school grounds, was a mural—a larger-than-life painting of Hitler with the words "Nigger Torture Chamber" displayed at his feet.

There was practically nothing the school could do. The janitors arrived at five a.m. to a horror show of World War II nightmares and Alabama neckties, and thankfully, some of them were old enough to remember. Solemnly, they brought out the brown butcher paper and they set to work covering the paintings; a sand blaster was ordered and the sidewalks were scrubbed clean from end to end. There was a small blurb the next day in the local paper—a note from one of the older teachers at the school; all it asked was "Why?"

I'll tell you why. Because it fucking hurts you, that's why. We could have walked into that school and drawn Disney cartoons using the same paint, the same grand strokes, and all it would have been was a pain in the ass to the clean-up crew—a cute, stupid prank that got out of control, but we didn't. We reached into the dark consciousness of the mind and we pulled out pain, and we used the logos of your hate against you. Do you think I believe in that shit—the color differences in your fucking skin? I live in the eternity of night, and the weak flesh you're draped in is nothing to me. Have you ever seen a soul? I have. I've seen the transition from death to life, the mass amount of energy leaving the body, and the small amount of energy left in the skin that slowly, through disintegration, returns to the earth, and I can tell you that when the soul leaves, its color is clear.

I picked symbols with a story, and I let your mind fill in the details.

I once saw a bumper sticker, and it read, "Don't ask why." What a ridiculous slogan, the *why* is everything, because the *why* is where the pain comes from. If you human scum didn't question, you wouldn't hurt. But when a tragedy occurs you want the details—the whole story, front and back. Who was involved, what happened to them, and why? I communicated with you in a simple language that you could easily understand.

I couldn't very well just walk up to strangers on the street and wail the fuck out of them with a hammer, could I? You wouldn't get it. Don't get me wrong, the idea of randomly walking into a grocery store and whacking the checkout girl in the head with a two-by-four is enough to keep me giggling for days, but you need a back story, to make it worthwhile.

A swastika and a death's head convey a message that's already been written. You knew the story when you saw the markings, you knew the pain, and just like that pattern of wavy white lines on a red aluminum can, you knew you were getting "the real thing." Actually, it's plagiarism on my part—but I've always been a bit lazy.

### I I I

Todd had a back room at his grandparents'—I think it might have served as a pseudo-guesthouse at one time—and we converted it into a clubhouse for wayward young adults. It was where we practiced, and it was called "The Studio."

The walls were covered in graffiti and dirty pictures; we had a wheel of fortune that we'd spin for our daily activities: drugs, robberies, booze, sex; whatever the arrow landed on, we'd do. Todd had also built a half-pipe for skating; it was plywood and decorated with two large swastikas. On the top of the ramp was a sign: Bergen-Belsen activity ramp.

Todd's grandparents rarely said anything.

There were mornings when we'd lay out all the things that we'd stolen the night before on the driveway. Musical equipment, bicycles, guns, and clothes—everything neatly ordered and ready for cataloging. Todd or I would stand on the garage roof with a camera—we loved the bird's-eye-view of our take—and we'd snap shot after Polaroid shot of our goods. (The Polaroid was also a gift from a burglary.) If Todd's grandfather or grandmother questioned the loot, Todd would play the spoiled baby, telling them to "get back in the house," or that "it's just stuff we picked up."

In between the cataloging, vandalizing, and the burglaring, we'd rehearse. The percussion gear had been baseballed into the neighbor's yard, and the stand-up bass had been jettisoned onto the freeway—a delightful throw off an overpass into heavy rush-hour traffic—but the marching drum we kept. It was spray painted black, adorned with my favorite logo, and turned on its side.

I would bang on the drum and yell obscenities at the neighbors as Todd strummed those two strings. Our first songs were simple— mainly covering the topics of hippie infestation, too much government, and racial tolerance. We were against racial tolerance and hippie infestation, but the government? None of us had ever been taxed, or poorly represented, and, as a matter of fact, there wasn't too much governing of us going on at all, but yelling, "Kill the President" to proud veterans was always fun.

We picked up a few other band members from the skate park and the high school. Todd switched to the drums full time after we acquired a very nice kit from a Mexican restaurant; Pat joined us on bass, and our friend Tom on guitar. I continued to scream—it didn't take talent—and since I was a master at extracting negative emotion through the spoken word, it fit me.

Tom was the muscle in our group. He looked like Clark Kent, yet behaved like Lex Luthor when aroused. Tom was not to be fucked with. I never saw him lose a fight, and for a human, his ability to black out and separate himself from pain was amazing. I watched him beat a man one night; I laughed as blow after blow expanded the features on the victim's face. At one point, Tom reached his arm around the man's neck and wrenched his body—in a police-type chokehold—to the ground. The victim, in a last-ditch effort to get away, sunk his teeth deep into Tom's arm, trying to force Tom to release. He might as well have been biting rubber. Tom calmly looked up at me—a trail of blood starting to trickle from the victim's clenched mouth and down the sides of Tom's arm—and asked, as if requesting a cigarette, "Jack, can you kick this fucker's head off my arm?" I happily obliged, with a steel-toed release on the arm biter's face.

We were a three-piece—guitars, drums, and mouth—and we called ourselves Johnny Koathanger and the Abortions, or JKA for short.

I was Johnny and we were absolutely unforgivable.

This was not art, and if, perchance, we were gigging before the Superior Court our first amendment rights would definitely not apply. Our logo was a coat hanger with a baby speared on it.

You might be questioning the three-piece, when I just told you there were four of us—and if so, you're paying attention. Pat sucked. He was a demon with absolutely no musical talent whatso-ever. The only thing Pat was good at was mayhem. If his IQ was above sixty, then you fronted him a few points. He was the stupidest demon I'd ever met.

One night, while leaving a concert, Pat was stopped by a police officer and questioned about his underage drinking. The officer asked Pat to exit his vehicle, but instead of getting out, Pat rolled down his window, grabbed the officer's arm, and held on as he drove off.

Pat dragged him through the parking lot and as he let him go, the cop's partner, who Pat ran over at the end of the parking lot, fired a few rounds into the back of Pat's car. When Pat was finally stopped—and brutally beaten for running—he asked the officers, "What's the matter, sir? Did I do something wrong?"

## I I I

Danni had called twenty times in two hours, and it was getting annoying. She wanted her guitar back, and I wasn't giving. We'd picked up plenty of guitars since we'd borrowed hers, and we really didn't need it—but what's mine is mine, and if you told me you wanted something bad enough, you definitely wouldn't get it.

"Come on, Jack. My mom says I'm grounded till I get it back. Bring it over."

"No." I hung up.

Ring . . . Ring . . . Ring.

"Come on, I'll do anything, just come over."

"No." I hung up again.

I could have done it all day—I loved fucking with people on the phone, but my dad was grumbling about the incessant string of calls.

Ring . . . Ring . . . Ring.

I picked it up, cupped the receiver with my hand, and whispered into the mouthpiece, "I told you no, and if you call here again, I'm going to drive over there and beat the living fuck out of you. Do you understand?"

I hung up. And for safety's sake, I took the phone off the hook and left the house. It was a nice afternoon—sunny and clear, a perfect southern California day. I walked a short two miles over to Todd's.

When I got there, Todd was pissed. His phone was off the hook. Danni had been calling him too. She was out of her mind. A fucking obsessive little skate-rat, going crazy, locked in her parents' cage.

I sat on the couch in Todd's room and we watched porn.

Todd was a bit of a defect sometimes. He was fun as fuck, but he was obsessed with pornography. Anytime you visited him, he was jerking off, openly, and he didn't care who knew it. I saw him chatting with his grandmother once, a hard-on protruding from the hole in his boxer shorts.

It was a pretty good film that Todd was showing that afternoon—*Tied up Teens*, one of my favorites.

I was just settling in, getting relaxed, when I heard Pat's voice outside. He was talking to Todd's grandmother about her birds. Pat thought that he'd heard one of the canaries talking.

"If he said anything, Pat," said a creaky old grandma voice, "he said, 'Ronald Regan for president! Ronald Regan for president!'"

I couldn't see how Todd continued to jerk off with that going on.

Pat broke into the room

"Danni's out of her fucking mind. She's been calling me all day trying to get me to fuck her or something."

Todd stopped jerking off.

The phone rang. It was Danni—Todd's grandmother had put the phone back on the receiver after translating canary speak, and now Danni was at it again.

I took the call while a semi-erect Todd yelled at his Granny.

"We're gonna drive over there and kick your fucking ass. I told you to fucking stop it . . ."

Danni cut me off. "Fucking do it then. Do it. Kick my fucking ass. I want it."

I hung the phone up and made sure she couldn't call back by yanking the cord out of the wall. Todd wouldn't care; he loved that kind of shit.

We waited until it was dark and the three of us snuck up to a window on the side of Danni's house. I took off the screen and Pat knocked on the glass. When Danni opened it, I grabbed her by the hair and dragged her out—tearing the skin of her stomach with a nail that was carelessly hammered into the sill. I threw her on the ground and kicked her—a shot viciously aimed at her ass. I didn't have a problem with this. Danni wasn't some Christian thinking she deserved punishment—she was just a bitch, a cousin of all the other fucking bitches I'd run into.

Pat lifted the shocked Danni off the ground, threw her over his shoulder, and carried her to the car—a teenage grocery bag being mishandled by the lot boys. He threw her in the backseat and jumped on top of her. I drove, while Todd and Pat took turns beating on her.

We took her back to Todd's and tied her up.

The studio smelled like mildewed carpet and stale beer. It was dark—maybe a small light or two throwing faint images on the wall, but for the most part . . . dark. It was a dungeon, and three fiends had just dragged a young girl into its mouth.

Danni's wrists were tied with cord and then pulled up over her head and secured to a hook hanging from the ceiling. We wrapped duct tape around her face, closing her mouth. Her eyes were frightened as she stabbed glances in our directions, but her looks did little to penetrate our intentions. I picked up a half-filled glass with what looked like orange juice and tossed it in her face, the orange liquid tie-dying her nightgown. Todd kicked her legs out from under her, and I heard the bones in her shoulders pop as she went down. She was hanging now, swinging from the ceiling. I leaned in and held her nose closed with my thumb and index finger, the duct tape blocking her mouth. Todd and Pat laughed as she struggled for breath.

"I told you what we were going to do, didn't I?"

She shook her head yes violently, trying to go along, get on our team, gain herself some leniency. But there was none.

"Should have kept your fucking mouth shut, huh?"

More shakes of the head, but they were stronger now, urgent pleas for release.

Todd jumped in. He took his hand and ran it up the inside of her thighs where he roughly grabbed between her legs.

"She's wet! The fucking bitch is getting off on this."

I was done.

The minute I knew she dug it I lost my groove.

"What the fuck are you doing?" Pat now questioned me as I cut her down.

"Fuck her." I said, "Let's dump her on her fucking lawn and go score. I wanna burn something."

I threw her over my shoulder and carried her out. She was hugging my arm as I walked. I opened the back gate and walked out to the driveway.

"What the fuck are you doing?"

It was Danni's mom. Danni's little brother had seen us driving off with her and he'd ratted us out. I put Danni down and started stuttering an explanation.

"I'm sorry, Mrs. Trainor. I didn't mean anything. I was . . ."

*Slap!*

Danni's mother slapped Danni in the face with a rocket ship blow.

"You little bitch! You whore! What the fuck are you doing?"

I almost fell over, and I had to hold hard to keep the laughter inside. This mother thought so much of her child that she believed her little whore had been up to no good. This was way better than the kidnapping. This was real. Danni begged.

"Please, Mom, you don't know what they did to me. They—"

*Slap!*

"Please, I'm begging you, Mom."

Danni's mother grabbed her rougher than we did, and she hair-pulled her to the car. The cries of her daughter went ignored, the tears forced into the backseat.

I was given a see-you-in-jail stare as they left, but I needn't worry. I was protected, and anyway, no mother like that would take the word of her daughter over us.

### III

My job at the paint store was beginning to be a real drag. I didn't mind working hard at some things—burglaries weren't always easy, but having to show up, four days a week, sometimes before ten a.m., was a real pain in the ass. I got cranky—sort of a male version of PMS—so as I was finishing up my Friday shift, I took a razor blade and started doodling. I didn't cut deep—not stitch-worthy at least, but I did cut deep enough to get the blood flowing. It was just lines at first, and then a small swastika, and then a two-word message . . .

"Excuse me. Do you work here?"

I looked up and smiled. I was sitting behind the paint desk, wearing a navy blue smock with the name of the paint store boldly displayed on the chest, but yeah, I guess it might have looked like I was a customer.

"Yes"—big smile—"how may I help you?"

She was your standard getting-paint-for-her-husband's-weekend-off housewife—she picked the colors, he laid it on.

"I was looking for a white—maybe a Navajo, or a Swiss Coffee."

"That sounds great. We have the Navajo pre-made, but if you'd like, I could mix you up a special batch."

I couldn't have been nicer or more ready to serve, but I was a fresh shit dipped in Godiva chocolate, and she was about to break through that thin candy shell.

"I don't like special orders—no offense, but they never seem to match, and I don't want to be a bother."

*Hmm, wasn't she nice. I bet she even made sandwiches and served cold drinks while her husband painted.*

"I understand. There's nothing like the consistency of a large batch of paint coming straight from the factory. You always know what you're getting when you grab it off the shelf."

I walked her down the paint aisle, even grabbing a cart for her. I was eager and didn't want her to struggle with her two gallons of the white Indian. She was walking behind me and when we got to her brand, I stopped and did a half twirl, so I was now facing her. My move might have been a bit too Fred Astaire, but she seemed delighted, even thrilled with her shopping experience. I reached out my left arm, my sleeve rolled up. A pro, not really needing to see what I was grabbing, I looked her straight in the eyes. She blushed and looked away to her right where she froze in disgust.

On my forearm, blatantly displayed at eye level—sleeve rolled back like a movie curtain—was the two-word message. The blood had smeared a bit and congealed in a few spots, but it was still very, very legible. It read: *Fuck Customers.*

It was time to get a new job.

## III

I knew my father wasn't going to like me getting fired, but there was no need to tell him. As long as I maintained a proper gone-from-the-house-when-I-should-be-working schedule, and I had money in my pocket, I'd be alright. Besides, the burglaries had progressed from residential to commercial, and I was doing well. I took whatever I wanted from whoever had it. If you had an attachment to something, and I knew it, I'd do my best to part you from the object of your affection—including your girlfriend.

Punk rock music was a perfect background theme for us to help you loosen your hold on the material. We'd listen to The Damned's *Machine Gun Etiquette* album as we burned down stores and ripped off restaurants—the songs playing in our heads as we danced. I remember an evening, a special, beautiful evening—the kind you cherish forever—where I stood at the altar of a magnificent church. The rectory was dark; I'd entered from an unlocked door in the back. I faced the statue of God—an image that looked nothing like Him—and in my mind I put on the record. Side one, song one was "Love Song." I held the long-handled axe that I brought with me, and I pictured the needle reading the grooves on the disk—static before the song, fuzzy crackles and pops introducing the bass.

I turned the axe in my hand. . . . *Ready . . . and here we go . . .*

*"Hey baby, what's happening?"*

*Dum-didda-dum dum . . . da-dum-dum . . . dum-didda-dadum . . . da-dum-dum . . .*

I took a swing. The first blow slammed into the lectern at 208 beats per minute. The head of the axe buried itself in the wood—a stage dive coming to rest on the pulpit. It was stuck and refused to release. It took me most of the first verse to get that fucking thing out of there, but I did, and I was ready for the chorus . . .

"*Just for you, here's a love song.*"

I swung the axe as I sang, smashing a statue here, a picture there—slashing and singing.

"*Just for you, here's a love song. And it makes me glad to say . . .*"

"*It's been a lovely day . . .*"

"*And it's okay.*"

I buried the axe into the image of God. It stuck.

"*And it's okay.*"

If we wanted microphones, or larger speakers, or even if we were just feeling a bit naughty, we'd burgle a church. Churches are easy. They usually leave a door open at night—sanctuary for the tired traveler and an opportunity for the industrious young thief. There was never an alarm. We'd walk in, splash holy water at each other, throw a few bibles around, and then load out the statues and the PA. Sometimes I'd stand at the podium and deliver a dark mass. I didn't know any real satanic rituals—those were for TV and humans trying to be scary. The not-quite didn't believe in that shit, but starting out with "You worthless fuckers" always got a great laugh from the boys.

If we were in the market for band gear, we'd hit a restaurant. You could always find a semi-classy joint with a top-40 band playing, and after closing, I'd just kick out a window, walk through, and take their shit. Restaurants were also good for liquor pick-ups. The bars were usually well stocked and an empty trash can made a perfect shopping cart—a handle on each side. I'd dump the trash all over the kitchen floor, and then I'd carry the can to the bar, load up, and wheel it on out.

Every night was like Christmas, but instead of staring at your gifts under a tree, your presents were displayed behind glass. We'd stand at the window—sweet little cherubs, waiting to unwrap the goodies. All it took was a shovel or a brick to remove what stood between us and happiness.

We even satisfied our creep-factor, searching out sex shops for leatherwear and toys, running down the darkened aisles with dildos and dog collars in our bags, squirting slippery oils in each other's eyes, and playing smack-you-with-the-studded-leather-belt as we shopped.

Anything that was or was not nailed down found its way into our hands. Most of it we didn't even want—throwing it from the car as we drove off. We just loved stealing—and better yet, I loved what it did to humans when they found their precious things had been so mistreated.

One night we burgled the restaurant that Jenny worked at. We took it all—including the safe, which we rolled out on a dolly. Jenny was terrified.

She called me the next morning.

"Someone broke in and stole the safe," she cried. "They took liquor from the bar, all the band's instruments, and the cook's bike."

"Was that the blue one with the—"

"It's not a joke, you asshole. What if they come back? What if they get me?"

Wishful thinking, Miss Jenny, *they* already got you—and you liked it.

If school was as exciting as stealing, I might have attended more often. It was fun when I did go, though—especially after a night of robbing and interior decorating at church—when I sat in class just like the other boys. My hands, freshly washed from the holy water bath, would gleam as I raised my right—offering an answer for the teacher just as I held up a rock to gain entry through a window.

Secrets are fun; stealing is more fun; but you thinking I was a good boy was fucking hilarious.

Todd had started "jacking off" in girls, using their real flesh bodies as a sperm receptacle instead of a tissue and the never-dumped wastebasket in his room, and he was getting a bit distracted. I called him one night and told him I'd be over as usual, about midnight, to go on a run, but he declined.

"What the fuck you mean you're not going?"

I was a bit angry at the big kid. His girl was coming by.

"Just fuck her, and then start a fight. She'll split, and we'll go."

I was a master at relationship advice.

"I can't, man. She's talking about breaking up, and I don't want her to go. She lets me do shit to her, stuff that I can't do with other girls."

She loved taking it in the ass. I didn't blame him—and although I wasn't a fan of that practice, I could see why he might like it. It is, after all, a bit, well, humiliating to some.

"Well, fuck you then. If I score, you're getting shit."

I hung up, and then I set about making other plans.

In our neighborhood, there was never a shortage of criminals in training. I knew Pat had wanted to go on a larger burglary with us, but I was always hesitant about bringing him. Pat was fine for busting windows out of guitar stores—that was noisy, quick work. Smash the window, jump in, grab a guitar in each hand, and jump out. It didn't take a whole bunch of smarts or sneaky skills to pull that off—but commercial burglary was something entirely different. Some of these buildings were kind of tricky to get into—there were alarms and armed security guards driving around, patrolling the perimeter.

Fuck, I wasn't going to not go just because Todd was ass-fucking some girlfriend.

I called Pat.

Pat was in before I could say, "Do you wanna . . ." It was a quick yes. While stupid, and dangerous behind a wheel, he was willing to please, that's for sure.

We picked up two criminals from the neighborhood—a boy who was two years younger than us who wanted me and Pat to tutor him in "having fun," and our friend Mark. Mark was one of us—down for anything—although he hadn't been involved in any large moves yet.

I wanted guns, and I needed a new surfboard. The last board I had was ceremoniously thrown off a cliff in hopes of better waves—I'd ridden it only once.

I'd staked out a large Surf and Sport, about forty miles from my house. It carried boards, guns, and sportswear—it was one-stop shopping for the late-night bargain hunter.

I laid out the plan.

It was a good setup, the store had a low roof, and there was some ground cover in the back. I'd usually go through a roof vent or chop my way through a side wall on these jobs, but it all depended on the alarm. I hadn't seen anything too solid in the way of security, and the store was fairly new, so maybe they hadn't yet protected themselves from thieves. I decided I'd go in through the roof.

I didn't need the axe.

I gave the guys the standard what-to-do-if-the-cops-come lecture: "Run like hell, and if you get caught, keep your mouth shut."

We climbed to the roof, and I pulled off a large vent. I kicked my way through the ceiling, hung onto a pipe, and dropped to the floor below. I took the young boy with me—he might be useful for something. Pat and Mark stayed on the roof.

I started handing the store inventory up.

Things were going well—I was a quick supplier. I knew where to find everything I wanted: surfboards, wetsuits, watches, and guns; inventory was disappearing with assembly-line precision up and out the hole in the roof. It was beautiful.

I'd loaded out what the cops would later call a thirty or forty grand haul, when I heard jumping and running above me. Pat had been laughing earlier so this was going to be the second time that I silenced him.

"What the fuck are you doing up there?"

I called in my quietest voice, and I got no reply.

"Hey, what the fuck are you doing?"

Silence—as a matter of fact, I didn't hear any sounds at all. If Pat was still up there, this was the quietest he'd ever been in his life.

I decided to give it a quick look around. I crept towards the front window of the store—checking for unwelcome visitors—and I came face to face, with an armed security guard. We were separated—adversaries divided by one quarter-inch of safety glass.

I was wearing a black suit, with a black stocking cap on my head, and holding a new unloaded shotgun in my hand. The armed security guard had probably been practice shooting at a target that looked just like me at the local range—but now the target was breathing, looming, and holding a weapon.

He panicked.

Suddenly his $21.50-an-hour pay rate had become extremely unsatisfactory. He did a Barney Fife, fumbled his gun and ran.

I ran back to the hole and called up. I needed help getting out, and I had the boy with me. They bailed on me. I was trapped.

I had two options: one, crash through the front window while waving the unloaded gun; or two, get out through the roof. The doors were dead-bolted. I went for the roof. I figured Barney Fife was probably radioing for backup, so I yelled at the kid to start grabbing racks. I made a quick pile of display stands—anything that could get me up to the pipe so I could pull myself out. I jumped up on this pile and leapt for the pipe. I got it, and the fucking thing held. I started pulling myself up, when I heard the kid crying. *Motherfucker.* I was going to leave him, but when I saw his face I knew that when the police yelled "Hands up!" he was going to answer with "Jack Grisham. Jack Grisham. Jack Grisham."

"Grab my fucking legs. Come on! Grab 'em!"

He jumped up off the racks, and when he grabbed me, I thought he was gonna pull me off that fucking pipe, but I held on and pulled myself, and him, up. We went back through the hole and up to the roof. He ran and jumped off the minute we got up there, but I took a quick look around. There was way too much shit on that roof. I don't know what the fuck I was thinking, this shit wouldn't have even fit in the car. I was laughing as I watched at least four police cars racing to the scene with their lights off; I knew the report was armed burglary, and it was going to get exciting.

I flew from the roof.

Police were everywhere.

They had already caught Mark. I saw him scuffling with a pack of hyenas dressed in blue with shining badges. He put up a good fight, at least as long as I could see it, but I knew he was done.

They were everywhere—polyester blue flames chewing up asphalt and sidewalk. I ran until I found shelter in the crawlspace under a mobile home. It was at best an eight-inch gap that I slid under. I had to exhale all my air out and suck my stomach in to make it, and even so, I tore my pants and cut my leg squeezing under the metal siding. I lay there for hours listening to the police cars as they drove by. I could hear the cops talking on their radios.

"We've got one back at the shop. He was clean. Security said there was at least two, maybe three."

I was waiting for a voice to say, "Come out of there, and get your hands up," but they never caught me. I disappear well when I need to, and of course, I was practically untouchable.

I waited until mid-morning, and then I walked away.

It's a miracle that I never did any real time.

### III

I've heard humans credit God on the craziest of shit. They claim Divine Intervention on narrow misses and close calls.

"God must have wanted me alive, because . . ."

"It was so easy; God blessed us all the way."

What crap.

I've given you tale after tale of my behavior and the worst that ever came down my pipe was five days—five boring bologna sandwich–smelling days—which I spent by playing dominos with a cell of fools. God didn't care.

I took the license plates off my car and chased children across the elementary school lawn with it—I guess God thought their little legs needed a little workout, hmmm? They were getting lazy.

In an extremely amusing display of brutality, I kicked a passing motorcyclist, face-first into a parked car—he slammed into the rear bumper at forty miles per hour. What's the story there? Did God want him to slow down?

One sunny afternoon, I climbed to the roof of the local pharmacy. I brought an extremely powerful $CO_2$ pellet rifle with me, and I played sniper. The pharmacy was directly across the street from the high school, so my vantage point was perfect. As my fellow students were walking through the parking lot to their buses, I got in two head shots and a couple of solid body pops from a hundred yards. God helped me keep my eye true, and my hand steady.

I never got questioned or even remotely harassed for these acts. They were cruel and amusingly fun; sport designed to hurt others, and they went off without a hitch. So you tell me, the next time something goes wrong—a senseless tragedy that befalls you and yours—are you gonna thank God for it?

I was sitting around the house one afternoon. My father was at work, my mother—well, who knew what the fuck she was doing? Anyway, I was watching cartoons when Dave stopped by. Dave was an older neighborhood thug who had recently been released from a two-year sentence—a gas station robbery that netted no money, but did leave the clerk with a consolation prize of permanent brain damage and blindness in one eye. I was never tight friends with Dave—or anyone else for that matter—but it was okay to see him. Dave asked me about punk—and the stories he had recently heard about me being, well, a bit violent. He didn't understand it. When he went in to pay his debt to society—not sure how that cures brain damage or restores sight—I was masquerading as a surfer. And yes, I was a trouble-making surfer, but I wasn't a fighter. Dave was intrigued.

**Vicious**

I told him I thought the suburbs encouraged my violence—created it almost. In the city, people are more tolerant and concentrated, forced to get along, but it wasn't the case where we lived. Everyone looks the same in the suburbs. It's like the horizon on a hazy day—up-close, the images are stark and clear, detailed and refined, but as you look towards the distance the colors become muted and flat with a slightly fuzzy outline. The city was the detail—the closeness—and no matter how near you got to the suburbs, they remained muted and washed out. They were the distance. If you took a punk with purple hair, black leather, and boots, and you dropped him off somewhere downtown in a city like Los Angeles, well, he'd be just one more speck of color in an already colorful world. He would be absorbed by the city. But if you took that bright flash of color and you dropped him into the watercolor world of the suburbs, then he would be instantly in contrast to everyone and everything around him, and all would be against him.

I learned to fight because I had to. Punks were hated in the suburbs, and we were constantly being harassed by the jocks, the greasers, and the police. The newspaper ran stories of little old ladies being held down and having swastikas carved into their foreheads—not true. They printed accounts of punks vandalizing churches and graveyards—true. We were looked upon as pariahs and lepers—trash that needed to be put out in the street. There were daily battles to survive.

I told you before that a great demon uses his mouth before his hands, but I would not sit back and let myself be victimized by those I came here to conquer. You talk, I talk back; you touch, I touch back.

"You got a problem with my hair? Fuck you."

"You don't like my shirt? Fuck you."

"Is this too loud? Fuck you."

There were weak punks—artsy little freaks that ran at the first sign of trouble—but there were no weak demons. Cowardly, yes, conniving, lying shits who would do or say anything to get out of trouble, of course, but if you angered a demon you were better off killing him because a demon will not stop.

After one or two fights, I got a taste for it.

I wasn't a tough guy; that wasn't my thing. Any bull could stand in a field and slam his head against a fence—it didn't take too much talent to kick ass, nor did it make one especially evil. I prided myself not in fighting—although I did love it—but in being a bull that could get the rancher to shoot himself with his own gun.

Punching someone in the mouth or busting a beer bottle over their head wasn't as sophisticated as psychological torture, but it was fun, and I liked it when they hit back. There is nothing like the sharp sting of a sock to the eye to make you appreciate the cool evening air.

Dave was laughing as I explained this suburban phenomenon.

"Do you want to get a Slurpee?" Dave was asking. "My mother gave me some money for being good." We both laughed and walked to his car.

The 7-Eleven wasn't too far and we had fun on the way. We swerved the car at pedestrians, bike riders, and stray dogs. I loved watching people jump out of the way, and if they weren't fast enough, they'd get clipped by the side-view mirror.

"Hey, check it out!"

Dave spotted a middle-aged man stepping into the street. He floored it, cutting real close—the man was forced to jump back or Dave would have hit him. As the man faded away from the car, he threw a bullshit kick and spit at the front windshield. Dave was furious.

"Motherfucker! Did you see that? He spit at my fucking car."

I started screaming.

"Go back. Go back!"

Dave swung around and the man was running—a slow jog at first, but picking up speed. I figured the bastard was on his way to night school—we were by the college, and he was running with books and papers in his hands. He cut back across the street, heading into the residential area, and it was there that we caught him.

Dave and I jumped out and fucked with him.

"What'd you spit at the car for? You think you're fucking bad?"

These questions were drilled into him, coupled with punches to the face and head.

"No, no, I'm not. I'm sorry. I'm sorry."

He was crying. I guess his old ass hadn't been beaten in a while. I grabbed his papers and threw them over my head—a heavy rain of B-grades and index cards. Dave kept hammering on him. He started calling out a name, and I don't know if it was his mother or his wife, but I couldn't have given a shit if it was his retarded daughter. He sickened me.

I wanted him gone, but the wet red tones of the blood that Dave had drawn from his lips had spoken to me sexually and made me hard. I looked into his eyes and saw weak pleading tears—crybaby bullshit. I grew lustful with rage. I threw five or six hard punches in succession, scoring on his face and throat, and then I jumped in the air and came down with both feet on his head. I tried to crush his skull.

Dave freaked. Kicking somebody's ass was one thing, but trying to open up their cranium with your cowboy boots was another. He grabbed my arm and pulled me towards the car. The man was lying still on the lawn—at least he'd stopped crying.

"Let's go! Let's fucking go!" Dave was hustling.

I got in the car and was instantly calm. It was like a garbage disposal that turned on, chewed up the refuse, and then instantly went off. I fastened my seatbelt.

"You gonna get banana, Dave?"

"What?" He didn't know what the fuck I was talking about.

"Your Slurpee," I went on, "what are you getting? Banana or Coke?"

"Fuck you. You're out of your fucking mind. We're going home."

It *was* a little strange—me getting emotional like that. I was normally real cool—cold, actually—but I got a little heated there. One time I was wrestling around with a guy at a party. I had a knife and I was poking him—just little pokes, breaking the skin, teasing the blade into his flesh, but nothing real deep—and he was getting angry. I cut him fifteen times before I realized he was fighting for real. If I got the chance, the next time I had a chat with the not-quite, I'd bring up my anger.

### | | |

I was getting ready to go out. My bedroom door was closed. Its back panels were plastered with a small mirror and news clippings of the world's latest disasters. I pulled up my leather pants—black and expensive, courtesy of a smash-and-grab at the Bondage Palace. I secured them in place with a leather belt and put on my boots. Some punks wore great big lace-up boots, but I preferred my cowboy boots. Besides, sharpened spurs looked stupid on work boots.

My shirt was tight, fitted, and black—always black—and I topped it off with a black jacket—one I designed myself; it was covered in zippers. The only nods to color were the yellow polka-dotted scarf I tied round my neck and the Nazi armband I wore on my sleeve.

I kept my hair close—shaved in a military-style cut; it was a two dollar and fifty cent buzz job, courtesy of the Navy barber. My father loved it. The first time I came home with my head shaved he thought I was getting squared away, growing up, getting ready to toe the line, but then he saw the pierced ears and the occasional black eye and his hopes went the way of my old blond locks—right in the trash. My hair was short because I didn't want anyone to be able to grab it in a fight; my head was also greased—a liberal amount of Tres Flores to deter hangers-on. I was ready to go. I was meeting the crew at the shopping center.

A young boy was in front of the liquor store leaning against the wall in a dress. It was a nice imitation silk—deep navy blue and almost sexual in the way the material clung to his hips. He was fucking the outfit up, wearing a pair of ratty old tennis shoes underneath. But if you didn't notice the footwear, he looked good. He'd been given a job; each time a driver pulled into the parking spaces out front, he was to force visual contact as they entered the store, but after fifteen or so visitors, he hadn't had any luck. He was about to give up when they arrived—four boys in a Mustang, looking to pick up a couple sixers of ice-cold Bud. The dude sitting in shotgun laughed at the boy, and then called him out to his friends. *Finally, we might have a nibble.*

The fishing had been bad lately. We'd gone to this well too

often, and it was getting harder to reel someone in, but these dudes weren't from here. I was worried that the old Chinese man who tended the liquor store was going to warn them, but he was too busy to notice.

They purchased their beer and walked out—a laughing band of four young studs ready to get it on. They thought they ruled the night; it was gonna be pounding brews and banging bitches for these boys, that is, after they teased the little punk faggot outside the liquor store.

The boy was still standing against the wall. He was small for his age and although a tough kid, he'd been picked on quite a lot due to his size. They made a crescent around him to block his exit in case he wanted to run, but he didn't.

I couldn't hear anything—I had the tape deck on and a dubbed copy of the Germs' "Forming" was ruining my cheap car speakers—but when I saw the driver of the Mustang shove the boy against the wall, I knew we had a bite. I got out of the wagon; I was followed by three demons.

The "wagon" was the nickname for my '66 Chevy Nova station wagon. It was my first car, acquired for two hundred dollars. When I got it, it was a light cream yellow—almost chiffon cake—but I'd taken spray paint and "fixed" it up. I'd drawn a middle finger salute on the roof and written the words *Fuck you, Sky Pigs* underneath the finger. But now, the wagon was all black—I decided to camouflage it after that lawn driving incident, the one where I'd chased those young kids across the front grass of the school. I didn't hit any of them, but the police still look down on that kind of shit. I'd even gone as far as to paint over some of the windows. It was threatening—if a car could be called threatening. I'd stenciled a death's head and a wreath on the back.

There were four of us that evening—well five, if you count the boy. We were looking to stomp the fuck out of somebody. I'd copied this using-the-kid-as-bait deal from an old greaser that used to gay bash at the shore. He had a cute younger brother that he'd perch on a fence, and when gay guys came up and talked to the kid, he'd rush up and demand money or give them an ass beating—it worked well for a while until the gays got wise and gang-banged him.

My spurs jangled as I walked towards the dudes. I love that word, "jangled," and I loved the way I looked—6'3", dressed in black, fresh teeth cuts across my knuckles, and, of course, my polka-dotted scarf.

"What's up, Jess?"

I addressed the boy, taking no notice of the four wannabe tough guys circling him. My companions stood back—a crescent around a crescent. The dudes knew they were fucked. If Peckinpah had directed this scene, you would have seen fast edit close-ups of eyes darting back and forth—concern and panic coupled with the stifling feeling of being trapped.

"We were just fucking with him."

The driver of the Mustang was trying to be cool—just one of the guys out having a good time—explaining their actions. I ignored him and kept talking to Jess.

"Your sister still working at Tastee-Freez?"

I knew she was still working there; we'd driven over and gotten ice cream before we came here. I liked that hard-chocolate-shell thing they do. I looked around at the dudes now, as if this was the first time I saw 'em.

"So what's going on here, Jess?"

"These fucking assholes are fucking with me. That one shoved me against the bricks."

He'd fingered the driver, who, at the time, was realizing his night of pussy and cold brews was about to be traded in for a beating, and if he was lucky, a very sore drive home.

I asked Jess what he'd like to do. "Do you think we should fuck 'em up, or do you want to do it?"

We were starting to draw a small crowd—neighborhood kids, mostly. I was digging this. Can you imagine? I was actually getting a reputation as a local hero. When younger kids started getting into punk they had a "protector" of sorts—"I'm friends with Jack."

Jess was confused. "What do you mean?"

He was thinking I might have been setting him up—my friends never knew when I was fucking with 'em—but I had a plan.

"You can kick his fucking ass, and if he lays a hand on you, I'll stomp his fucking throat out."

How's that for being a good guy?

The driver stood there as Jess threw his first punch. It was funny; Jess practically had to get up on his tiptoes to hit the dude, and when he swung he had a smile running ear to ear; his whole face was lit up—years of being picked on were trickling out of his memory, crawling into his knuckles, and expressing themselves on the driver's head. The crowd was laughing and cheering. The driver covered his face.

"Get your fucking hands down."

One of my partners was telling the dude to take it—stand there like a man and pay for attempting to be tough. This wasn't going to last long—after seven or eight solid blows the driver turned to run. I tripped him, and he fell into a pole, hitting his head hard. The driver's friends took this as a cue to also take leave, but they got nowhere. In an instant, there were four stacks—a body lying at the bottom of each one—the focal point for the kicks and blows that rained down upon it from the neighborhood kids. I loved it when everyone jumped on.

Depending upon which end of a fight you're on—the beater or the beaten—a fight can be over in an instant or last forever. To me, it was seconds before those dudes had gotten to their feet and run off bloodied, leaving the car behind. But to them, they'd spent an eternity on the ground—a long slow year feeling each punch telegraph into their eyes, their noses, and their mouths.

I walked over to the Mustang and opened the door. I had the keys—found 'em on the ground after the fight. Someone else had grabbed their beer. Luckily, the dudes had bought cans—a few of them had popped open when they dropped the bag, but for the most part, they were still drinkable.

## AN AMERICAN DEMON

We pulled the radio out and slashed up the seats. We could have taken the Mustang for a joyride then set it on fire, but I expected the police to arrive any minute. I shut and locked the door then threw the keys on the roof of the liquor store. Jess was getting mobbed by kids—he was a pint-sized heavyweight whose standing had just gone way up in the world. Once this story got around, he was never picked on again.

### | | |

You might have noticed the infusion of demons into the story. I'd told you earlier that it was rare to meet others of my kind, and now I was beginning to be surrounded by them. If you remember, I said that in times of great change or social upheaval, the demons would be concentrated like flies on the carcass of a cow. Well, that's what we had here. Great change—change in attitude, appearance, and in society's reaction to the world at large. Punk rock was an angry voice for revolution—but unlike the hippies of the sixties, punks were willing to use muscle to force change. Any change, good or bad.

### | | |

Vicious Circle was created in 1979; it was my first real band. Todd had actually developed on the drums—I think all that jacking off had something to do with his quick, powerful hands—and I was still tossing verbal at anyone who came near me. Our friend Tom had dropped out, but we got a replacement—two, actually. We got a guitarist named Steve, who came from a band called the Klan, and a bassist named Laddie, who more than filled Pat's inept shoes.

We were instantly popular. It wasn't hard. We were the craziest, meanest idiots from the area, and we started a band. Our friends were just as fucked up as we were, so we had a whole bunch of crazy fuckers running around, and if you were in the area, and you liked punk rock, well then you'd better like a band like ours that was surrounded by a bunch of crazy mean motherfuckers. You sure as fuck wouldn't want to disagree with them . . . would you?

Whatever the logic, the Vicious Circle was a maniac attractor.

I hadn't gotten any messages from the not-quite. I was waiting—thinking some written-in-blood sign would be dripping on my wall when I woke, but it never arrived, so I just stayed on my path. If I had the chance, I lied. If it was lying around, I took it, and if it came at me, or tried to beat my ass, I stomped on it. It was pretty simple, really.

I was having fun and playing around with aliases. I liked being different people, and with the right amount of thought, I could blur my features and become the names my face suggested. There were people outside the punk rock world who knew me as Anthony. When I was Anthony, I went to the local college—the university on the hill. I'd ride up there on my bike and chat up coeds in the student center. I never gave out a phone number. I was sweet and shy. It was good practice being kind and gentle because, to tell you the truth, I was really digging hurting people, and I didn't want to blow my cover. I'd done a lot of work learning to fit in with you, but like any discipline, if you stop practicing it, you'll revert to where you started. The violence was intoxicating, and if my short venture into Pam use was any indication, if I didn't watch out, I wouldn't be able to control it.

Vicious Circle's first show was at the Fleetwood in Redondo Beach.

The Fleetwood, a club near the harbor's edge, was one of the few local venues willing to take a risk on punk. I think it might have been a grocery store at one time, and if so, the manager's special was about to be violence and mayhem in aisle nine. I walked onstage wearing a straightjacket, cowboy boots, and leather pants. I was also sporting my favorite spurs. I looked and acted like an escaped gay cowboy from a mental hospital.

I was surrounded with a phalanx of criminals—a crew with the average life expectancy of anytime now. We were barely more than children wearing the skin of eighteen or twenty years, but the eyes that floated around that stage were old. This crew was the body-guard of the dead. Demons, for the most part, but there were one or two human boys—consorts, whose responsibility was to watch over our gear. You couldn't lay a hand on me if you had tried—not that you'd want to; I love biting hands.

There are numerous books and eyewitnesses that recall Vicious Circle shows turning into bloodbaths and ambulance conventions, but it's a bit overblown. Yeah, the shows were crazy, and it was junior gladiator school for demons, but you didn't go there without knowing what you were getting into. Blackjacking, brass-knuckling, and razor knives were the tools of the day.

That night I walked onstage and wrapped my hand around the microphone. We'd never played a show, but there were cheers, and the crowd was ready. We started with a James Bond theme and the dancers on the floor moved in a fluid circle—smooth, slow motion . . . sinking down an imaginary drain on the dance floor . . .

The band held, paused, letting the last smooth note reverberate into the ceiling of the club. The tension built. The dancers were frozen in place—primal and evil in their intentions, waiting to spring . . .

Armchair reviewers can condemn Vicious Circle all they want, but most of our victims were tough guys looking to beat up on punks. These clowns would show up with no fucking idea of where they were heading—it was almost as if they painted targets on their chests. They wanted to stomp a piece of punk ass, and where better to do it, they thought, than this club? They should have paid attention to the crowd as they walked in; these weren't cute little kids spraying wash-out crazy color in their hair—these were monsters, outcasts, and sadists. These were the kids that were willing to take a beating to be different, and these wannabe punk killers had just walked right through a group of them to stand before the stage . . .

I squeezed the mic and felt the scream start to rise from my stomach through my chest to my throat . . .

One, two, one-two-three-four!

We tore into our first song—and the fans tore into their first victims. Vicious chainsaw guitars accompanied flailing arms and box-cutter stabs. Teeth were knocked loose with pounding drums and slashing boots. In the fury, the band was forgotten and the dancers drove in a circle around the floor—a procession of terror with their would-be attackers strung up before them. This was demon business and, as I said before, the unlucky visitors picked the wrong night to come.

Do you know what this was, these idiots being lured into an ass-whipping? It was the use-a-cute-boy-as-bait tactic, but on a much larger scale. The first punks in Los Angeles—of whom we were an offshoot—were inventive, reckless, and wild, but they were also smaller. And except for the odd few, they weren't really equipped to go toe-to-toe with a drunken fag-bashing construction worker. They were the bait.

And then there we were: large, strapping beach kids; our tanned bodies were built from years of surfing, swimming, and skating. Basically we were the field hands in this evolutionary cycle—we were the muscle, or the "hook."

Drunken would-be punk-attackers had run into a lot of bait—they'd snatch up those little morsels of scared punk and they'd grown accustomed to a free meal every time they ate . . .

### I I I

I was with the Vicious Circle crew at a party. We were celebrating. The first show was a great violent success and our reputation as maniacs was spreading. The boys were lounging by the keg—animals waiting for a feed—and I was chatting up a couple of punkettes on the patio.

We were a close-knit group, and in honor of the now dead, I will remember them.

I've mentioned Todd and Pat—more like brothers to me really—and Tom and Mark, but there was also Wild Bill and his brother Jim, Scott Stewart and Rick the Animal, the loud-mouthed Worm, Hole and Verts, Vince and John the Nazi, Russell the Terror, Dave the Lady Killer—literally—and the two Brads. There was Vinnie and Borzu, Bozo and Britt. There were more, so many more, and each of these names is a part of a lineage of terror and destruction that still trickles down today. Some of them were demons, and most of the names have been altered, but I know them, and I won't forget.

"Sherri says you're in a band."

"What?" I'd forgotten where I was and the conversation I was having with these little punkettes wasn't helping. Mark was standing next to me laughing. I don't know why the fuck I bothered talking up chicks sometimes. I could just walk up and say, "Fuck me?" If they shook their head no—which they never did—I would just move on.

"Sherri said Cindy's brother saw you at a show and you hit a guy with a—"

A bottle broke at my feet—brown glass thrown with force.

*Crash!*

*Crash!*

Two more. I looked over, thinking my friends were fucking with me, when I saw Pat go down. He'd been hit in the head with a beer bottle—they were flying through the air from the direction of the street.

The party was at the only house on Huntington Beach. It was the old head lifeguard's quarters; the secluded house was on the borderline of Newport and Huntington, a double rock jetty ran along the river channel near the edge. The house was literally on the sand. There were no neighbors.

There were a group of toughs that had run through Orange County beating on punk kids. They had a name for themselves, but I won't give them the pleasure of citing it here. Their Mohawk lynching parties and leather jacket ass whippings had netted them quite the reputation. I'd talked to smaller punk kids that were actually afraid of these guys—to the point that they camouflaged their look while out. I refused—I'd travel to the market in a dress at eleven a.m. on a Tuesday morning, I didn't give a fuck.

I heard a kid call out this gang's name. He was running with a scared look on his face. I enjoyed watching this boy freak out—shitting his pants in front of his date—but I was gonna enjoy hurting these "punk killers" more. It wasn't even a question of wondering how many or how tough they were, I was figuring they'd met nothing but weak defiance so far, and besides, I never lost a fight.

This might seem like wishful braggadocio to you, but I can assure you it is not. You see, you have to define what it is to win—what's the end goal, what are you trying to gain? I fought in a dress whenever possible—it helped that I usually wore one—and I always won. Let me give you an example.

"Hey faggot."

This was the opening salvo to the majority of fights I was involved in—although I did hear "please don't" and "I didn't know" a few times. I usually followed this with "What?"

"What?" is not as good as "fuck you," but it was polite and appropriate.

They answer, "I'm gonna kick your fucking ass."

A statement most absurd—unless the would-be attacker was actually going to put his shoe against my rear end, and that wasn't going to happen unless he knocked me out or paid me for it.

My turn. "No, you're not."

Yes, I know, it's childish and argumentative, but it is fun. It's also a great tool for confusing the IQ–challenged combatants. After a short pause where their brain tries to catch up to the dialogue, they would usually throw out a very confused "Oh yeah, why?"

Now, if you know anything about the way humans think, then you've realized I've already won this battle. He had just asked me to explain why I was going to beat his ass. If someone ever comes to you with a statement like "I'm a piece of shit," never ask them why, because they will give you all the reasons why they're a piece of shit, reconfirming in their own minds that they are indeed shit. These idiots were already thinking that they might lose, and now they had just asked me to list the reasons why they would. Now, if the combatant would have said, "What makes you think that, faggot?" I'd prepare myself for an ass kicking because that statement puts me in the position of having to present a case in support of what I thought would be a futile battle on his part.

My turn.

"Well, I'll tell you why. First of all, I'm wearing a dress, and I'm out in public. That should lead you to the conclusion that this is not my first rodeo. The dress fits me and I'm comfortable in it. Men wearing dresses in our present society is frowned upon, so you've got to imagine that I've been called 'faggot' before. However, if you look at my face, you will see that my nose is straight and my skin is clear—untouched by combatants' hands. Now drift your eyes down to my knuckles—notice the healing scars, they look like they've recently been used to knock a tooth or two out of a mouth. So, you've got a man in a dress, with a beautiful face, and hands that look like they've seen the wrong end of a meat grinder standing before you. Now, let's look at the issue of pride. If, and I do mean if, you 'kick my ass' as you say, you've accomplished nothing—all you've done is beaten up a man in a dress. Surely anyone can do that. However, chances are, taking in all accounts, you're going to get the living fuck beaten out of you by a very vicious 'faggot' wrapped in a Christian Dior evening gown, and how would that look to your friends?"

So you see, win or lose, I always win. If I get my ass beat it's just one more story used to confirm the fact that I'm a complete psycho nutcase—a maniac, loose in the world.

But back to the party . . . a bottle just flew past my head.

We went into action fast. Throwing beer bottles at a party was the teenage equivalent to mortar attacks in Vietnam—on contact the broken glass could split a head open and take out an eye.

Pat was bleeding down the front of his shirt and onto the sand. He was looking at the blood as if he'd never seen it before; I heard him giggling and commenting on the warmth of the liquid. Fucking Pat, you never knew if he was really injured, or if he was just being himself.

My crew and I ran towards the bottle throwers. There was no communication between us to do so, but none of us would have run the other way.

They were standing outside the chain-link fence that separated the beach from the parking area. Seven or eight polo shirt–wearing fucks were about to get their collars straightened. The minute they saw us, they knew they were fucked.

There were kids that were scared, and there were kids that walked the border between out and in—that invisible line between jumping in a fight and running. Under the right circumstances, these polo-shirted fucks could've terrorized that whole party— maybe a hundred kids. But under the wrong circumstances, they were vastly outnumbered. My crew's willingness to attack turned those kids sitting on the fence into soldiers, and the seven or eight attackers found themselves looking down the barrel of a fifty-punk gun. We over ran them and we swallowed them whole. They tried to bolt, but everywhere they turned they were met with opposition. I will give them this, though: they threw their share of blows. I took a hard bottle break to the head from some asshole wearing, of all things, a light pink knitted shirt. But they couldn't last.

I sure as fuck wouldn't have wanted to be them—lying in that dirty, sandy parking lot, no chance of being saved, years of wearing braces destroyed by one or two quick kicks from a Doc Marten, and . . .

"Get him! Fucking get him!"

One of the fucks had somehow slipped away from his abusive captors, and he was making a run down Pacific Coast Highway towards the Newport Bridge. I was on him.

I took off running, pulling along a few eager stragglers in my wake, including, of all people, the fourteen-year-old son of one of my neighbors. I don't even remember how we got the kid, but he was doing an authorized ride along. His father was a great guy—an ass-kicking long-shoreman that fenced stolen goods for me. He even gave me a bailing hook for a birthday present. It was handed over with the pleasant wish of "I bet you can tear some shit up with this, huh?"

The kid was on my heels when I caught the fuck. We were on the bridge, in the slow lane. The Newport Bridge is not high, and a jump from the top into the dirty water of the Santa Ana River won't hurt you, unless of course, you don't hit the water. The rocks on each side of the channel are sharp and there are gaps between the boulders—if you land on these, you *will* get hurt, guaranteed.

I dragged the polo-shirted fuck up to the rail of the bridge. He still had some fight left in him, so I popped him a few times in the mouth. I wanted to toss him off the bridge, but I couldn't do it with him struggling like that—he was big. I had him against the railing, but I was having a hard time throwing him over, so I asked for a bit of help.

It's a question like this that separates the demons from the humans.

"Hey, could you guys help me throw this fucker over?"

Fucking A, you would have thought I'd just asked for a blow job. All I wanted to do was give this fuck what he came for. He wanted to see somebody get hurt. He wanted blood, and he wanted pain— I didn't blame him, I wanted the same things. And who better to give it to him than me?

I was worried it was gonna be an all-night thing throwing this fuck off the bridge, but then a few of the Vicious Circle boys caught up with us and the worrying stopped.

He begged like a little polo shirt–wearing bitch as we tossed him off.

*Shit, he isn't anywhere near the water—well, maybe if you count what sprayed up on the . . . ouch . . .*

He landed right on the fucking rocks.

I thought I heard his leg snap, but I was laughing so fucking hard it could have been his arm. Either way, motherfucker hit hard, and then kinda bounced down into the channel.

I guess he thought we were gonna come down after him—being as how we were enjoying ourselves so much—so he took his maimed punk-killer body and started lamely swimming up the channel to the sea.

I felt a touch on my shirt. It was the fourteen-year-old kid. He was looking up at me with a pair of adoring eyes. He was sure proud of his friend Jack. I wanted to do something for him, something nice, so I grabbed a semi-cold beer out of an onlooker's hand and I gave it to him.

"Go ahead, buddy. I won't tell."

He was stoked. I was a real friend. "Are you sure, Jack?"

"Yeah, I'm sure, and if you throw it real hard, you can probably knock the fucker out."

My new little buddy cocked back his arm and let that beer bottle fly. And you know what? I'll be fucked if that little prick didn't score a head shot. He was a natural.

It was all fun after the bridge incident. I wasn't even bothering to pretend I was human anymore. I made jokes about being a demon and the Vicious Circle followers swallowed them whole.

It helped that I'd been desecrating graves.

### III

Long Beach is a seaside town, and buried under the harbor and the piers is the remains of an old amusement park called "The Pike." I guess in its heyday The Pike was something to love, but now it was more like an old beauty queen that'd gotten long in the tooth. She was still sort of pretty, but the company she kept—hookers, sailors, and IV drug users—had made her something a little less than desirable.

Todd and I cruised down in the wagon. There were only a few shops left on the midway—a tattoo parlor and a cheap gambling establishment. Todd wanted to get another tattoo. He was as uncomfortable in his body as any demon would be, and he'd found a shop that'd cater to his underage flesh.

She was standing outside when we got there. She was ancient, and if I had to give you a hair color, I'd go with a lavender-blond-gray. If she told you she was eighty, I'd say she lied.

Todd walked into the shop to see who was around, but I chose to stay outside. The old woman had nodded to me as we pulled up, and to tell you the truth, I was interested in her—what the fuck was this old lady doing hanging around in front of a tattoo parlor? There were state-run boarding homes nearby, so maybe she'd wandered out for a little unauthorized stroll, or maybe she was looking for a tattoo—but being as it was close to midnight, and I didn't see any ink on her arms, I figured she was up to something. I looked directly into her eyes—she was a ways away from me, but the distance wouldn't affect my sight.

I saw her death—it was six hours from now, and she was wearing my sweater. I was pissed at first. It was my favorite—a long, thick mohair that I'd recently stolen. The old woman—although dead—had a smile draped across her face. She was lying on what I took to be her bed. There was an open bottle of pills next to her—Haldol. I knew these pills were used to treat dementia—my grandmother was taking them before she died. The old woman's hands were dirty and, other than my sweater, she was naked and covered in gray ash. Lying next to her was an old military photo of a handsome man in a Navy uniform.

I smiled and walked towards her—I was trying to be disarming, but there was no need. She spoke first.

"Would you help me?" Her voice was stronger than she looked, and it had a Midwestern, maybe Iowan, accent. I wasn't surprised, my grandmother used to call Long Beach "Iowa by the Sea." The old woman had been drinking—not much, but enough to leave the scent of stale whiskey on her breath. "I need to pick someone up, and I don't have a car. I'll pay you."

I liked money and I had no trouble taking it—especially from the elderly. Besides, she wasn't going to need it after tonight. She handed me an envelope, which I assumed held directions, but it was stuffed with bills. I didn't count it—there were criminals about. And besides, I didn't want to split it with Todd.

"It's close, real close," she said. "I would've taken the bus, but it's late and last minute. I need to get this done."

I let her wait in the car—she had a large purse and she was wearing a long black skirt, tennis shoes, and a flimsy tank top. She was short on style, and she had the overdoing-the-lipstick-and-perfume thing that the elderly are prone to. I gave her the quick sniff-test before she got in—old folks are known for shitting themselves, and I didn't need some bitch in leaky Depends snuggling in on my nice vinyl seats. She was clean—a little too thin, but clean.

I walked in and got Todd. He was grumbling—he liked hanging out at the tattoo shop, and the idea of us taxi-cabbing around with some old woman didn't sound like a great time. I broke it down.

"She gave me forty bucks—I'll give you some—and she said she'd buy beer."

*It's nice that I can lie three times in two sentences.*

She'd given me money, alright. But unless it was made up of all ones, that stack was surely more than forty. And as for giving Todd some of it, he didn't need money—he was a kid and he put the pinch on his grandparents whenever he was short. Buying beer? She hadn't agreed to that, but I'd guarantee you she would; you get these old fuckers away from their houses at night and you threaten them with being dumped off in Nowheresville and they'll do practically anything you say. I was positive she'd buy.

The old woman had her face practically pressed against the passenger's side window as we walked out, and it was freaky. Mind you, I've been dealing with visions since I was a kid, but to see that old lipsticked skeleton sitting shotgun and eager as a mutt getting ready for a car ride to the park was a trip. I laughed as Todd recoiled.

We jumped in, and she gave me directions to a spot not far from there. I knew the streets, but I couldn't figure out where the fuck we were heading. The scenery was mostly industrial on the outskirts of Signal Hill—oilfields and a cemetery. She leaned back, smiled, and settled into the seat. Her skirt rode up on her legs and it was a rough view. I wished she'd pulled her stockings up higher—they were above her knees but the four or five inches of gray varicose-veined flesh that remained was a bit much. I decided I'd coax her into covering up. I took my right hand and set it on her thigh—right below the hem of her skirt.

Fuck, she covered my hand with hers. The skin on her palms was rough and dry, and then she guided my hand up under her skirt between her legs. She had on panties and they felt thick, but she wasn't diapered. I was tripping on how loose her flesh was, and I was wondering if she was able to have sex. I was going to find out.

"Who we picking up?"

I forgot Todd was in the back, until he spoke up.

"My husband." She kept her smile lit and her eyes closed. "He needs a ride home."

She was fucking out there, and when we pulled up to the gates of the old cemetery I thought about the Haldol. Fucking old bitch was demented. *Oh well, I have the money.*

The cemetery wasn't gated—there was a wrought iron fence around it, but it wasn't keeping anybody out. We drove in and parked the wagon on a tree-lined path. She got out and purposely tottered off in the direction of a crypt.

I love this place. I'm sure that when the Sunnyside cemetery was planned, the city founders picked a quiet spot outside of town to lay the bodies of the dead, but they'd discovered oil here, so now, the old civil war veterans and the first mayor of Long Beach were forced to lie a hundred feet away from foul smelling black sludge and nymphomaniac oil wells who furiously pumped 'round the clock—respect goes only so far.

Todd jumped down into an open grave and I threw dirt on him. I didn't think they buried people here anymore, but it looked like somebody was going to get tucked in. We fucked off for a while—kicking over tombstones and pissing on a few graves, but I kept my eye on Granny. She looked all right; she was sitting on a bench in front of a small house of the dead—sort of a one-room flat built of imposing mossy granite blocks and a metal door. I walked over and handed her my sweater—my favorite mohair.

It was a mumbled thanks and then back to her vigil.

I walked up the lane where I saw a crypt of my own. It was larger than hers—newer, more formidable—but there was no door. Instead there was a wrought iron gate barring the entrance—I could see through it.

A large bronze cross hung on the inner wall of the crypt, and I wanted it. It wasn't worth anything, but it'd look good glued on the back of my wagon. I grabbed the edge of the door—the hinges were rusty and old—and I leaned back hard. It gave. I managed to pull a corner away from the wall and I squeezed in.

The streetlights on the highway sent beams of pale light streaming through the stained glass windows that bordered the room, and the cross was lit, almost as if staged. I paused in that white marble body-pantry, and I looked at the cross. It was majestic. I didn't care much for Jesus, but that bloodied cross thing was genius—a perfect logo. I thought of the family that had come there to mourn—their tears puddling on the crypt floor, their eyes resting on that large bronze symbol of eternity. *What comfort it must have given them.* I stood up and tipped my head in acknowledgment of its splendor, and then I ripped it off the wall.

I was walking back to the car with it and could hear snickering laughter and what sounded like headstones breaking. I figured Todd was busting grave markers on the driveway. My old lady was gone.

The bench was empty. I was pissed; I was really looking forward to sampling that.

"Help me."

I looked over, and she'd opened the door to the crypt—she had a key on a chain around her neck. I walked up and slid my hand down the back of her dress grabbing what was left of her ass. She ignored me and walked inside. The room was larger than it looked. There was a bench about three feet wide—sort of a shelf or built-in table for flowers or candles. I put one hand on each side of her waist, sliding her dress and her thick panties to the floor. She stepped out of them, and I lifted her up to sit on that shelf. It was perfect; I spread her legs and positioned myself between them. Her skin hung and clung to me—soft, gray folds that wrapped around my fingers and my legs. Her breath was dusty, old and sprinkled with booze—like putting your mouth on the floor of an old western saloon. She didn't fight. This was a trip; it was intense for a second—I was really into it, but I didn't last. It was "Think about it, think about it, stick it in, done." Oh well, she couldn't tell too many people that I was a shitty lover in the four hours and sixteen minutes she had left.

"What the fuck?"

Todd had walked in and caught me as I was pulling up my pants. He might have been jerking off to some pretty creepy shit, but I think this was too much for him.

"You're fucking sick, big man."

I was gonna offer him some—share the old lady, but then . . .

"Help me. He's here."

Thank God for my eighty-year-old girlfriend; she took the heat off me by grabbing Todd's attention. She was up and pointing at a niche in the wall. It was a twelve-by-twelve white marble square with a date in brass—you know, the standard "born here, died there."

She had a rounded kitchen knife in her hand. Where she got it, I'm not sure, maybe she'd had it in her purse. I should have patted her down before I gave her a lift. She was sticking the blade in the edges of that square, trying to pry it off, but she was crazy. She wasn't gonna get that thing opened with a knife.

"Let me help."

I was once again the gentleman. I might have been quick on the trigger but I knew how to score.

I held the brass cross by the foot—it was heavy, real expensive work, and I used it as a hammer. I slammed it into the cover. The marble cracked on the first blow—it was thinner than you'd think. A couple more swings and I had it. It split in half and then I was able to remove it completely. There was an urn behind it—her husband's almost-final resting place. I grabbed it before she could. I wanted to check it out. I opened the urn and took a pinch, setting the urn down after I'd got my sample. The old woman grabbed it and held it tight—I wondered if her old man knew she just cheated on him. I took the pinch of ash and put it in my palm. There were small fragments of bone in it.

"Fucking A, Todd, check this out."

I held my hand towards him, and as he bent down I blew it in his eyes.

"Motherfucker!'

We were laughing as I followed him out.

We drove the old lady downtown and we dropped her off at a low-income boarding house. I didn't kiss her goodbye. I knew what she was going to do. She was gonna take all her pills, lie down on that shitty little bed, and try to rub the scent of another man off her with her husband's ashes. I was surprised she died in my sweater; maybe she got cold, right before she went out.

I was at home taking my clothes off. I could still smell the old woman on me. The cross was lying—somewhat beaten up, but still beautiful—on my bed. I pulled my pants off and felt the envelope in my pocket. The money; I'd forgotten.

The envelope must have held a letter once, because there was both a sending and return address on it, but I didn't give a shit about that, I only cared about the contents. It was money, a lot of money, fifty-three stuffy old hundred-dollar bills—lying, one on top of another, like bodies in a crypt. It must have been her life savings. What the fuck she was doing with it, I don't know, but she wasn't about to tell me. As a matter of fact, she was probably five minutes into telling her deceased husband why she was such an easy lay. I would have to be sure Todd got his twenty.

I picked up a black roadster with the cash. It was a two-seater convertible, an old Datsun 2000. It was small and fast—a little go-kart of a vehicle. I tied a raccoon tail to the antenna, and I had my friend airbrush a picture of death on the hood. It didn't look anything like him, being as death wasn't visible, but it was one of those straight-out-of-hell things that you see in movies. It was inspired—bony hands coming out of wide sleeves and wrapping themselves around the headlights, a cloud of fiery red smoke and flame surrounding the upper torso of evil. And the eyes? The eyes were perfect. The artist said he'd gotten the inspiration from mine—cold and green, eyes that were happy to hurt you. I wish I could have driven with the hood up, given my fellow travelers something to see as they glanced in their rearview mirrors. That car and that painting were a calling card for me.

Your world was like a candy store with the owner hogtied in the back with a dirty sock stuffed in his mouth, and I took what I wanted. I gorged myself on violence, on sex, and on every pleasure of the flesh. I became drunk with satisfaction, and I became reckless.

Passion is a disease to the damned. A pure demon is without feeling—cold, emotionless. Yes, I enjoyed hurting you, but if I didn't hurt you, that should also be okay. It was just a job, and I was never supposed to really enjoy my work. I should get satisfaction, yes; enjoyment, never. But I was developing a true zeal for selfish infliction of pain on others. Maybe it was a touch of humanity that had seeped in through the flesh—when you step into a host body there are certain attributes of that host that you acquire. Maybe I'd picked up a human trait. But whatever it was, it was dangerous. When you become focused on the self, you become your own man, or own demon if you will, and your needs begin to become more important than the needs of others. My needs were starting to come before the needs of the not-quite. And if they overshadowed his plan, one way or another, I would either toe the line, or the repercussions of my misbehavior would force me back to service. But I couldn't stop.

There was quite a long rope of pissed-off humans dangling behind me. Pissing off humans wasn't as bad as pissing off demons, but they could still fuck you up. Many demons spent their last seconds at the hands of an angry mob, and there weren't too many people around me who weren't angry. When I left the house it was now dangerous. I always traveled with others; it was a real rarity to see me alone. I wasn't prejudiced with my terror—spreading the pain equally among many realms of society. I never knew from which group my would-be assassin would crawl: pissed-off boyfriends, husbands, bikers and greasers, gang-bangers, business men, surfers and teasers.

The catalogue of people who wanted me dead sounded like an amendment to that Julie Andrews number in *The Sound of Music*. There was no shortage of humans that would like nothing more than to see me put to rest. And they tried—always unsuccessfully, but they did try. There were shots taken by cowards at my parents' house; there was the morning I woke up to a pickaxe sticking out of the front windshield of my car and there were parties and clubs targeted when attackers thought I might be there—it was a real game of hide and seek, with me being the dirty needle in a haystack world.

Thankfully, I had my share of supporters, and without them I would have been fucked, but my detractors far outweighed my defense. It wasn't that I'd just beaten people; I'd humiliated and broken them.

One drunken evening I kissed a man on the lips in front of a crowd. Now, you may find nothing wrong with this, but if you're a supposedly straight male trying to prove his machismo and sexual prowess in front of the ladies, being treated as a bitch could put a real crimp in your ability to pull trim.

He was threatening me.

I don't know where he got off, but a challenge was issued to fight. I laughed at him and called him a little girl.

"Why would I fight you?" I asked. "You're a bitch, a cute little bitch, and I'm going to give you a kiss."

I grabbed him behind the neck, pulled his face to mine, and shoved my tongue in his throat. Everyone laughed. He stormed from the club—his cock shriveled and tucked between his legs like a little pig's tail. I went back to entertaining the crowd; he went home and got a twelve-gauge demon killer and waited outside my house. Luckily for me, it was a long wait—I didn't go home, and the morning found him reverting to his cowardly cocksucking self.

### III

I walked out of the house, opened the garage door, and looked at my baby. The garage was never locked, and I was going to take a drive. I took her cover off, admiring my painting and the shine from that glossy black lacquer. She was beautiful and ready to play. It was then that I caught the scent of another man. It wasn't a clear scent; it was just as if something had been touched. I didn't see anything out of place. The seats had not been adjusted, there was no graffiti on her doors, and the gas tank, to my knowledge, had not been tampered with. I started the motor and she was as responsive as always—coming straight to life with no trepidation. I pulled out of the driveway and shot down the street, taking the first corner on the edges of my wheels. I stomped on it and headed for the highway. I was going to the beach. I had the top off, it was a nice morning, but even if it had been cold, I would have taken a ride with it off—there's nothing like a convertible with the heat on and the top down on a cold day.

I loved driving this car—playing Racer X, dodging and drifting around my fellow drivers—I'd speed up to the car ahead of me and swerve viciously in front of them, narrowly missing their front bumper, and then I'd hit the brakes, sometimes forcing them off the road.

I took a corner—fast. I downshifted, letting off the gas and then as the tachometer dropped, I . . .

*What the fuck? I just filled this baby up with gas and now my gas gauge is dropping almost as fast as my RPMs, and . . .*

There was rain or water hitting the window. *No, it's fucking gas! There's gas all over the front of my . . .*

I felt the heat before I knew I was burning. A great flash of flame enveloped the front of my car—a fireball, pushed forward by the roadster—an explosion that lit the day with its light.

The whole front of the car was engulfed—I was choking on the acrid smoke that rolled over the windshield and down into the cockpit of the roadster. She was burning.

I pulled sharply to the side of the road and jumped—rolling on the ground, extinguishing the hitchhiking flames that'd jumped on my body.

A truck pulled in front of me—a large commercial vehicle—and two men jumped out. At first I thought they were assassins coming to finish the job, but they grabbed hoses off their truck and immediately started firing water onto my car. They were mobile truck washers, and traveling behind me, they watched as I caught fire.

*You've got to be fucking kidding me.* I mean, I was almost embarrassed to write it down,'cause it sounds like bullshit. Who the fuck has mobile truck washers roll up behind them the instant they explode in flames? Well, that's what my guy is good for. He controls the flesh, and he can put anyone anywhere in this world whenever he fucking feels like it. Including mobile truck washers behind a burning demon—thank the not-quite.

They had my car extinguished in moments. Only the engine compartment had a chance to burn. The image of death was gone—the paint had peeled and blistered from the hood—but the majority of my car was saved, and soon towed to a shop.

It was a day or so later that I got the call. The mechanic was giving me the damage report on my toasted roadster—it didn't look good.

"Is there any reason to think your car might have been tampered with?"

*Not at all, buddy, unless you call me being the most selfish, brutal, remorseless fuck that'd ever touched down on earth a reason.* I played dumb.

"What do you mean?"

"Well, it looks like your gas lines had been tampered with. Who'd do that?"

*Great, I got fucking Dick Tracy for an auto mechanic. Just fix my fucking shit and get me back on the road, asshole.* I needed to curtail this detective shit.

"You know what, it might have been me." I was apologetic and acted embarrassed at my own supposed stupidity. "I was fucking around under the hood, and I probably fucked something up. I should have just had you fix it in the first place; it would have saved me a few, yeah?"

"Yeah," he replied. He bought it. "Next time call first."

*Fucking idiot. Next time, I'll cut your gas lines.*

### III

Vicious Circle ended where it started, back at the Fleetwood in Redondo Beach.

It was a show like any other show: violent, but nothing out of the ordinary. There were scattered fights on the dance floor and there was blood in the parking lot outside, but so what?

We were in the middle of our set; I was digging it, really letting myself go, when I saw one of my crew getting choked. A long-hair had his arm wrapped around my man's neck, and my man was starting to go limp. I jumped off the stage and I kicked the attacker in his face. It was a flying side kick—180 pounds of cowboy boot–wearing bully stopper.

My heel caught the long-hair above the eye, and my razor sharp spurs left a trail of torn flesh up his cheek. I was pretty sure he'd be getting a new nickname—old "One Eye" was knocked out and bleeding profusely from the left side of his face. I thought nothing of it—and why should I? He was just one more idiot taking a beating for showing up.

I jumped back onstage and the band launched into the next song. The violence and the blood on the floor had inflamed the crowd—an inhalant of evil that had just given us all a head-rush. A security guard dragged "one-eye" off the dance floor and threw him outside.

As we played, the music and the violence intensified so much so that the walls of the club shook and One Eye woke up. He stumbled to his motorcycle and grabbed his pistol out of his saddlebag. It was a .45—a gun big enough to stop a demon in spurs. He came back to the club intent on killing me.

I was oblivious to the action—so involved in the music that I wouldn't have ducked if he stood before me, aimed, and fired—but I was pulled off the stage. A young towheaded demon grabbed me by the arm.

"You've got to go," he said. "You're done this time. You've got to go."

It was then that I heard the commotion—police ordering someone to drop their weapon, but that someone wasn't complying. I ran out the back, hopped in my friend's car, and headed home.

I think, at one time or another, everyone has a moment of clarity, or a chance to see ourselves as we really are. Most of you pass up that chance. You look in the mirror, see your own reflection, and you get scared. You turn away before the introspection can propel you to change.

I walked in the bathroom, looked into the mirror, and I was proud of what I saw. Yes, I'd gotten a bit out of hand, and I'd served myself maybe a bit more than I needed to, but on the whole, I'd created change—for the worse—and I had a good idea that the not-quite was proud. This band thing had been real good, maybe too good. I was either gonna be taken out by some coward with a gun, or I was gonna get popped for accidently killing somebody. It was time to move on. I'd let my parents, family, and friends clean up the mess. I decided to take a trip. I hadn't received any new messages from the not-quite, but I didn't think he'd begrudge me a walk into the wilderness. Christ wandered off for a few days; why not me? But I wasn't going into the fucking Sinai; I was going where it's nice and cool—maybe I'd do a little polar bear hunting near the Arctic Circle. I got a ticket to Alaska, and I split town. Vicious Circle was through.

Alaska was a drag.

Fairbanks, the city I was closest to, was okay, if you liked that sort of thing. But there was no night—in the summer time they've got twenty fucking hours of daylight—and the town is loaded with a thousand times more mosquitoes than people. Thank God malaria can't live in the snow.

## A Short Rest

I was living north of town in a log cabin with no running water. We carried our liquids to the house in five-gallon jugs. There were bugs everywhere.

Now, you might be wondering why the fuck I picked Alaska—me, a southern California surfing punk, running off to the land of grizzly bears and frozen tundra. Well, I'll tell you. Sometimes, when I needed to make a quick move, I'd just stab the wildest idea I could think of and roll with it. You humans call it "making a decision based on panic and poor judgment," I call it "Who gives a fuck? I just gotta get out of here."

Alaska might have been pretty, but I'm not remotely close to being a woodsman, and I'd had enough after a few weeks. *What the fuck was I thinking?*

My move to the land of the midnight sun reminded me of a movie—*Young Frankenstein*. There's a scene where Gene Wilder (Dr. Frankenstein) locks himself in a room with the monster he just created. He tells his assistants, "No matter what I say, don't let me out. Even if I'm crying for help, begging to get away, don't let me out!"

Well, he soon realizes that he fucked up, and that he needs to get out as soon as possible—like now.

Two weeks later I was pounding on the bars of the wilderness demanding release. *Why the fuck didn't I pick Vegas for my vacation getaway?*

I was living with Dr. Jim—he was my own Dr. Frankenstein—and his family. Jim was the brother of my older sister's husband. He was some sort of orthopedic surgeon who delivered door-to-door medical assistance to remote locations. Jim was a trip. I'd walk into the kitchen—thinking I might like a light snack—and Jim would be boiling the skin off a human foot he'd just amputated. It wasn't a big deal to him. It was, after all, just a foot. And besides, he was pretty sure he'd remember to wash the pan before cooking dinner.

I was polite and gracious, but I was also packing my bags. I didn't mind cannibalism—having practiced it in another life—but I preferred skewering my own victims and boiling them alive. I had to get out.

I told Dr. Jim I was going to the market. I asked if he needed anything—a rope, a knife, maybe a new bottle of chloroform—but he didn't. I went to the market and never came back.

Every now and then you read about these cats that just disappear—people surmise that they've been abducted by aliens or kidnapped and tortured in the woods, and I'm sure some of them have been. But I'm also sure that some of them were just like me—not necessarily a demon, but a person who doesn't owe you a fucking explanation, doesn't give two shits about whether or not you're concerned. When I didn't need you, or could no longer use you, I left.

I got on a plane and got my ass back to Long Beach.

The flight home was a bitch. My assigned seat was too tight and the fucking plane was all over the sky. There was a storm and the darkened cabin came to life during intermittent lightning flashes. That was the only thing I did enjoy about that trip. Every time the lightening flashed, I got a flickering glance at the fear playing across the faces of my fellow travelers. It was like a silent movie, but instead of old-time piano accompaniment, it was thunderclaps and screams. The stewardesses weren't even serving—there had been an "incident," a cart being lifted and slammed to the floor, so they'd folded up shop to ride it out with the rest of us.

I got up and moved to the back of the plane. The seat belt sign was on, but it wasn't like they were going to do anything. No one even asked me to sit down. I'd seen a row of empty seats when I'd gone to piss, and I was thinking I could throw the armrests up and stretch.

The seats were still vacant, so I sat down, put the dividing arms up, and prepared to get some sleep when a stewardess plopped down next to me.

"You think that's funny, kicking his fucking eye out?" Her voice was low, raspy, and sleepy. Her vocal chords were being manipulated by an outside force. It was him: the not-quite. She started laughing—more like slow croaking, really. She would have been hot if she'd shut up. "I think it's funny; I think it's fucking hilarious—almost as funny as you running away like a little bitch. You have a nice rest, baby? Is my little Jackie all refreshed and ready to go?"

As if the flight wasn't bad enough already.

"I didn't know what the fuck to do. You didn't tell me. Get involved. That's it; that's all you said. So I got involved, but I couldn't keep it up, could I? Somebody was gonna end up killing me. What the fuck good am I dead?"

"Oh, you are a willful one, aren't you, big boy?" she cooed, then put her hand on my arm and squeezed. "You want a hand job?" More croaking laughter followed as her head lolled back and forth. She was possessed.

"Come on, man . . ." I would have been down if he wasn't inside her. But having him controlling her hand was like jacking off in front of your grandma. Thankfully, he didn't push the issue.

"Yeah, well, lucky for you, you did everything I planned. When you're fucking up, I'll tell you. Until then, if I say jump, you just jump. You don't ask how high, how far, or how long—you just do it. Now, here's what's going to happen. You're going to go home, and you're going to lay low—keep the heat off. Get yourself a job, a shit job that you can just blow off when I tell you to, and you're going to sleep, and you're going to forget for a while, and just lie low." She stressed the low while her hand grasped my crotch; she squeezed again, but this time she held on—fucking tight.

"Ow, fuck. Come on, let go." I tried pulling her hand off, but he had it locked on.

"I need you reborn when you roll back out. By the way, I think you just lost the engine on that wing."

She got up and wandered off. My crotch hurt—and that engine *did* look a little loose.

I got off the plane and took a cab home. I wanted to surprise them. I was expecting to be welcomed like an old campaigner coming home from the war, but as I rode down the street, I heard the sound of the doors and the windows of my neighbors' homes slam in my wake.

I was shocked that my family wasn't happy to see me. I guess they thought they were getting a break when I left, but two weeks was long enough. I decided my mother needed to whip me up some dinner without the aroma of human flesh. I sat at the dining room table and outlined my plan. I told my old man that I was going to get a job and "go straight." I wasn't going to hang out with that crew anymore, and I was going to grow my hair out. They sat there listening like kids in a doctor's office waiting to get a shot—they knew it was coming, and they knew it was gonna hurt, but they didn't know when. To them, it was only a matter of time before I started fucking up—if I hadn't done so already.

I finished my meal and went to bed.

### I I I

I got a job in the harbor painting boats.

My boss was a maniac; he was a vegetarian, and he had a black belt in some form of martial arts. He was supposedly disciplined, but he'd been kicked out of every marina he'd ever been in for either assault or pure lunacy. He had one rule: we don't eat anything with a face; other than that, anything goes.

He sat me down on my first day—I hadn't even started working yet, and I was already getting a talking to. He reeked of patchouli and marijuana.

"Look, I know you belong in the jungle or jail; I've heard about you, but I'm willing to give you a shot. As long as you try to show up on time and you don't eat anything with a face. Okay?"

He didn't give a fuck if I dumped a one ton drum of pollutants in the harbor, as long as I wasn't eating "souls." According to him, the water in southern California was a fucking garbage dump anyway.

What the fuck did he think I was gonna say? I agreed and ended up serving six months under the crazy motherfucker.

I didn't mind working, but don't get me wrong, I disliked having to be there when he said; I disliked not being able to leave until he said; and I disliked doing what he said. But I loved the physicality of that job. The sun felt good on my body, and my muscles, after a hard day's work, would lie quiet at night. My hair even grew longer—to the point where I wore a turban to keep it out of my eyes—and my hands became calloused and hard. I started to forget the past, and my consciousness as a demon drifted in and out with the tides. Some days, I could recall with vivid detail my plan and my path, but on other days, I remembered nothing and I seemed almost human in my reaction to the world.

### III

It was a Saturday—a day when I would usually work, but not today; I had money in my pocket. My roadster had been repaired—repainted a solid black without death on the hood. I was thinking of taking a drive when the phone rang.

"Grisham, where the fuck have you been?"

The voice was familiar—one of the old crew members—but I couldn't put a name to it, so I just played along.

"I've been working. I got a job in the harbor as a boat slave."

"Yeah, fucking Todd told me you bailed on the scene. He said he'd seen you 'round though."

"Yeah, I guess he did." I didn't know who I was talking to and the name Todd sounded a bit strange. I waited for him to continue—the pause was awkward and long—I was going to hang up and walk away, when he said, "There's a party in Huntington. The Vandals are playing. Why don't you come?"

I felt my mouth moving and the sound coming from my throat. My voice was slow, raspy, as if controlled by an outside force. It was the not-quite, and he answered for me.

"I'd fucking love to, man."

I woke up.

It'd been so long since I'd been out that I wasn't sure what to wear. My old uniform seemed outdated and ill-fitting—out of character for who I was now. Black didn't seem the right color for rebirth. I went upstairs and got in my mother's closet. She had a nice pantsuit—dark blue with light gray piping. It was short in the legs, too wide in the waist, and a bit loose across my chest, but somehow it fit me—if not in body, at least in mind.

I put on a pair of golf shoes that I'd bought in a thrift store—the steel spikes still intact. The cleats made noise when I walked, and I'm sure they weren't too kind on the floor, but I liked the thought of holding a weapon—on me or beneath me. Around my neck, I tied a pink scarf. And hanging from my ears were two dangling gold hoops. I wasn't exactly sure what I was going for, but I didn't feel the need to advertise my intentions with a hard, dark look.

There are warriors who try to make you fear them by the markings on their faces. They pose, bulging eyes, outrageous hand gestures—all moves that say "stay away." I had friends like these warriors—tattoos on their faces, blue-inked warnings of their ferocity. But I didn't want you to fear me; I wanted you to see me as a flower.

I got in a fight at the gas station.

I was filling up, minding my own business, when two guys in an old Cadillac pulled up behind me. They were dressed like punks, and I heard punk-type music coming from their car, but I'd never seen them before. There were a lot of these guys around now. I didn't pay them much notice when I was working on the boats—I was a civilian, not interested in military business, but I noticed these two.

I didn't like them.

I'd forget how big I was—6'3" and 180 pounds. Sometimes I saw myself as 5'3" and 113 pounds—as I've told you before, the body feels strange.

When these two got out of their car, they laughed at me—I'd smiled at them and they mumbled something smart-assed as they walked by. I was offended. I noticed their pump was running by itself—they'd prepaid and were getting snacks. I walked over, pulled the nozzle out of the tank, pulled back the gas station foreskin from the nozzle head, and I squirted gas all over their car. It wasn't a lot of fuel, maybe ten or fifteen seconds worth of spray—a dollar fifty of regular unleaded—but it was enough, sort of like a dog pissing on another dog's territory. I dropped the nozzle on the ground, walked back to my car, and was driving off when they came out.

They came after me.

You might say I looked afraid, and you wouldn't be altogether wrong, but I wouldn't use that word. It'd been a long time since I'd beaten on someone, and my stint on the boats had caused the viciousness in me to sleep. I could feel a tingling in my body, like that part of me was starting to wake, but I couldn't be sure I'd be ready to perform. But it didn't stop my nature, and it certainly didn't stop me from doing what I did to their car.

I tried to get away but they were too close behind, so I pulled into the golf course parking lot and stopped. They were right behind me. I quickly got out of my car, thinking I might be able to reason with them—the almost-humanness I'd showed working on the boats still clinging to me. I'm not exactly sure how I was going to reason dousing their car with gas, but I was hoping they'd take it as a joke. *I do love jokes.*

They both came towards me.

They weren't as vicious as I'd been in the past, because the driver was yelling and not yet trying to hurt me. I wondered how I looked standing there—seeing it through their eyes—a big, good-looking guy, with blond hair, a nice tan, wearing what unmistakably looked like a lady's pantsuit, with the look of a guilty child on his face.

It got quiet as they yelled—a vacuum of sorts surrounded my body, and I became an observer. The sound in the world had been turned down. I was staring at their mouths. Their lips had taken on the characteristics of the green and brown clay lines that formed Gumby and Pokey's mouths, and I didn't like it. The passenger of the car was studying my face as the driver yelled—it was that look you get when you think you might know somebody, but you're not sure. It was right then that a boy on a bicycle rode up. He was a familiar face and waved and called me by name. The passenger suddenly realized who they were yelling at. He reached out and put his hand on the driver's arm, but it was too late. I'd already decided that the driver's mouth needed to stop moving. I kicked him in the balls as hard as I could. When he doubled over, I came with a fist from below—a long uppercut that concluded in his mouth. I felt a sharp pain in my knuckle that I knew came from his front teeth, and I smiled—it was a warm tickling little cut that made me think of sunshine. The driver went down and I stomped on his hand with my cleats. He wasn't nice, and I didn't like the way his mouth looked. I kicked him repeatedly as he lay there. He tried to cover his face, but the cleats found their way between the gaps in his arms. His friend, the passenger, had run away. I saw, before I felt, my friend on the bicycle grab me. I looked down and his fingers were digging into my arm. I turned towards him, and it was as if someone turned the sound back up mid-word as he was yelling. "You better get the fuck out of here! Come on, Jack, come on!"

He was pulling me towards my car, and I followed.

I didn't say anything; I just jumped in the roadster and drove off. There was a cassette in the tape deck—I hadn't listened to that thing forever, and I wasn't even sure what it was, but I pushed it in and turned it up. The song that came on was "New Rose" by The Damned.

The party was in a Huntington Beach tract home. It was nice and new, but still just another version of the same old cookie-cutter shit that home builders were erecting all over the southland—I think they only had five different models. I pulled up and it was like a ripple started at the curb and rolled into the house. Kids were nodding and smiling. Behind my back I heard whispers of "Do you know who that is?" and "It's Jack from vc." I'd only been gone six months, but the scene had grown, and my exploits were legendary. There were guys that bragged about being on the bridge with me when that fuck in the knitted pink shirt was tossed off—shit, if everyone who said they were there actually was, the bridge would have collapsed under the weight.

I wandered into the living room like I'd wandered off into that colored park so long ago, but now that small dark prince, who had once abandoned his grandmother for an afternoon stroll, was older, stronger, and darker. However, I treated these kids just the same: like they were mine. I assumed loyalty and allegiance. I suddenly realized what the not-quite had wanted. I was to establish a reputation that could never come into question—one that would grow even without any other action on my part, one that fed on itself. You don't need to keep sticking your hand into a lion's mouth to know it has teeth—people knew I bit, and that was enough.

It felt good, figuring out the not-quite's intentions; I was proud, borderlining on cocky. I was really gonna dig the rest of this life. I reached out to a young punkette that was standing in the kitchen and I waved her over. She didn't hesitate or play shy. I kissed her deeply on the mouth—tasting the malt liquor she'd been nursing on.

"Do you have a name?"

She started to give me some bullshit punk handle—"Lucy Nuclear" or something—but I stopped her; it was fucking embarrassing.

"No, your real name. Don't waste my fucking time."

I let go of her and she quickly answered me.

"Amber. It's Amber."

"And who's that? Is that your boyfriend?" I pointed to a young dude who was skulking away; he looked beaten—a small dog that had his bone taken and there wasn't shit he could do about it.

She nodded yes.

"Go get him," I said. "And tell him I want to fuck you in front of him."

She ran off and came back with a boy that couldn't look me in the eyes. I grabbed her by the hand and led her into a back bedroom; he followed. It was the master suite—large with a dressing table and chair. I told him to sit down in the chair, and I took off her clothes. I slid my hand and my mouth all over her, making sure nothing was untouched. She had a few hickies on her neck and one on her breast. I figured the boy had at least had her before, but I was gonna ruin it for him. I pushed her back on the bed and spread her legs. He tried to look away but I threatened him. And then I took her. I was selfish: I didn't give a fuck about her or how long he loved her; she was five minutes of a good time, and then I left them to sort it out.

### III

It was a few days later that Todd showed up at my parents' house—and if my parents were unhappy to see me return, you should have seen the look on my mother's face when Todd showed up. She was practically holding the door closed as she greeted him. There was only one reason Todd would be coming by—he wanted something—and my mother had a good idea that I was all too willing to deliver.

"It's good to see you, Big Man. You know Ron and Mike, huh?"

He formally introduced the two guys he had with him. I knew them from around. The early beach punk scene was very incestuous—you'd either played in a band with someone, went to jail with them, fought them, or slept with their girlfriends. Surprisingly, I'd only been in one fight with these guys, and we were on the same side.

It was about a year ago, at a performance of the Vicious Circle and a band called the Hoods—Paul and Ron's band. The show was in Signal Hill near the oilfields and the graveyard. Paul, one of our crew members, had a dad who owned a machine shop, and he organized the gig.

It was a great place for a show. The Signal Hill police were more concerned with hanging black football players in their jail than they were with arresting teenage white boys with weapons, so we never saw them. There were no neighbors, and besides a few windows, nothing in the area was really breakable. You could take a bat and wail on one of those oil derricks all night—or, you could just beat each other's head in.

The fight was actually pretty stupid, and if we would have been in a battle zone somewhere, they would have called it injury through friendly fire. It was the black leather beach punks against the black leather north-town punks—two crews that looked alike, liked the same music, hated the same government, and slept with the same teenage prostitutes. Some of them even shared the same needles. I wasn't even sure what the fight was about, other than the fact that we all liked fighting, and there was no one else there. It started as all fights start—pushing, shoving, a bit of peacocking. I was smartassing the early combatants, trying to get 'em to turn their attention to a bigger target—mainly the police—when the fight sparked. I'd never seen so many concealed weapons come out at the same time—it was like one of those bricks of fireworks on a Chinese New Year—bang, bang, bang-bang, bang.

Knives, pipes, blackjacks, pieces of wood with nails in it—you name it, anything that didn't fire a projectile was fair play. There were guys literally blackjacking the fuck out of someone they'd just shared a beer with. I tried to stay out of it, but it was hard to do when I was being swung at.

I got punched once or twice and then I punched back. I knocked my attacker into the street where he was immediately run over by a vc member in a small truck. It was over as fast as it started, and the street was littered with bodies—seriously. The not-quite found the whole thing quite amusing—us beating the shit out of each other. He told me that he made it happen because I looked bored—and he hated the opening band.

But that seemed like a long time ago, and I was trying to remember Ron as he was that night. They had a band now, Todd, Mike, and Ron: a three-piece with Ron doing the screaming.

We couldn't talk privately, so we took a walk—I wasn't sure what they wanted, and if it was something fun, I didn't want my mother getting all nosey. We walked to the school—home of the bungalow fires and the rooftop hotel. Todd was the first to speak.

"We want you to sing for us, Big Man. It's a great band and we need you."

I didn't think Ron was wearing the same look of "needing" me, being as he'd been doing the screaming, but Mike and Todd were pretty adamant about me joining.

"It'd be great, man. With you and Todd, we'll fucking kill it."

I didn't take much convincing. I knew the not-quite planned this. It was all coming together, the rep, the band, everything. I was in. The name of their group, well, now my group, was TSOL—the True Sounds of Liberty.

The boys had stolen the name from a late night evangelical tv show—what they were doing watching it is a point of contention, but while doing so, a Christian band took the stage, and the name of that musical tribute to God was the Sound of Liberty Band.

I learned the songs they had and then started writing lyrics for new ones. The songs and the lyrics were a bit more intelligent than my last project; the themes were basically the same—a lot of noise about hating the government—but they'd cut out half the "fucks" and dropped the racism completely. I was glad. Being a demon, I liked fucking with people, but I was a bit of a snob when it came to the quality of the attack. A racial slur is an idiot's attempt at inciting anger—I'd use it, sure, but only when I'd exhausted every other avenue, or if I was among company that found it extremely offensive.

We practiced at Todd's studio, and I could smell old crimes on the walls. The backyard was littered with tombstones and the broken goods of past robberies. If we stole something, and we couldn't be sure of its purpose, we'd either fuck with it until we figured it out, or we'd take turns throwing it off the roof until it was destroyed.

It wasn't long before we made our first recordings. Vicious Circle had never made a record, but we had fooled around making ghetto blaster tapes of our practices. These tapes were great for kids, but you couldn't really hear the songs and nobody was going to press a record from them. TSOL's first recordings were going to be of real quality—at least as much quality as you could get in a studio that charged ten dollars an hour.

I was a bit concerned that the band would be unhappy with me after they'd caught me on tape, but if they were, they never said anything. Hearing my recorded voice was strange—I didn't think it sounded like me, but it worked. The good thing about punk rock is that you don't have to sing anything, you just have to scream with conviction, and I had plenty of that.

On those first recordings, I sounded like I was from Long Beach via England. It was hard to listen to, but I mimicked the bands I loved; Siouxsie and the Banshees, Adam and the Ants, and The Damned were all English bands. There were some very cool American bands I also adored, but something about a British accent made punk rock what it was. It reminded me of pirates, and being from Long Beach—a harbor town—I'd dabbled in piracy a few times.

I loved playing buccaneer.

Dressed in my best evening wear—black pants, long-sleeved black shirt and a black eye-holed stocking cap, machete at my side, I'd hop in a dinghy and row out to the bay. Large yachts would be tied at their moorings and I'd cut them loose—and, as they drifted through the channel, I'd load up on cameras, TVs, and weather radios. If you were really lucky, you'd find cash.

Sometimes there were people asleep on the boats.

I climbed up the side of a beautiful yacht one evening. I admired my look in the white gloss mirror of the hull. I cut a dashing figure: I would have made Bartholomew Roberts proud—although, he wouldn't get to be captain if I was aboard. As he himself said, "Better being a commander than a common man."

My machete was in hand—I'd spent all afternoon sharpening it—and it was sure to make my work easy. I was humming a sea shanty and just heading below when I came face to face with a common man . . . holding a gun. No blunderbuss did he carry, it looked like death. Grade-A steel, a handgun with a full chamber of pirate-ending bullets. I probably could have split his head clean open with my machete before he squeezed off a shot, but I was not the murdering sort; instead, I used my mouth.

"Where's Tony?" I asked. He was taken aback.

"What the fuck are you talking about?" he said and then continued his questioning. "Who are you? How'd you get on this boat?" He wasn't shooting, so I knew that after a bit of calming chitchat I'd be off—kind of a drag, really, having to work when you knew you weren't going to get paid.

"Phillip? Are you okay?" It was a woman. On second thought, I might split his head and grab his wench.

"Is that Jane?" I asked.

"Look, you're on the wrong boat, guy. I'm Mike and my wife's below."

"I'm sorry, man. I must have scared the fuck out of you guys. I thought this was Tony's boat. He and his wife Jane are taking me and my girl to Catalina for the weekend. Fucking A, I am so sorry."

I started walking back to mid-deck, where I climbed over the railing to my dinghy. I guess he thought all visitors dressed in black and carried machetes.

"If I see you on the island," I yelled up at him, "I'll buy you a drink. Shit, I am really sorry about all this."

And then I rowed off—cutting them loose from their mooring along the way. The fog was coming in thick, and it'd be a fine night to be adrift. I rowed ashore empty handed, but without a smoking pistol hole in my body. I continued humming my shanty.

The TSOL recording came out well. No pirate songs, but as punk music went, it was pretty good. Kids started passing it around, and as far as I heard, they were stoked. Of course, for the most part I'd get nonchalant "Hey, that tape's pretty cool" comments to my face, but then I'd find out that the same kids had dubbed fifty copies and passed them around. One night, I was on my way to a burglary, and I was listening to my favorite Sunday radio program, *Rodney on the Roq*. It was the same program I was listening to when I was inspired to invite the parishioners to "Cum Worship" at the church. The DJ, Mr. Rodney Bingenheimer himself, played a track from our demo. It was just as the not-quite planned—a perfect career for a young demon.

TSOL had an instant following.

Todd and I attracted all those Vicious Circle fans, and our old reputation for ass-kicking got us shows. Our onstage chemistry didn't hurt either. We looked wicked. Some of those fuckers in punk bands would dress like ghouls, and although we did wear stage make-up, we pulled off wicked, as in "cool" and "tough."

I liked bands that looked tough.

I couldn't stand wimpy little rockers in kimonos, jumping around and squealing about killing dragons and shit. *Yeah guy, and your little four-foot frame is gonna hoist that hundred-pound sword and kill a dragon? What the fuck are you gonna do after it eats you?*

TSOL had just the right amount of tension, flavored with a hint of larceny. And, as individuals, we were physically huge. There wasn't one guy in our band under six feet. Todd was the shortest at six feet even, but he was behind the kit. Ron was 6'2", I was 6'3", and Mike was doing the Lurch thing at 6'4". When we hit the stage, it was an offensive line of good-looking thugs.

Funny as it may seem, we actually caught a little behind-the-back heat for being *too* good looking. There was a little contingent of inner city kids that thought all punks should be wormy little pussies who caught daily ass beatings for their "art." Well, that's fine for you boys, but I preferred being in shape and pulling prom queens—surfing, skating, and punk rock was way better than cringing, crying, and running any day. And besides, this little contingent of "artists" never said anything to our faces—at least not more than once.

Sometimes I wonder why there're demons at all. I mean, you fucking humans basically do my work for me—if I wait long enough. Take punk rock. Here's this really cool music scene—close knit, non-conformist, rebellious, and wide open for experimentation, right? Now, toss in a couple of controlling, classifying cunts who start trying to run the show. They start deciding who's cool and which bands are "real" and which aren't. And then maybe they decide that only bands that come from a certain area or a certain country are really punk. Now, let's bring in critics—the fanzine writers who start pigeonholing the sound so it's easier for them to do their work. They start coming up with shitty little classifications like "hardcore" and "punk," or "new wave" and "noise." In just a short amount of time you have this really cool family scene that's been dissected, classified, and controlled into the gutter and we, the demons, never even raised a hand.

Do you know that sometimes the not-quite gave me credit for shit I had nothing to do with?

I read some quotes from these artsy clowns about them not understanding why *we'd* be into punk rock. "They're all such good-looking beach kids," they'd say, "what could they possibly have to complain about?"

Personally, I had *nothing* to complain about; I was having a blast being a total fuck. But if I was to speak for the kids I knew, I'd respond, "Those artsy fucks never lived in suburbia."

In the suburbs, being a teenage punk was a terminal disease.

The suburban "dream" families were plagued with as much abuse, drug use, divorce, suicide, and violence as anything those old inner city pricks had ever dealt with; they just endured it in a more idyllic setting. Did these idiots honestly think that if you were in good shape and lived at the beach, then you trusted God and Country? If you had a tan, the Contra issue was non-existent? If you surfed, Vietnam was a slight inconvenience? Did they really believe that you had to be a scrawny art student to realize Reagan was a terrorist and you'd been lied to for years?

Look, don't get me wrong, I liked those old chicken hawks calling us good looking, and I strutted my tanned, handsome shit by them every chance I got. But the bottom line was, it ain't fun being a scrawny little art student trying to sway to the music when you got animals in the pit. They were just too scared to dance.

### I I I

We got an offer to make a record. It was shit money and a shit deal, but what did we care? The initial contract got flushed down the toilet at Sammy Wong's hotel when we were playing a gig in San Francisco, and we didn't even bother signing a new one. We made a verbal agreement with the Fagin of punk rock.

Robbie, or the "Posh One," was an ex-Brit, a sometimes substitute teacher who minored in punk rock exploitation. He was the perfect host for our first disc. Robbie had his own record company, Posh Boy Records. Jesus, even the name sounded like a scam.

The EP, as it was called, was a five song extended play version of four kids hating the government and refusing to get real jobs. It was muscular and threatening, anarchistic and confrontational. It was a straight up attack at the government of the United States and those involved with it. The Posh One went way out of pocket on this one—he spent five hundred dollars making that disc—and the quality showed. You can even hear the sound of an uninvited motorcycle going by on the highway during one of the songs.

It didn't matter, though; it was the feeling in the music and the lyrics that counted. When you're standing in a crowd and getting ready to toss a Molotov cocktail at the police, your fellow rioters never questioned whether you had super unleaded or regular in your bottle.

As with everything I touched, the record was the success it was meant to be. The kids ate it up like candy, or cheap booze, and the shows grew in size. There weren't very many clubs that catered to our kind—especially in the suburbs. You had the Whisky a Go Go and the Starwood in Hollywood or the Fleetwood in Redondo Beach. All we had down here was the Nest. I say "all," like the Cuckoo's Nest was something less than those other clubs, but in my opinion it was much more. The Nest was a hangout for demons, and its name was fitting.

It was an Orange County stronghold of evil, and its owner, Jerry, was in full support of our dealings—at least he fully supported the revenue we generated from kids flocking through the door to see us.

The thing I liked most about the Posh One and Jerry was that they were men after my own lack of heart. They profited off the fringe, therefore making them as creepy as the music they came to promote. I could picture either one of them running a concentration camp. Jerry was the sadistic commandant standing in the guard tower and directing his henchmen to round up the skinnier prisoners—the ones with thin wallets, who wouldn't drink his over-priced beer—and dispose of their skeletons. And the Posh One was the liaison officer for the new female prisoners; he offered them a rockstar career, casting couch included, or a trip to the showers. I still admire them both.

I changed my name for the record. The disc has me listed as "Jack Greggors," but as I've said before, I had a thousand names—and I used them all.

Huntington Central Park is a great rambling park with large trees and dimly lit paths, a duck pond, a library, and a nature center smack in the middle of the city. It's a wonderful place for an ambush; if you're out at night walking the family poodle, I'd suggest a more well-lit venue.

I was getting ready to take a cruise through the park to see what sort of trouble I could dig up—there's nothing like playing forced hide-and-seek with an unwilling victim to get your evening going. There were six of us that night—a demon gang of midnight pic-nickers. We had just gotten out of the car when a small four-door sedan pulled up—its occupants consisted of two men and their dates. It turned out they weren't big fans of the punk sound, and their dis-pleasure was registered by one of the ladies yelling, "Punk sucks!"

*Indeed it does, my dear, but a secluded park with an audience of vicious thugs is not the preferred forum for such a critical review.*

I walked over to introduce myself and the driver of the sedan extended a very large knife in lieu of a handshake. If there's one thing I can't stand, it's a critic without good manners.

My boys were on them before the driver could do any cutting. They were dogs, snarling at the visitors. I calmly walked back to our car and grabbed a pair of large metal shears that I had under the seat. Tin snips—you never know when you might have to fashion a tool. I walked back to our guests, asked my boys to step aside, brandished the tin snips, and said, "Stab away, my friend."

"Hey, fuck, man." The driver was now being polite. "I was just fucking with you. I dig Devo."

Devo was a wannabe safe word for guys that hated punk but

didn't want to get the fuck beaten out of them for not being "with it." Devo was the only band they knew. It's like someone about to get his ass kicked at a Black Panther party blurting, "Hey, I had a black friend in high school." Idiots.

His attempt at escaping a beating was so weak that I actually let him go, figuring I'd just take the women. My friend Hole walked over and showed the critical young lady something *she* could suck as he ran a used sixer of beer out of it at her feet. She wasn't impressed. I could tell they didn't really want to play, and I was actually thinking we could pursue something more exciting when they hopped in their vehicle and rudely departed. We said our goodbyes with a bottle or two thrown at their car, but what do you know? The driver left us with a parting remark. He rolled down his window and yelled, of all things, "Fuck you! Fucking punk scumbags!"

I knew in an instant that he was not a frequent parkgoer, because the way he was heading lead to a dead end. He was going to have to pass us on his way out.

Oh, I could just imagine the excitement in that car when the ladies realized his mistake. And then—just as a child clings to the sides of a roller coaster as it climbs, the anti-rollback device clicking its way towards climax—the car turned and sped for the exit. The ladies hung on tight in the back. This ride had a very different outcome, however, and no safety marshal walked this track before they plunged.

I picked up a loose parking block—this may seem unbelievable, given that it was about four feet long, six inches high, made of concrete, and it'd been anchored to the ground with two pieces of rebar, but I'm a big man. As I said before, a tool always appeared when I needed it.

When they drove by, I used the long cement block as a javelin, throwing it through the back window of the sedan. It took the glass out in a beautiful, shattering musical display accompanied by screams in the back of the car as the block slammed into the passengers.

It was time to leave.

Their car swerved drunkenly out of the parking lot and came to rest on the front lawn of a house across the street. The occupants that could walk jumped out and started screaming, "Rape!" and "They're trying to kill us!"

Neither one of these statements is very comforting when you're speeding away from the scene of an assault, and I was angry at Hole for showing the critic his business. It would have been a simple assault charge if he hadn't flashed his cock. I took off for the highway, and I'll be fucked if the police weren't already on me. They'd been called when we'd rolled in—pre-assault—and after an hour, they'd shown up in time for a car chase.

A few of my companions were asking to be let out of the car— *fucking demon pricks, they're always in for the action, but they never want to help clean up.* I informed them that if they wanted out they could jump, at which point, I rounded a corner and one of them bailed out the back door. I tried to run over his legs as I turned but he was rolling too fast. The police chased me the wrong way up Beach Boulevard, in and out of traffic, for about a mile, before I crashed through a wooden fence and came to rest in a field.

I was instantly ordered to lie face down in the dirt, spread-eagled, and then was hand cuffed. My vehicle was towed to the impound yard and my remaining companions and I were transported to the Huntington Beach city jail. I was to be booked for assault, evading, and reckless driving.

We had a great time in the cells—getting arrested with your friends is just a minor inconvenience; you have to stay where they put you, and that's a drag, but at least you have someone to fuck around with while you're waiting to be arraigned.

The police were photographing me and getting my aliases. I figured I'd fuck with them, so I just kept rattling off names: Johnny, Anthony, James, Eric, Alex, Xerox, and the Crusher. I started making them up after a while, but the police thought they had a line on every punk-related crime committed in the southland. After I'd given the arresting officer about twenty names I started laughing—I couldn't help it—he was so fucking intent when he was writing them down. He got pissed; he knew I was fucking off.

"Are you fucking kidding me? Do you really use all these?" he asked, pointing to his lengthy list of noms de plume.

"Yep, every one of 'em."

He put down the pen and walked me down the hall. On the way to my cell, we passed a drunk that was being held in cell number two—the drunk recognized me.

"Hey, it's Big Man," he shouted. "Hey Big Man!"

That was one name I hadn't given them.

As I walked down the hall, I thought I was fucked. I needed to call somebody but I didn't know where to turn. I sure as hell couldn't call my old man. First off, he didn't have any money for bail, and secondly, he sure as fuck wasn't gonna put his house up for me.

"Grisham! You made bail."

*What the fuck?*

An officer handed me a business card with my booking papers. It was for a lawyer—a Mr. Roberts, practicing out of Santa Ana, California. There was a number written in ink on the back and a scribbled note read, "Call me."

I was gonna blow him off—not on purpose, but because I usually waited until the police picked me up on a warrant to deal with court matters. I decided against that strategy though, and I called him a prompt two weeks later.

"It's Jack." I assumed that since he bailed me out without asking, I didn't need further introduction—I was right.

"I'm glad you called, son. I talked to the DA, and he's gonna let you plead guilty to tampering with an auto and give you credit for time served. You're going to have to make some victim restitution, but it's probably only going to be a few grand and I'll cover it. I'm going to need you to come in and sign some papers; do you need a ride?"

"No, I have a car, but I was just wondering how you got involved with this."

"Mutual friends, son."

He hung up.

I knew the not-quite had gotten me out of this one, and it wasn't strange that he was using a human to do it. There are humans who knowingly and solely consorted with demons—kind of like guys that date only Asian chicks.

The lawyer's office was small and dirty—a rundown Santa Ana storefront that would have been better suited to a shooting gallery for heroin addicts—but beggars can't be choosers. It also looked like somebody had been storing empty Popov bottles in there—he didn't seem the type to keep a secretary so I figured I just picked up a lawyer that loved cheap vodka. He was dressed just as my mind had pictured him—a cheesy three-piece suit with coffee and food stains on the top two pieces. It was a miracle that this guy had enough pull to get the DA to . . . *what the fuck?*

He was human, but I couldn't see the manner or the time of his death. His future was blank—clouded—as if someone had rubbed Vaseline over the lens of the next few years of his life. This wasn't like the phone call that the slutty blond gave me, the one where her man had died; this vision was strange, like it'd been tampered with.

He offered his hand and, after a brief introduction, he laid it down.

"I'm going to be handling anything you need along these lines now. I don't do music business, but based on what I've heard, neither do you."

He smiled a sleazy old drunk's smile; it went along perfectly with his slicked-back hair and crooked teeth. The fuckin' not-quite was slipping. *You'd think he could have given me some chick counselor with a Newport Beach address.*

On second thought, if someone like me would have shown up with upscale counsel it would have been strange.

I signed the papers as asked, and I promised to show up on the date he gave me. I also promised to call him when I got in trouble again—two days later, I got picked up for resisting arrest. It was nice to know I had representation.

TSOL didn't stay long on the Posh Boy label; as a matter of fact, we jumped ship before the vinyl records had even hardened and we found ourselves recording for Frontier Records. Not much of a group, really, just one young woman who lived in the valley, I think, and as before, with Jerry and the Posh One, I could imagine Lisa working at a concentration camp—the San Fernando she-wolf in black leather and stiletto heels.

The record we gave her was a bit of a switch from the first one—although the recording contract was of the same quality. We went darker, with fewer songs about hating the government and more about insanity and creeping about. There was even a track entitled "Code Blue" that made reference to having sex with the dead. It was a joke.

Have you ever tried to have sex with a corpse? If you catch them right after they expire they're still fairly malleable, but once they've sat a bit, the body gets stiff—and not in a good way. Also, when they first dump the soul, they dump everything else, whatever waste they were carrying in their little poop-shoot comes creeping out. So, if you really want to ball a corpse, you gotta get 'em quick, throw 'em in a shower, and cum quick—before you're left with nothing sexier than a pile of compost.

And anyway, why the fuck would I want to do that? If I wanted to try old, old was easy—shit, I got that old broad in the cemetery without even trying. And if I wanted creepy or ghoulish, there was no shortage of freaked-out little punkettes that would have loved a taste of me—I could dress them up in a skeleton suit if I felt like it, or just throw a little embalming fluid and some light blue make-up all over their faces. The song was a joke, just a creative way to say, "I would rather go through all the hassle of fucking a corpse than I would to ball you, my dear."

It didn't matter, the record sold well, and the live shows were as intense as ever. If people wanted to think we'd gone creepy, let 'em. I didn't give a fuck: I was robbing, pillaging, and plundering as always, and the majority of the punk kids adored me—Alex Morgan, the punk rock hero. Oh, I'm sorry, I forgot to tell you that that's what I was calling myself now—Alex Morgan. And sometimes, when I went out, "Jim, the King of Shrubbery."

The other boys in the band thought it was time to take our act on the road—give America a little taste of what TSOL was serving to the punks in the west—but as far as I was concerned, it was a mistake.

I don't know why we ever wanted to leave the West Coast. Do you know what we ran into? We ran into a bunch of controlling, classifying, and decriminalizing wannabe punks that thought they knew what was best for "the scene." Yeah, okay, guys, as you went through your week as Joe-citizen ice cream scooper, substitute teacher, and part-time punker, *you* were gonna tell America through your fifty-cent fanzine what *real* punk is?

Real punk is not being able to hold it together for your college degree, or for your long term, forty-hour-a-week day job. Real punk isn't fun or glamorous; real punk means that, against all your best intentions, you're sitting in a lonely empty apartment with your head in your hands wondering how the fuck you destroyed your life again. Real punk means that whatever you love is gonna be gone unless you get a touch of divine intervention—and as I said before, God doesn't give a fuck.

Real punk *does* suck.

You might have been a punk rock aficionado, and your bands might have sounded real tough—with a few cool tracks—but you weren't anything but a sissified square masquerading as hardcore on the weekends.

Now, don't get me wrong, I can smell a masquerade because I'd been starring in one my whole life, and there were some unbelievable punk bands out there that weren't faking it. Bands in New York, Boston, D.C., and Chicago. We hit plenty of cities where the "real thing" shared the stage with us, and shared drinks with us, and

I could see their lives and how they ended. Not many of them were pretty. There *were* real punks on the road, but you had to find them.

As another word of warning, remember, history is rarely written by those creating it. So, I'd be careful of what you read and believe. Time makes it easier to hide what was real and what was not, and more often than not, history gets changed by the written word—Columbus didn't discover America, Edison didn't invent the fucking lightbulb, and your favorite old-time real-cool punk band or singer wasn't.

I liked seeing the country, but starving myself to death in the back of a fucking box van with no windows wasn't exactly my way to do it. There were weeks when the four of us and our crew were spending ten bucks a day on meals—between us. We split White Castle burgers into four pieces to make 'em go further. If you've never had a White Castle, they're tiny; I can fit four of 'em on the end of a fork. We didn't see a lot of hospitality out on the road either—there were a few bands that took us in, but for the most part we were on our own.

If Todd and I hadn't been stealing everything we could get our hands on, supporting our living conditions through larceny, I would have been eating kids at the shows. When we rolled into a club, the first stop would be the pinball machines or the video games. I'd grab a screwdriver and pry the covers off, and then I'd take the quarters out. I'd head to the bar, grab what booze I could, and then I'd go to the back room for leftover musical gear or a bit of the club owner's property. They always left shit lying around. I wasn't planning on coming back to any of these places, so I wasn't too worried about maintaining any reputation of honesty or integrity. They were all short-time scams anyway, so I didn't need to pretend to be cool. I made more profit ripping off clubs than I ever did from music.

Of course, there were the times that I only profited by keeping my scalp. There may not have been roving bands of hostiles sneaking off the reservation looking to kill whitey anymore, but the

Midwest was a trip back to the fucking Dark Ages. The police, or troopers as they liked to be called, practically rode around with a lynching rope in their patrol cars.

Lawrence, Kansas, was an out-of-the-way stop any time, and we were there during tornado season. The sky was a beautiful lime green—pouring rain one minute, hailing the next. There was a river running down the boulevard in front of the club, run-off from the storm. I would have been thrilled if anyone showed—whether or not they got swept away after arriving—but the club stayed empty.

We played to about twenty people, including us, and when it came time to settle up, the promoter was gone. He'd run off and left his security guard to clean up the mess—one fucking corn-fed fool to throw out six animals. We could have ruined the guy's evening, taken our pay in flesh, but we decided to be nice instead, and help him clean up. We took the promoter's sound equipment out to our vehicle—microphones, cables, and anything else that wasn't nailed down. It was a fair trade.

We drove out of town.

We went through a tollbooth and our driver sensed a problem. The guard on duty had picked up the phone as we passed through and had started dialing—it was a look-in-the-rearview-mirror-and-see-the-civil-servant-freaking-out kind of thing. Our driver told us to throw whatever drugs we hadn't already swallowed out the window, and the boys complied by swallowing a few more. We were red-lighted a mile out of town. The police stopped us but didn't approach. It was a few minutes later that I noticed traffic had stopped coming down the opposite lanes. They'd closed the freeway.

It seemed like hours before they walked up, and when they did, we could hear fear in the trooper's voice as he talked to his partner.

"Take it easy, Billy. . . . We don't know what we got here. . . . Go easy."

They shined a light on the side door and ordered us out.

Human was the first to exit. Human was an old vc friend and at present was the designer of TSOL's merchandise, which consisted mainly of T-shirts sporting the image of an upside-down Jesus on the cross and the words "Ignore Heroes" and "Fuck the System" at his feet. Our system was about to be fucked, as soon as the troopers caught a look at Human—6'3", Herman boots, boxers, and bright pink hair.

"Oh. My. Gawd," a trooper exclaimed, each word its own sentence. "What. Do. We. Got. Here?"

The troopers were scared and confused. These southern Baptist coppers had never seen creeps like us—and it didn't help that the promoter had called the police and told them we were heavily armed. Luckily, we'd just mailed home a box of stolen guns we'd taken from an earlier show—if the troopers had stopped us three days earlier, we would have been climbing out of the vehicle with six-guns stuffed down our underpants.

The troopers laid us face down in a ditch on the side of the toll road. They proceeded to get us up, one by one, for a search—first, of our person, and second, of our effects. I was the first; a trooper patted me down and then marched me into the vehicle, holding a shotgun against the back of my head.

"You talk out every move, boy. I wanna know what-cher doing."

I was not to surprise or confuse him, or the vehicle would be wearing my blood on its seats. Not surprising him would be easy, but this fucker thought Ronald Reagan was doing a great job, so I was fucked when it came to not confusing him.

"No surprises, boy, no surprises. I'll blow yer head off."

"I'm reaching for the bag, sir. I'm opening the bag."

"Keep talkin', boy, jus' keep talkin'." His words were punctuated with shotgun jabs to the back of my neck.

I came up clean.

We were each searched, individually, in the same way, and they tore our vehicle apart looking for contraband. They should have taken a knife and opened up a few stomachs—I could have told them who was holding the Valium.

After the freeway opened up and they had emptied and rifled through every pillowcase and cabinet, they decided to arrest just one of us. At first they wanted me, but Mike, another friend who was acting as band manager, suddenly got the balls to tell them he'd stolen everything and the boys knew nothing about it. I was stoked; I wasn't looking forward to a Kansas territorial prison.

The rest of us were released to the night, with a helpful trooper giving us a caveat about the roads ahead.

"You boys are lucky this didn't go down in Missouri; you get hung for stealin' chickens there."

I was glad to get back home to the land of surf and sunshine, where the police were kinder and more sympathetic to our plight, and where I had easy access to an attorney.

With the coming of spring we switched record labels again. We were three for three—three records, three labels—there was no need for us to wear out our welcome. Alternative Tentacles in San Francisco was the headquarters for our latest release, and Jello Biafra, the lead singer of the Dead Kennedys, was the founder of the feast. If I was sticking with the "imagine if they were in a concentration camp" theme, which Biafra would surely hate, I would cast Jello as the mad doctor who experimented on the campers. Jello owned Alternative Tentacles, and I was surprised he even accepted us on his label. We weren't as politically correct as he liked his bands to be—he preferred art students, not pirates.

The disc wasn't bad, but it wasn't especially good either. It was another EP, like the first TSOL record, but the songs were a bit more experimental, and we fucked with the packaging. Records are like wrenches: people know how to use them according to their size. If a record is large—meaning 12" or 10" in diameter—one plays it at the turntable speed of 33 1/3 rpm (revolutions per minute). If

you're playing your grandma's records, you play the record at 78
rpm. If a record is small—a 7" disc—then one plays it at 45 rpm. It's
pretty simple, really. But we decided to make a 7" record that was
made to turn at 33 1/3, thereby fucking up the listener's whole
concept of what to do with the fucking disc. If you think it sounds
confusing here, think of the little punk fucks all hopped up on black
beauties and malt liquor trying to figure out what the fuck happened to the music.

### I I I

At six a.m. on July 22nd, I was at the liquor store. I rode up there
on my bicycle and bought a big bottle of Jack Daniel's. I'd just purchased my first legal drink.

Now, I wasn't completely honest with you as this story unfolded.
You see, there were times when I drank, took drugs, or both, and I
didn't mention them to you. I've spent so many years lying and
hiding that it got to be a habit. I would have told you if it'd gotten
real out of hand when I drank, and I'll admit to a few instances of
insanity.

One of these times, I drove from the hood of my car. I pushed
the roadster to sixty or seventy miles per hour, and then climbed
over the windshield as I continued steering. All the while my terrified female passenger—who'd just lost a brother and a father to a
drunk driver—was screaming and crying in terror as I laughed. And
if I had to give you one more example, I could tell you about the
time that I dared a man to shoot me, walking towards his shaking
pistol hand until the tip of his gun was buried in my stomach—his
soon to be ex-wife was pregnant with my soon to be ex-living fetus.
I'd gotten a bit loose, I'll give you that, but the booze and the drugs
never got a hold of me, and I remained strong. If I hadn't, I probably would have told you, and I probably wouldn't be writing this
book. And we have a party to attend.

I was hosting a party at my house that day. It was my twenty-first birthday, and I was ready to roll. My mother and father left early—they knew they couldn't stop me from indulging this day, and they were probably afraid to see what might happen to their home. They didn't even ask me to be good. Why bother? They saw me wander in early with the bottle, and they guessed where it was heading. It was funny how they clutched their things when they left—like a mother trying to protect her child from harm—but in this case, it wasn't the child that needed protection. My father muttered something about not burning down the house, but we wouldn't be playing with fire that morning; it wasn't on the agenda. Today was a water sports day.

I knew better than to let my crew in the house; I'd been to enough parties with those guys and I didn't need them pissing in my mom's shoes or cutting the phone lines. It wasn't a matter of disrespect. It was a matter of "Fuck, Jack, whattaya expect? Your mom's necklace was just laying out and all; I had to take it."

We stayed by the pool.

The backyard at my parents' house wasn't large, but the builders packed a whole lot of pool in there. There was hardly any room to walk around it safely—it was so tight that we had to stick the barbecue in the side-yard. We had two cases worth of patties and matching buns, all courtesy of a late-night kick-the-door-in at Tastee-Freez.

The street was packed with cars by noon and there was no-through traffic—kids just double-, triple-, and quadruple-parked their cars in the street. The neighbors weren't about to call the police—for fear of retaliation—so it was "Fuck you, drive around" to any outsiders that tried to pass through.

The first injuries came early. We were drunk-diving off the roof into the pool and people were climbing out with huge goose eggs and bloody foreheads. I was sauced. Shit, I don't know why I kept the cap after I opened that bottle of Jack, because I sure the fuck didn't have any intention of putting it back on. I was guzzling that shit like lemonade on a hot day.

There was a Jacuzzi in the yard, and I suggested we try to fill it with as many people as possible. I coaxed them by giving them the pitch often used to shove people in a phone booth, or pack students in a V.W. bug—I was acting like the Guinness record people were gonna show up for verification and the kids crowded into that small pool and jammed in tight. When I was sure they couldn't put one more kid in there, and it was nearly impossible for any of them to move, I dropped my trunks and pissed all over them.

If you came into the backyard, you were going to be swimming.

It didn't matter if you had a leather jacket, spiked hair, or an eight ball of cocaine in your pocket, everybody got wet. We were even dragging innocent passersby into the backyard and tossing them in.

It was over before the sun went down.

There were hamburger patties and kegs floating in the pool, underage kids were passed out on the lawn, and trails of puke were drifting off in a hundred different directions.

### III

Most people will never know what it's like to do whatever you want—short of intentional murder—and not worry about the outcome. I just urinated all over fifteen kids and nobody did a thing about it. I was at a point in my life where anything I did was cool to somebody. Maybe not the person I was doing it to—but somebody else *always* thought it was funny. Do you know that since my first existence, there was only one other time that I feared no reprisal?

It was a few thousand years ago. I was living in this fucking hole of a village in the land of Uz—and when I say village, I'm stretching it. Anyway, there was a man that lived there and his name was Jacob—he knew me by the name of Akhar, or the Butcher—and you might know him as Job.

Job was the most unselfish man I had ever met. He was kind to everyone, not a complainer or a crybaby; he loved his God and he demonstrated it with his actions. He fucking sickened me. Job was one of those nice guys who had a kind word for everyone—no matter what you said or did to him.

I was asked to look out for guys like this—God lovers. The not-quite was always interested in the real nice ones—the pious and the penitent—so I told him about Job, and how nothing I could do would shake him.

It was one of those standard desert days when the not-quite came to town—the wind was drifting subtly over the dunes and the sun hung, unashamed, in the sky. I was proud that he was coming—a visit from a father would surely straighten out this desert saint. I ran to see him when he arrived, but he quickly stopped me in my tracks. He told me that he wasn't there to see me and I would have to wait. He was there to see *the Man.*

I watched them talk—two swirls of dust dancing back and forth across the sand. It was hours before they finished. One of the swirls scattered to the wind, and the other solidified into the not-quite. He was wearing the skin of a small boy, and he came to me.

"Do whatever you want to him, Akhar. Take everything he owns and everything he loves, kill his children and all his beasts, cover his body with sores and give him to the night, but you may not take his woman or his life—these you must leave him. I guarantee he will curse God. I give you my word."

It was like my father told me to drink, smoke, and do anything I wanted to the house—burn the fucker down if I felt like it—and I would not be punished in any way, not by him or the authorities. The not quite and God himself just gave me the green light to go ape shit on that fucker. And ape shit I went.

I started with the house and his land—a sandstorm took them both in an hour. Job hit his knees and thanked God that no one was hurt. I moved to his animals, laying disease on them, and they all perished but one small lamb, which I spared to remind him of what he once had. The next day, Job offered his last lamb as a sacrifice to

God—he slaughtered it on an altar and touched none of its flesh. I was furious; I couldn't believe I needed help.

A wagon rode into the village the next day. It was a gang of demons—reinforcements. There were eight of them, vicious and old, experienced in turning the blessed into the blasphemous. We killed Job's children and we drove his wife away.

The next morning found Job on his knees again, he was crying about his loss, but he was thanking his God for the opportunity he had to know them. He thanked God for the blessings that He had bestowed on him, and he prayed that he would come to know God's will in the trials that he suffered. I walked up and kicked Job as hard as I could in the face—his head snapping back so violently that I thought I might have gone too far and broken our deal with the Man, but I hadn't. Job just looked up at me from the ground, and said he was sorry if he'd angered me, or if, in his misfortune, he had failed to pay a bill that he owed me—motherfucker.

We did everything we could to him, and he would not break— we pushed his body with sickness and disease beyond that which would kill any other man, and Job never cursed God for his woes.

I was contacted by the not-quite. He came to me as my reflection in a pool; he told me stop, pack up, and leave town. I was never to touch Job again, and the not-quite didn't apologize for breaking his word.

### III

Two thousand years later, I was now calling myself Jack again, Jack Delauge. TSOL had just finished our fourth record—our second full-length disc. Unsurprisingly, we'd jumped ship again, and this record was financed by yet another company, Faulty Products. I never saw a face behind the label. We were moving up the ladder of corporate punk and we were now dealing with the gentleman that might fund the concentration camps—if you were sticking to that fantasy. We'd gone from the sexual liaison officer and the sadistic commandant, to the evil she-wolf, to the mad doctor, and now, we were dealing with the financiers—those nameless faces that supplied the money, but took none of the blame.

We pushed the edge on this disc—not with any attacks against those outside the scene, but on those within. We conscripted a fifth member, Greg, who added keyboards—piano and synthesized strings—to our sound.

Punk rock had become too complacent, as far as I was concerned. The West Coast needed to expand and become inventive again—the boundaries that the scene had set for itself needed to be opened up. The scene disagreed.

Humans hate change and I love them for it; it makes my work easier. They're so easily disturbed. When they wanted something that they'd grown accustomed to and were comfortable with, I gave them the opposite. If they wanted me to wear Levi's, I gave them Chanel. If they wanted me to have short hair, I gave them long. If they wanted hard guitars and anti-government lyrics, I gave them a soft piano, strings, and an ode to unrequited love.

I fucked with them every chance I got, and I fucked with outsiders to our scene by changing my name on each record—reviewers would write that the band was getting worse with each new singer.

However, the live shows were as spontaneous and as crazy as ever, and I started to expand my role as a messiah of hedonism to the youth.

Riverside is about sixty miles from the beach. It was part of the Inland Empire, a piece of old California that refused to change with the times. The advancing climate of teenage dissent against the government had never crossed the small mountain range that separated the Inland from the sea—a conservative viewpoint hung like smog in the sky. But there were a few small pockets of resistance that were eager to be fed with a dose of the true sound.

## Punk Rock Messiah

We booked a show at a nightclub/disco that had "Saturday Night Fever" Sunday through Friday, but ironically, Saturday was "new music" night. The promoter was a freshman in the punk scene, and he wasn't exactly sure what to expect; he figured maybe a hundred kids would show in total, and he'd get a pretty good take from the bar. He ended up with six hundred rabid fans in a line that wrapped around the block, and a wallet full of nothing.

Our man Mike—the guy who managed us and took the rap for the stolen microphone in Kansas—offered to collect the cash at the door and help run the show that evening. The promoter gratefully accepted his generous proposal. There was no way that the club could handle the crowd; the legal capacity was maybe three hundred, tops. But as long as they were paying, Mike was taking their money and stuffing them in.

The promoter lived in the upstairs section of the club; his bedroom doubled as a dressing room—and to us, it also filled the role of toilet and ashtray. While we waited to go on, I piled the promoter's dirty clothes on his bed and lit them on fire. We were laughing and attempting to piss it out when security showed.

The promoter hired these two huge black bouncers—they had never attended a punk rock show, and to them, our antics and our general demeanor resembled those involved with voodoo and demonic possession. I was surprised at their clarity of perception, and I did my best not to let them down.

The first band was awful. Not only were they lacking in talent—we could have stomached that—but they thought they were God's gift to crotch-stuffing rock and hair-flipping roll. Our friend Human, our T-shirt guy, was in attendance that evening, and he asked me if I'd like him to stop their performance. I didn't give a fuck—I didn't attend shows, I just played at them. I was curious as to how he was going to arrange their finale: so yes, I thought it would be nice if they were through.

During one of their songs Human walked onstage, grabbed the neck of the guitar player's guitar, and casually said, "That's it, you're done." The voodoo-fearing bouncers promptly escorted them from the stage, assuming Human was in charge, which really wasn't far from the truth, and we were on.

Before we began our set, one of the bouncers made an announcement about the disco ball that hung from the ceiling directly over the middle of the dance floor.

"Don't touch it," he said. He was adamant, and he was large, flexing his muscles and wringing his hands together as he made his pitch for the safety of that rhinestone orb. The crowd took a step back from the prized object.

Mike started our first song—the bass low and driving—calling out for the band to answer; I grabbed the mic, pointed at the disco ball, and said, "Rip it down."

The crowd went crazy—monkeys climbing onto backs, and then climbing onto more backs, as they made a human ladder towards the ball. They were fighting for the honor of destroying it. The ball was reached—twelve pairs of hands hanging and pulling simultaneously until it was ripped from the ceiling—and then carelessly dropped to the ground. The glass shattered on impact. The dancers waited for another command from me; their eyes rolled back into their heads, the ecstasy of abandon slashed across their faces. Anything I asked would be done without question. Any order I gave at that moment would have been followed. I ordered them to dance and not stop, and they didn't until the band was through. The show and the pleasure of control turned me on.

After the set, the bouncers cornered our drummer, Todd, and Human upstairs. They were told there were damages, and someone had to pay. It was going to be a mash-up, and my boys had no chance of beating these two.

I was running upstairs to help when Mike stopped me.

"Let's go!" he yelled. "Let's get the fuck out of here!"

He was grabbing me by my arm—pulling, while holding me back.

"I can't leave Todd," I said "He's gonna get the fuck beaten out of him." I wasn't worried about Human—he could handle himself.

Mike kept pulling, "Fuck Todd, get in the car!"

I'd never seen Mike like that—he was panicked. And he was usually pretty cool. Something was definitely driving him. He wasn't going to let me go—I decided to trust him, and we ran to the vehicle.

We drove off, gravel flying from the tires as I fishtailed the car out of the parking lot. I could imagine Todd screaming as they beat him. I was a fuck for leaving my friends. I demanded an explanation, and Mike supplied it.

"Look what I have." His smile broke into that naughty boy grin that I'd felt on my own face numerous times. I looked down, and between his legs, riding safely on the floorboards, was a brown paper grocery bag. It was filled with money.

"I took the fucking cash, Jack. I took the whole fucking door. I'm thinking five or six thousand dollars. We're fucking stoked, man!"

He'd taken all they had.

I tried to remember who we'd abandoned at the club, but I couldn't think of a name or a face that'd been left behind. Everybody we needed was sitting right there on the floor, and I was gonna drive, real safely, home.

We took the money back to my parents' garage and started counting. It was as he said: five hundred and seventy two people at ten dollars a head made a whole bunch of nice green bills lying on that floor.

An hour later, Todd and Human came in. Todd had a freshly delivered black eye, and he was furious—they'd tortured him, but he didn't break.

"I can't believe you fucking left us, man. They slapped the shit out of me, and they—"

He saw the cash.

Thousands of dollars stacked in piles on the floor, beautiful little green faces and they were smiling back at all of us. I didn't have to offer an apology of any sort; the money did it for me.

This was a turning point for the not-quite and myself. I was now openly giving commands to my followers, and they were being performed without question. The army was in place. The groundwork for loyalty had already been laid.

I was becoming the Jim Jones of punk rock—a trusted leader who cared about the kids and who was willing to stand up for what he believed in. A leader built on the back of the criticism of the American political machine. I was going to be in government one day—I would be the candidate of the disaffected youth. I'd never been convicted of a felony, and I'd never marked my body with ink or pen—I was scarred, yes, but they were the scars of a hard childhood that would endear me to the populace. I was perfect for the coming change in the American political climate—when someone with a background that at one time would have been too dirty, would now be considered colorful and tough in his bold ideology;

a maverick whose willingness to stand alone on the lines of change proved his strength . . .

And besides that, chicks dug me.

To be a leader, you have to have what my old friend Jerry of the Cuckoo's Nest called "fuckability"—the attractiveness that draws both men and women to you sexually, making you the kind of guy that anyone or anything might want to sleep with. Being a demon, I had it in spades.

Some reviewers said that TSOL brought street-hot women into punk rock. I don't necessarily disagree; if you wanted to pick up some ladies, you sure as fuck didn't go to a Black Flag show. You came to see us.

I treated each person I fucked with the same respect . . . basically. As long as I was with you, you were mine. I was never yours. But the minute either you or I walked away, I took the next girl, and you vanished. I was like an infant: when you disappeared from my sight, you ceased to exist, and all benefit and memory of our association was lost.

I screwed this chick in the parking lot before a show. She'd been hanging around, batting her eyes at me all night, and laughing at everything I said—it was sad, really. I'd pointed it out to a crew member, and then just to show him how stupid she was, when some-one asked me a question, I just answered back with random words.

"Hey Jack, did you see the Crowd play last week?"

"Blow-dryer."

She loved it. Cooing and giggling with every non-sequitur.

Normally, I would have considered her too stupid to fuck, but something about her reminded me of a sex doll I once knew— maybe I could tape her mouth shut or hold my jacket over her head.

I grabbed her hand and told her to come on. She started to question where I was taking her, but I gave her a glance that conveyed what she feared in one stab: "If you don't shut the fuck up, I'm not gonna fuck you." She understood, and for the first time that evening she was quiet—I realized I might not need the gag.

I led her over to my car where I politely held the door open for her. I climbed in on top of her and pulled up her skirt. I figured we'd had enough foreplay already—what with her laughing at my jokes and all, so I got right to it.

She was quicker than I was: some women like being used.

We got out of the car, and she was hanging on me as if we were now dating. I was getting ready to inform her that the past tense of dating is dated; we'd *dated*, and as far as I was concerned, we'd just broken up. She saved me the trouble when she excused herself to "clean up."

It was then that my date's best friend walked up—her protector, confidant, and close companion was not about to let her get used by the likes of me.

"You're a fucking pig," she scolded. "If Kathy thinks you're anything more than a slut, she's an idiot."

"Who's Kathy?" I was serious.

"Fuck you, Jack. I bet you'd try to fuck me if I gave you the chance."

I looked her over, top to bottom. She was cuter than Kathy—at least I think that the girl I'd just dipped into was Kathy—and I read between the lines. She was saying, "Jack, fuck me, I'm giving you the chance."

I opened the car door and gestured to the seat. It was still reclined—and warm.

"You're a fucking asshole," she replied.

I read between the lines again—she must enjoy being invaded from behind. I grabbed her and forced my lips on her. She fought for less than a second, giving me a sharp bite on my tongue that she almost instantly "kissed better."

I turned her towards the car, and she climbed in. I figured the girl before her had already taken care of the foreplay, so I just dove in. She was wild, aggressive; I thought she was going to kick the windows out as I fucked her. Kathy was lucky to have such a strong, protective friend as . . . hmm, I didn't catch her name. Oh well. Kathy was lucky to have a friend as trustworthy as Kathy's friend was.

I was just about to finish when I heard shouting outside the car. *What the fuck?* It was Kathy, and she was now pounding on the window. I took a quick look around, thinking she might have forgotten her purse or something. I opened the car door. She wanted to talk.

"What the fuck's wrong with you? I was in the bathroom you piece of shit."

She was drawing a small crowd of amused onlookers.

"You're fucking my friend? You fucking asshole!"

I wish she would have said, "You're fucking Maria?" or something. I was kind of digging this girl, and it might have been nice to know her name.

The onlookers were having a great time—this was punk rock theater at its best, and their presence at this event didn't hurt me one bit. As a matter of fact, my reputation as a ladies' man was increasing with each sexually charged word she spat.

"Slut."

"Fucking whore."

"Asshole."

I was flattered.

When Kathy got tired of pumping up my ego, she ran screaming into the night.

What the fuck did she think she was doing, considering me property? She slept with me twenty minutes after meeting me, so what did she expect? Why the fuck was she crying? I was the one that didn't get to finish. Her friend was concerned about her.

"I need to go get her," What's-Her-Name said. "She's got my keys."

As if that was my problem.

I was scheduled to play at midnight, so I had a few hours to waste. I decided to be kind. I asked a friend to drive us around a bit, so Kathy's friend could look for Kathy.

He drove; I sat with my pants down in the backseat.

The friend of Kathy sat facing forward on my lap, so I could screw her while she looked for her buddy.

It would be no exaggeration to say I often slept with four or five different girls a night, and most of them were like horror-movie bimbos; they just kept wandering outside while the killer circled the house. However, there were a few ladies that were almost as frightening as I was. The punk rock revolution did create some good: it sexually liberated those that were looking to be freed. I think the phrase "I've got a pussy and I'm gonna use it" was coined at a TSOL show, and to say some punk girls were liberated—meaning they were as trampy as the boys—would be an understatement.

My parents didn't have an answering machine, and it was years before voicemail, so when I was out, I'd dial home every half-hour or so just to see who called. It drove my folks crazy.

I rang home one night, just checking in, and my mother said she'd just caught two young ladies setting up a tent in the front yard. She said she'd invited them in, and they were now having lemonade and getting ready to go through the baby book. I was horrified. I couldn't imagine what my mother might be saying. I was at a party, but I got home as quickly as possible.

When I walked in, two of the most fucked-up looking ladies were sitting at the bar having a drink with my mother. It wasn't that they weren't cute—because they most definitely were—it was that their choice of attire wasn't proper for visiting one's mom. Both of them were wearing torn-up lingerie, extremely short leather miniskirts with no under-britches, and they'd tied previously used condoms in their crazy-colored hair.

My mother was acting like it was nothing and chatting them up.

"You know he's really not flashy enough onstage, I sewed

sequins on all his shirt collars, but for some reason he pulled them off. Maybe they should set down the instruments and do a little dance number. . . . Now *that* would really get the crowd going."

I thanked my mother for her hospitality to my guests, and then I hustled the girls out of the house and took them back to the party.

"Goodbye, mother," they said in unison.

The party was a high school affair. It wasn't a punk party, so to speak, but it was filled with younger kids who weren't against us either: supporters.

I brought these chicks in and the virginal high school girls were spooked, and maybe, deep inside, a little attracted. I saw these young girls look at me as I played with my ladies, and sometimes their tender young eyes would not look away when they caught my glance. I could read their thoughts as they watched: *I'd do that, if he asked me. . . . I want him to touch* me *that way.*

One of my little punkettes spread her legs, and I openly played with her as I sat on the couch—she was giggling and enjoying my attention—the other was kissing me as I played.

The evening ended with me bringing them back home for a little two-on-one action, but it got ugly. I was taking turns—balling them both—when a fight broke out over who would get the seed. They started arguing and then punching and pulling each other's hair. I was trying to keep them quiet but it was impossible, I had two drunken punkettes screaming and beating each other's asses at two a.m. I was finally forced to escort them, somewhat unlovingly, towards the door—without the seed.

Girls were always coming on to me; they'd grab my crotch, straight out, without a thought of rejection or judgment in any way, and they'd say, "I want you."

I always obliged.

I didn't mind being used one bit.

| | |

No one doubted my maniacal leadership skills, my charisma, or my sex appeal. However, my ability to sing hadn't improved much. It wasn't as noticeable when I first started out, but as TSOL's music progressed—developing a cleaner, clearer sound—my voice began to be a bit of a drawback. I was never going to be a pop star, and the number of people that I could touch playing hardcore music was limited. There had to be another way to reach more kids.

I knew what the not-quite wanted, but don't ask me how I knew, because I couldn't tell you. It was just a feeling that drove me, almost instinctually, towards the goal. Expand the market, expand the fan base, and expand the army.

The perfect opportunity soon came.

Penelope Spheeris asked TSOL if we would like to appear in her new film, *Suburbia*. It was going to be fictional, about a group of homeless squatter punks, and TSOL was going to be one of three bands featured.

Penelope had a solid underground reputation as a director who was honest with her portrayal of the punk rock scene. She'd recently directed *The Decline of Western Civilization,* a documentary chronicling the rise of punk in southern California and *Decline* was as close to the real thing as possible.

*Suburbia* was exactly what I needed. It was the perfect vehicle to reach a larger audience. We accepted her offer and performed as asked.

Most films and television shows about punk rock frustrated me. The films were usually a joke; I'd seen a few prime-time takeoffs of what the movie world thought we were like, and they portrayed punks as stupid, club-wielding savages. I didn't want to be part of that. I didn't mind the savage part, but I refused to be portrayed as stupid. I needed to be seen as suave and cool.

To her credit, Penelope made me look good. There was even a moment when we were onstage—being filmed—and two smokin' little girls jumped up and tried to kiss and hug me. Penelope recreated the reality of TSOL, and thankfully, the lurking danger and mayhem that followed me was held at bay by the bright lights of the production.

Appearing in Penelope's film was just one more step up the evolutionary ladder of domination.

### III

It was time to tour again.

The standard procedure for any working band was: make a record, go on tour, shoot a movie, go on tour. It was bullshit. Now that we were about to get national attention with *Suburbia*, why the fuck would we want to leave home? I'd seen the USA, and as far as I knew, it wasn't any different from the last time I'd been out.

I went along with manager Mike and the rest of the guys, because although my inclination to stay home was strong, it wasn't like I was being forcefully driven to remain. My wanting to stay home was probably about comfort and laziness, and not a feeling generated by my man. At home, I had a warm bed and any company I chose to take. On the road, the sleeping arrangements were dodgy at best—and the sleeping companions were sometimes dodgier.

I'm not sure if the boys in the band were trying to appease me, but when they pulled up in a thirty-five-foot motor home equipped with large soft beds, a toilet, and a working generator, I was a bit less reluctant.

The RV had been rented through a newspaper ad. The renters were supposedly a young couple out for a honeymoon trip, not five punk boys and their friends who would be traveling, heavily armed with drugs, guns, and drink. I sort of wish I was there when Mike brought it back—the concerned leasing agent asked, "Is that blood, or semen, on the bathroom ceiling?"

"Gee, I don't know, it looks like it could be . . . a little of both?"

We set up a going away show, or fundraiser, at the local youth center in the park. We rented the building for the fee of fifty dollars, and we gave the recreation department the promise that no alcohol would be served. We didn't say anything about drugs—we *were* serving those; however, being men of our word, alcohol was not on the menu. It was a special request item, available to those inquiring, and the kids always inquired.

We stocked the bill with local bands. We didn't need help on the draw, so why not kick a bone down to the up-and-comers? We paid them well.

Our people ran security and the door. The five hundred or so who showed had no problem with the five dollar cover, and our fifty dollar investment netted us about two thousand after paying the opening bands. It was an almost-perfect war chest to start our tour.

There were no real problems during the show—unless of course you count the hard time my sacrificial gift had finding her clothes. I guess the kids on the dance floor wanted to give me a going away present, so they thoughtfully stripped a young woman and passed her above their heads to me. It reminded me of an old Busby Berkeley number—maybe from *Footlight Parade* or *Dames*—as she spun around over the heads of the dancers. It was black leather and bandanas, white T-shirts and muscular necks surrounded with choke-chain dog collars: a kaleidoscope of testosterone and alcohol, drugs, and dementia—an X-rated musical.

The kids stood in the street as we waved goodbye. Our pockets lined with their money, my body covered in the scent of their gift to me.

The youth center lay silent like an old used towel—its windows broken out, its bathroom sinks kicked off their pedestals, and its nicely finished wooden floor scarred permanently by the steel-toed boots of the dancers. Somewhere in the office of the Parks and Recreation Department lay a credit card slip covering the deposit. The name on the card was one Kenneth R. Pearl—who the fuck that was, I'll never know, seeing as how I'd picked up the card during a burglary. Mike had used it to secure the building.

## AN AMERICAN DEMON

We left Los Angeles and pulled into New York.

I'd love to tell you that the middle of the United States had become a wonderland for punk bands, but it had not. If anything, most of the bands and clubs I liked had disbanded or been destroyed by lack of support. I *can* give you a good report about the flourishing business being done in cowboy belt buckles and confederate flags, though. They were through the roof in sales; the not-quite would have been proud.

It was a Friday afternoon and we rolled into New York City for a show at CBGB's. We parked the motor home right out front. It was instantly used as a shelter for human cockroaches—old homeless men trying to stay warm slid under our vehicle to suck up what heat they could. Fucking parasites. There ought to be a limit to how long you live when you're a failure. It's one thing to be fucked-up and homeless when you're young, but at eighty, the chances of you getting your shit together are pretty low. Might as well use that flesh for something beneficial to the public—maybe grind the old homeless up and feed 'em to the young homeless. That way we're killing two birds with one bum. We get the old ones off the street, and we give the young ones incentive to get their shit together. . . . I'll have to work that into my platform.

The gear was unloaded inside the club, and I had time to kill. It was six hours before the show.

I was sitting in the passenger's seat of the motor home, flipping the pages of one of Todd's magazines, when I saw the guy come around the corner. He was ancient—had to be close to a hundred if he was a day. And he carried his body as if the weight of the world was literally on his shoulders.

He was a demon, although in all my lives I had never seen one like this. He sat down on the ground in front of the club and pulled a bottle from his coat pocket—your standard brown paper bag sidewalk cocktail. He didn't so much lift the bottle to his lips as he did hold the bottle straight up in his lap and then drop his face upon it—almost like he was giving himself head. And then, when his mouth was securely fastened around the neck of that drink, he lifted the bottle and his head slowly back, with his eyes closed, until the wall he sat against stopped their movement. From there, he opened his throat and just let the liquid slide down.

I got out of the car and sat next to him. He looked up at me and the whites of his eyes were the color of urine—he looked as he smelled.

"Motherfucker won't let me die."

"Who won't, pops?"

"Him; the man you work for."

I didn't need to ask twice; he was talking about the not-quite. I didn't understand what this demon was still living for. When demons come to earth, we're usually around for a set period—the time it takes to do our work, whatever that may be—and then we're cut loose to start over. There were old demons, yes; but they were useful demons. This thing sitting beside me was done. He wasn't good to anyone or anything.

I thought about killing him, and he laughed with a great rolling roar that fought the noise off the avenue. He held up wrists that looked as if he'd tried hacking them off with a chainsaw.

"You think I don't want it?"

I was confused. "I don't get it, man."

"You don't get it 'cause you're still doing like he says. I used to be like that, doing what you do, getting what you got, but I quit on it, and he turned on me. I tried to make it better when I first hurt, but he won't listen no more, and he won't come. When I first tried taking myself home, I woke up in the hospital with him standing over me. 'A miracle,' they said, 'a fucking miracle.' But I knew it wasn't nothing but him wanting me hurt more."

"What'd you quit doing, pops?"

"I just quit it when I got this." He held the bottle up. "It jus' didn't seem right anymore, it jus' didn't seem good hurtin' anymore."

He turned the bottle up and finished the last, and then he held it up to his eye and laughed.

"There's a spider in there, there's always a spider up in there."

A single drop fell and landed on his now outstretched tongue. He started sobbing.

There wasn't fuck I could do for him, and that whole shit about not doing what was asked of him freaked me out. Shit, I could make it a bit easier for him today though. Normally I didn't give a fuck about the homeless, but this was different.

I remembered we'd stolen a case of Ancient Age whiskey and it was in the vehicle. I took a fifth out and handed it to him. He was done talking. We sat and we took turns pulling off that bottle. I watched a small bit of comfort creep down over his shoulders, but for me, there was nothing. I might as well have been sipping water. I couldn't quit thinking about him not being able to die. I remembered that night on the beach and how the not-quite wouldn't let me go—waking me up all blue and cold. I could see him keeping somebody around because he needed them, but to keep this old fuck alive just to hurt him was fucked.

After a few drinks, I got an idea.

Ron was lying down in the vehicle, so I asked him if he'd go get us some Dixie cups. He did, and when he came back I started pouring booze. The old boys underneath the car crawled out and got some, and then the bums on the corner drifted down and filled their cups. It turned into a soup line, except instead of soup, I was serving pure Kentucky blue.

Word traveled fast through the Bowery and the sidewalk around me was soon crowded with new friends. The case of Ancient Age seemed to be everlasting—it filled a hundred with its warmth.

The police showed just as things were getting fun. A few of my acquaintances had wandered into the street, and traffic was forced to break, swerve, and hold for a parade of inebriates. The police were not pleased. They wanted to know *who* and they wanted to know *why*.

I didn't stick around to supply answers, and I wasn't too worried about anyone else being implicated. Ron had ducked back inside the motor home and the police would probably just figure that one of these bums pinched a case of booze and ended up sidewalking it in front of cb's.

I walked up the street to get my head together. I didn't drink that much—maybe half that fifth, but I needed to shake the thought of that dude.

"You dating, baby?"

She was hot—sleazy as fuck in a red plastic skirt and torn-up nylons—and just the thing I needed to help me forget.

"Where you wanna go?" I asked.

She turned towards an alley, and I followed her in. She was probably just looking to suck me off, but I was planning on pounding her against the bricks and not paying for it. She leaned against the wall and spread her legs.

I stepped in and pulled her to me. I had friends that didn't kiss these things, but I wanted the whole experience—black lipstick and all.

"I don't like the company you keep."

Shit, it was *him*—the voice an octave or two lower with that raspy tone.

"Mother fuck!"

*Why couldn't he just say hello* . . . before *all the preliminaries?*

"Do you want to end up like that sack of shit back there? Maybe I could get him to make space in his box for you. Is that what you're looking for?"

"No, I was just wondering, I've never—"

"You never *what*? You never want to go back to California?"

"No, I just—"

"You just continue driving the way I steer. And stay away from the booze. I can smell your fucking breath, and you stink."

"That'll be twenty, baby." What the fuck, he was gone and I was left with this whore. I turned and walked away.

"Hey, you owe me twenty." She started screaming, "Roger! Roger! This motherfucker just walked after I loved him. Roger!"

I was figuring Roger was her pimp, but if so, he better come heavily armed; I was in no mood to haggle, and I was late for the show—which, by the way, sucked.

I was never leaving California again.

Home was everything I knew it would be. There was a swell in—a nice four- to six-foot south-by-southwest created overhead peaks that twisted and spit up and down the beach. I walked out onto the sand and knew I was home. That day I surfed the pier, the north side of Huntington Beach. It was usually a zoo, but I was a returning hero, and the boys in the lineup welcomed me back with cat-calls and whistles.

## Riot on Sunset

This was more like it. I dug being an invading army—the feeling I got on the road—but to be home and adored was perfect. This was what I deserved. *I wish there was some way I could work from here, put the world on a Lazy Susan and then just spin the venues in front of me—I'll have to ask the not-quite if he can arrange that.*

I lay on the sand after my surf session, breathing in the sea air, and thinking about the evening to come. There was a party that night, and it couldn't have been more perfectly timed. Welcome home.

Everywhere I went, I was either feared or adored. When I went to the liquor store to grab a bottle of vodka, it was like being in a parade—friendly honks on the highway as I drove to the store, a cheering shout from a passing car as I exited the roadster, a few girls in the parking lot giggling and waving and whispering to each other as I walked by. The old Chinese man behind the counter smiled a big yellow cartoon grin when I walked in.

"Mr. Jack," he said, "it's so good to see you."

He was happy I wasn't beating people in front of his market, or robbing his deliverymen when they showed.

"I'm a little short, Lee." I pointed to the vodka—not an expensive brand, because no matter what the fuck you say, it all tastes alike. "Do you think you can spot me on this one?" I had plenty of money, but some of these old Asian guys didn't really feel like they were doing business unless they were getting extorted in some way. I was doing him a favor.

"No problem, Mr. Jack. Good being home, okay?"

Yes, it *was*; it was everything a demon could ask for.

I drove to the party with the bottle of vodka tucked between my legs—it was safer there than it would be if I left it to ride all alone in the passenger seat, and besides, it was turning me on having my legs wrapped around that booze.

The party was already rolling when I arrived. The driveway and the street were jam-packed with cars, so I parked on the lawn. Before I got out, I poured a bit of vodka down my throat. It was like making out with a girl—I could've brought her inside and openly displayed my feelings for her, even shared her if I felt like it, but I didn't; I wanted something for later. So, after a few loving swallows, I left the bottle in the car and went inside.

I could feel the party light up as I entered. The energy in the room pulsed and got brighter; *I was going to turn this fucker out.* I headed to the kitchen.

If you want to have fun at a party, the kitchen's the place; this is where the booze waits for its owner, where lonely old sixers of cold brew are kept chilling in the fridge, and dusty cupboards are cradling fifths of the good stuff.

I didn't have to wait for a drink.

A boy—maybe eighteen at most—walked in with a fucking half-gallon of Old Grand Dad whiskey. I didn't have to ask where he got it—nobody but parents bought booze in those bottles, and I knew that his father's liquor cabinet had a big lonely gap in it. I questioned his selection.

"What you got there, little man?"

If you're going to make new friends, it's good to let them know right off that you think they're beneath you.

"Whiskey."

*Hmmm, shaved head, pock-marked face, homemade punk rock T-shirt, and smart as a roof shingle—this boy is gonna go far after he gets his ass kicked for stealing his father's booze.* I held my hand out for his bottle—he was proud, this boy, a junior king of the drunks.

"You give it back when you're done?" He said it as an order, but I caught the hint of question in his words.

"Yeah, are you kidding? You and I are gonna have some drinks."

He was smiling now; at least until I took the cap off and threw it.

"Hey, what the fuck?"

"You don't need the cap once the bottle's open. That's for transportation purposes only, my man." *It was my favorite line.*

Whiskey's not my first choice, but free booze is. I tilted my head back and poured the liquid down my throat—an eighty proof disappearing act for a gathering crowd. There were always people gravitating to me when I was out.

I took a few real big gulps and then I hurriedly handed it to him and encouraged him to hit it—quick.

"Come on, buddy, hit it! Hit that shit!"

He grabbed the bottle gulped and sputtered, but he got a fair amount down. I snatched it back and took another greedy turn and then passed it over again.

"Yeah, come on, guy," I pushed him. "Get it, that's it! Get it!"

He was swallowing fast, and now the small crowd in the kitchen was cheering him on. I yanked the bottle back—I took another splashing pull and got booze in my eyes. It stung—I shoved the bottle into his hand.

"Drink, motherfucker, drink!" the crowd inflamed.

He took a strong pull and then a hesitant drink, and then . . . he blew.

The whiskey and his dinner—a two for ninety-nine cents taco

deal at Jack in the Box—flew out of his mouth and onto the kitchen floor. I grabbed the booze. The boy hit his knees, and yesterday's breakfast followed the tacos, and then Thursday's lunch, and Wednesday's dinner also ended up on the floor. *For a small dude he sure had a lot of food in his stomach.*

The onlookers in the kitchen were going crazy—I was a whiskey-drinking gladiator, surrounded by cheering fans. I bowed to the room; spinning in a slow, gracious circle, so as not to offend my audience, I saw her: a beautiful blond girl, laughing as loud as anyone. I'd just found my date for the evening.

Vickie was a seventeen-year-old version of the Saint Paulie Girl: long blond hair, semi-virginal smile, and green eyes. She could've been the poster child for Dutch beauty. Vickie was so sweet and innocent that when my father first saw her, he shook his head and felt sorry for her.

"You're gonna ruin her, Jack. Come on, let her go."

He was just jealous, and I was insulted by his judgment. "You should see her in a swimsuit, Dad."

Vickie was a lamb in a tight shirt who was about to be lying with a very deviant shepherd.

### I I I

The next afternoon, I got a call from Mike the manager. TSOL had been offered a show in Los Angeles. This was good news. I loved playing close to home—the money was large and the crowds were huge. However, we'd been getting some static from the police. Our name was prominently displayed on at least two blacklists—as were a few of our individual names, most notably Jack "Whatever the Fuck He's Calling Himself Now" Grisham. Yes, there really are blacklists. The local authorities didn't want us in L.A.

The show wasn't going to be held in any of the usual venues. For one, they wouldn't have us, and two, we were getting too big for our own good. You'd think that big was a good thing, but punk wasn't meant for bullshit arena shows. You had to be able to get up-close, touch the band, feel the hard chords cranking manically from the amplifiers. You gotta get spit on you. Not from the crowd—fuck those little rabid bastards hocking loogies on some guy's dress—but from the singer. You had to be so close your forehead got dented in by his mic stand and your face got wet from every authority-hating drop of spit that shot from his lips. Punk was made for dive bars and house parties.

We did our best to accommodate the crowds, but anything over a couple hundred kids just wasn't punk.

When we *were* forced to play larger shows, we chose a production company that, at least, *kinda* kept it real. Maybe not with the small and intimate venues—but the company delivered punk when it came to the tax evasion and government hatred that we'd all come to love.

Gary was a promoter of the punk rock sound. He rented warehouses and large arenas, and then he put on guerilla shows. He knew how to do it: bribe whoever he had to, launder what money he had to, and then get the fuck out. Gary paid better than any promoter in the country—although the money often smelled of marijuana and had never seen a bank. I liked Gary. We played one of his first shows—it was in Santa Barbara. I remember it fondly.

Santa Barbara was a well-manicured artist's hideaway. It's nestled near the beach, surrounded by gentle rolling hills and long stretches of pristine California coastline. It's the perfect place to set up an easel and start a career in the arts.

TSOL rode into Santa Barbara like Patton rolled through Germany.

We got rooms at an upscale beach hotel. The lobby was filled with Bengay-coated octogenarians in white pants and straw hats. I think it was a shuffleboard convention. I was never questioned when I booked rooms or checked into places. Why would I be? I knew when to fit in, and when to turn up the charm. When I checked into this fucking place, I was wearing a pair of beige khakis and a white cotton shirt—it was long sleeved, but I had them rolled up and neatly cuffed. I also had the thing tucked into my pants and secured with a canvas belt. Around my shoulders was a loosely tied light pink sweater, and on my feet, a pair of Top-Sider tennis shoes. I looked like a Palm Springs homosexual on a beach holiday.

The show was fine; it was what you might expect from Santa Barbara—a few hundred polite punks and one or two fucked-up kids whose parents wished they'd move to L.A. I enjoyed their company. The venue was La Casa de la Raza, a community youth center. The staff at the center were fairly open-minded; however, they were not fans of stage diving. So I had the dancers drag a table up front and they dove off that into the crowd—until the table broke and it had to be replaced. I was glad the casa had a large supply of folding tables, because we tore through quite a few.

At the end of our show, I gave our hotel address and our room numbers out to the crowd—some nights, I don't like the show to end. I figured we'd just switch venues. Besides, the hotel looked like it could use some life among the AARP clientele.

Practically every one of the several hundred attendees accepted my invitation.

Our rooms were on the second floor and our television and couch were in the street—they didn't start there, but it was getting a bit crowded, and I needed to clear space for our guests. I also crawled across the balconies and entered the rooms to the left and to the right of me—I was sure that when these hotel guests returned they wouldn't mind sharing with my friends. I also had to make their rooms a touch more accommodating, so their TVs and couches joined ours.

It was a freak show.

I'm not sure who, but someone didn't appreciate the livening up I did, and the police were soon called. They arrived, two getting-ready-to-retire-in-a-quiet-little-town cops who'd never seen anything like this: dyed hair and spiked belts, black leather and swastikas, couches and chairs now residing in the street outside, and nudity—you can't have a hotel party without destruction and nudity.

One of the cops started crying.

He was walking up and down the hallway stuttering, "But this is Santa Barbara . . ."

I tossed an empty beer bottle at him. It ricocheted off the wall and connected with his head. As he went down one of our crew yelled, "That's Long Beach, motherfucker!"

You gotta love hometown rivalries.

I was in Hollywood and promoter Gary was yelling at me—not angrily, he just wanted to be heard over the crowd—it was show night, and the SIR studio was filled way beyond capacity.

SIR was a sound stage/equipment rental place on Sunset and Gower in Hollywood. They supplied studios with recording equipment, but they also offered a rehearsal room service, and the rooms could be quite large. We rented one that had the ability to hold a thousand people—twenty-five hundred if you were a crafty punk rock promoter trying to bring in cash.

"I think we got three more feet in the back," Gary yelled. "We can get another three or four hundred kids in here."

We had passed the twenty-two hundred mark about an hour ago, and the line to buy tickets wasn't getting any shorter. I laughed.

"I don't know, Gary. You keep stuffing those fuckin' kids in here, and you're gonna be dealing with the fire marshal *and* the IRS." Gary walked off counting numbers on his fingers.

There were other bands on the bill that night, but this was our show. I couldn't wait to go on.

I crawled up a backstage ladder to the ceiling of the building. There was a catwalk running the length of the room. I walked out over the crowd; I was wearing a black suit and a cape—a modern day phantom—and I looked down to the stage. No one could see me; it was dark near the ceiling.

The crowd swirled and swayed beneath me—they were warming up to one of the opening bands—it looked violent from here, but I knew they weren't really going to turn up the heat until we came on.

I had time to think.

Thinking isn't always a good thing, and for a demon it could be dangerous.

Everything was going as intended. There hadn't been a hitch or a snag in any of our plans for a long time. Mr. Roberts was handling all my legal entanglements, and for all the "fun" I got into there had been only been six or seven arrests—the majority of them were minor traffic offences. I had enough money for what I wanted, and if I didn't, I'd just steal the object of my desire or have one of my friends steal it for me. I had a beautiful roadster and a room at my parents'—I didn't need my own place; why would I? I was able to do what I wanted, anytime I wanted, and I had no bills to pay—unless you counted the hundred in pocket change I gave my mother once a month for rent.

If I wanted a girl I took her, and if there was nothing of physical interest to me, I had Vickie—I could call her in an instant. I'd placed her on the you-check-in-regularly-to-see-if-I-need-you plan, and she was always available. It was great: sometimes she'd be out on a date and in the middle of the evening, she'd tell the fool that she needed to stop by her aunt's or grandma's for a moment—the eager-to-please date was always willing to comply. They'd pull up at my house and Vickie would tell him to wait in the car, and then she would come in, take care of business, and leave. Her date always drove her home.

I had everything I wanted . . . and I was bored.

There was a pretty fucked *Twilight Zone* episode that I watched one afternoon, called "A Nice Place to Visit." It was the story of a small-time criminal who died and went to "heaven." He got everything he wanted—girls, a nice hotel, a flashy car, money in his pockets, and when he gambled he never lost. It was a gangster's dream. Or so he thought. After a while, he got tired of winning—

he wanted to lose, and he couldn't. It turned out he wasn't in heaven after all—he was in hell.

The concept of hell is an interesting one—and given that the souls of all humans return directly to God, I wonder, when did you humans think this stop in a brimstone pit was going to take place? Do you believe everything you read? Your spirit will be purified, but not by fire. When you leave the decaying flesh that you now occupy, the pure energy inside your body will return to the Creator of the Universe. You will not be tortured by Him, however; that's your job. If there is a hell, you've created it.

You humans have certain ideals and standards by which you base success or failure in this life—and when your surroundings fail to live up to the standards you've set for yourself or which you've allowed someone else to set for you, you suffer.

Hell, in reality, is not the sulfur pit that a desert mystic envisioned. It's your vision. You fill in the blanks: the pain, the sorrow, and the want.

I'll tell you something funny—although you might not find it funny. Sometimes, your world can be overflowing with everything you ever wanted—your wildest dreams splashed across your life. Success in business, in having a family, nice things around you—all the ideals and standards that you set for yourself have been met. And then one morning you realize: it's just not enough. You find yourself in a four-star hell because the emptiness that you feel inside can't be filled.

Now, I didn't know anything about wanting family, and I didn't know anything about emptiness inside because I had nothing to compare it to, but something just didn't seem right. I was . . . unsatisfied?

I was waiting, up on the catwalk.

I heard them announce the band, and from above the stage I watched them walk on. They were waiting for my arrival. Greg sat at his piano bench and dropped his hands to the keys—a chord as black as the darkest heart on a winter's eve drifted off the stage and prepared the crowd for an assault. I didn't hurry. I took my time climbing back down the ladder to the ground—the chord still hanging in mid-air, waiting. I slowly walked out from the wings, and when I hit the stage I lit up with a smile, grabbed the mic, and said, "Let's roll, baby!"

A sun burst on the crowd.

Todd laid down a heavy tribal beat on the drums—but faster than any savage besides himself had ever played—and then Mike, with the bass jumping over the beat, drove Todd faster. And then, finally, Ron chainsawed his way into the chorus with tough driving chords.

I danced. Rolling and swaying across the stage—at times, staggering—drunken grand movements that invited the people on the floor to wash up and over the barricades and become part of the band. The stage was swallowed by kids.

I've always loved the smell of leather pants and Tres Flores, the sting of a quick punch to the back or an elbow to the ribs as a stage dancer crashes into me. The physical pain makes me feel alive. To be onstage when the audience erupted around me was fucking brilliant, and if I could have cranked it up any harder I would have. I wanted to hurt, I wanted something to help remove the boredom that I felt; even now, as I was lovingly attacked by the dancers, I could sense the mundane waiting patiently offstage.

Towards the end of our set, the riot squad appeared. They were in full force outside and they were ready to dance. I wasn't surprised. I kinda figured word would have gotten out. There were flyers all over town. All it would have taken was one cop to pull down a handbill advertising our band—they had the day, time, and address of the show neatly printed in front of them. I wouldn't have minded them coming—if they were going to purchase admission—but these fucks probably wanted in for free.

One of the SIR employees jumped onstage to deliver a message from the police; he had a heavy French accent, which was just begging to be fucked with. I acted as though his pidgin English needed translating and I told him to go ahead.

"I've got your back, buddy, let's do this."

He wasn't exactly sure what I was trying to do, but he delivered his version of the message.

"Zee police are outside, and they wish us to leave."

Oh, no, that wasn't clear at all. I translated.

"He said there's a busload of raging homosexuals outside and they want our asses!"

The crowd went crazy. The Frenchman was not pleased.

"I'm not fucking around," he said. "Zay mean business."

I translated word for word.

"Zay mean business!" The crowd turned its energy up to ten and beyond. Cheering and yelling, egging me on.

This intercontinental bantering was fun, but it sure as fuck didn't change the cops' intentions. We were on the verge of an explosion—you could feel it. The cops outside had to see the building expanding with the energy from within. They had to sense the tension, the pure anger welling up from inside. It was time to act. I had to do something before it broke.

"If we all sit down on the floor, they'd have to pull us out one by one," I yelled.

The crowd collapsed.

Twenty-five hundred people fell to the ground in unison as if the switch for their lives had just been shut off.

It was unbelievable.

I don't know why I said it. It wasn't like me to practice "civil disobedience." I was more of a stand-in-the-middle-of-the-crowd-and-throw-bottles guy, but I gave an order and they fell—an army of soldiers that dropped at my command.

Anything after that was going to be anticlimactic.

As the crowd sat, we played a few more songs. They were without life or purpose. The bomb had already dropped. The war was over. The rest of our set, and even the police outside, were nothing but a few straggling skirmishes that needed to be cleaned up.

We finished with a shitty rendition of Lennon's "Give Peace a Chance" while the Los Angeles riot squad tried to figure out what to do about the twenty-five hundred bodies that were lying in state.

They found their answer.

The police started dragging kids out of the hall one by one. They would have kept it up all night; however, I gave them another problem to solve. I proudly stood before the microphone and yelled, "There are more of us than there are of them! Let's get 'em!"

Twenty-five hundred people emptied out into the street, and the cops got what they came for.

Bottles were thrown. Heads were smashed.

The police gave their share of blows, and we gave ours.

The combatants turned into a river that ran this way and that. Sunset Boulevard was a flash flood of violence that rolled over cars and over lives.

And almost as soon as it started, it was over.

The street cleared.

And all that was left was a sidewalk littered with broken glass.

I called Mike and the boys a few days later and I quit the band.

If you've stuck with me for this long, then you must be thinking, "Why the fuck would he quit?" And to tell you the truth, I can't really give you a good answer. I just quit.

The boys in the band didn't bother putting up a fuss when I cashed it in. Greg and Todd quit with me—out of respect, I'd like to think—and Mike and Ron chalked it up to me being an egomaniac and a lunatic. They expected as much from me. Our manager, Mike, tried reason, but I wouldn't listen. The only one I was curious to hear from was the not-quite, and it seemed he had nothing to say.

**My Way**

I didn't know if I was fucking up, or if this was part of the plan. And once again, I wished that I had a detailed list of directions to go by—stay here, go there, do this, say that—but I had nothing. How the fuck was I supposed to go solely on instinct? My instinct was to fuck up and to destroy. It was all I knew—let people build their dreams around me, and when they had hope, when they thought that everything was going to be okay, then it was the right time to smash everything into the ground and stomp on the broken pieces.

I did that.

TSOL had fans around the world who loved us, and I guess I'd just let them down. I hurt both Mike's and Ron's aspirations for success, which I didn't even realize they had until after I'd quit. I hurt our manager, and the record companies who were counting on us to sell their product. In one way, I had succeeded as a demon, but I was wondering if I didn't shoot my wad too soon—if I pulled the trigger before I had enough victims in my cache.

Oh well, fuck 'em.

I didn't need those guys anymore, and if the not-quite had a problem with it, I'm sure he would have let me know by now. If he wanted me to go back, I would, and I'm sure those fucks would only be too glad to have me—probably come begging for it. Anyway, life was still good; I just had to find another way to round up the beast called money—being that I'd just taken my cash cow out into a field and bashed its fucking head in with a rock.

I decided to start another band. Something nice that would appeal to the masses and the ladies. I was tired of having a front row of young boys in leather at my concerts—don't get me wrong, young leather boys are fine, if you enjoy that sort of thing. But I preferred skirts—perfume, soft skin, lipstick, and skirts.

My hair had grown to the length where I could curl it—it was dyed a very brassy blond, and it hung to my shoulders. I put on my lipstick—a light shade of pink, just a bit darker than my nipples—and I hooked on my earrings.

I was beautiful.

I'd gone shopping that day, and I'd picked out a gold tube top and a long skirt to match. The skirt was blue with gold swirls and when I wore it as I liked—hung low across my hips—it flowed to my ankles.

The only thing that fucked me up was the footwear. It was the same problem that Marty had at the liquor store when we were fishing for victims. Skinny, androgynous guys are stunning in chicks' clothes, but women's shoes just aren't made for dudes—or we're just not made for them. Either way, guys look fucked in spiked heels.

But what are you gonna do? You put on a tennis shoe and you ruin that whole going-out-for-the-evening look.

I decided to wear bowling shoes—yeah, they were a bit fifties-kitsch, but with a rolled-down sock it wasn't so bad. I looked exactly like a woman—that is, if you liked your women with a large cock, which I refused to hide or camouflage in any way. I didn't wear underwear, and a tight, clingy skirt is a boy's best friend when you're trying to show off your wares.

I called my mass-market, chicks-are-going-to-dig-this pop band Cathedral of Tears. The name was sensitive and emotional; it summoned up feelings of reverence and loss, and to the young ladies who crowded into our shows, it hinted that the boys in the band might be the kind of boys who would write poetry and go on moonlit walks. Or, actually, they might just be the kind of boys who would take you out to a secluded movie lot and gang-bang you.

During the final year of TSOL, our bassist, Mike, suggested that I expand my musical horizons. "The Damned was fine," he said, "and the Sex Pistols were great for inspiration, but have you ever listened to Roxy Music or T-Rex?" I hadn't, but I gave 'em a try. And I loved them.

The voices on those records made me feel a bit inadequate, but I dug the sound. And, as I practiced singing along, my voice got better. I was learning the rolls and flourishes that these great singers gave to their words, and I was learning emotion. I started digging old soul records. T-Rex led me to Bowie, and Bowie led me to Luther.

Luther Vandross was the greatest singer I ever heard.

I first caught his voice on Bowie's soul-inspired *Young Americans* record. Luther was a back-up singer and he co-wrote one of the songs. The crew members would tease me sometimes. They'd chastise me for being "soft" as I played Luther after a burglary or after viciously beating some idiot in a parking lot. I don't know why they thought Luther made me soft—the lead character in *A Clockwork Orange* liked Beethoven. At least I wasn't listening to classical music as I beat someone's ass; I preferred soul.

I got to see Luther once.

A "friend" of mine had an extremely sweet and willing girlfriend whose mom worked for Universal Studios. The girlfriend knew I liked Luther, so she got me four tickets to his show.

I didn't think it odd that she included herself as one of my guests, but didn't include her boyfriend—my "friend." Some girls needed time apart from their man; it helps recharge the old love-making battery.

Todd and our old Vicious Circle friend, Paul, held the other two tickets. I was surprised that Todd wanted to go, being as he used to wander around Washington Boulevard in a shirt that read "Shoot Blacks." I hoped he wouldn't wear it that night—he might offend Luther.

The show was great. We were sitting in the orchestra pit, and Dionne Warwick was sitting right in front of us. The girlfriend's mom had scored us killer seats and backstage passes. Luther walked down for a duet with Dionne, and I was so close that I could have reached out and touched his sequined jacket.

Paul and Todd thought my attraction to Luther was amusing, and a trifle odd, but our date for the evening thought my love of soul music showed that I had great depth of feeling.

I did tell you her boyfriend stayed at home, right?

The backstage area was a who's who of soul. I wandered around smiling at people, and as I saw each face, their radio hits played in my head. But we were way out of place: two solid punks—Todd and Paul—one semi-cross-dressed, starstruck demon, and a very soon-to-be ex-friend's ex-girlfriend.

When we were leaving, I realized that we were on the studio lot. There's no real security *inside* Universal's gates, so I drove the car down the tramway and we took an unauthorized tour.

It was like driving through a deserted city at night. The streets were laid out like Small Town, usa, but there were no neighbors running about—there wasn't a light on or a barking dog to be seen or heard anywhere.

On the outskirts of the movie lot town, on a small hill, was a life-size replica of the house from *Psycho*. We broke in.

The house was a shell—frightening on the outside, and empty within. It was the opposite of me.

As we stood inside, hidden behind the flimsy walls, I took my friend's girl and I pulled her to me. She didn't resist. I kissed her and then undid her pants. Todd and Paul were watching—it was our date, and she was putting out. I leaned her against the banister and we took turns sliding into her: first me, then Todd, then Paul, then me. She didn't tire.

After the house on the hill, we drove to the "town" of Amityville to see the Jaws exhibit. I banged her again on the causeway. We were in the movies.

On the way home we took turns screwing her. I put the car on cruise control, and I laid the passenger seat back. After one of us came, we would rotate around without having to stop. Todd or Paul would hold the wheel from the back, and I'd crawl over on top of her, leaving the car driverless for a while.

When we dumped her off you could tell she'd been used. Lipstick was smeared all over her face and there was dried cum in her hair. My friend tried to fight me over the condition of his girl, but it was no use.

"You knew what she was when you started seeing her," I told him. "But I'll give you a free shot." As he punched me in the face, I instinctively kicked him in the balls and he fell to the ground, beaten.

When I got home, Vickie was in the driveway waiting.

"How was the show?" she asked.

If you've ever seen one of those cartoon women tapping her foot, questioning her husband with a rolling pin in her hand, well, then you just got a good idea of what Vickie looked like. Just add bigger boobs and a prettier face.

"They made me do it."

*What the fuck, I can't believe that just shot out of my mouth.* There I was, all 6'3" of me claiming that my companions forced me to participate in a gang-bang. *How the fuck does she know I was fucking off?* Some women are better than demons at seeing the future—or the recent past.

I kept it up.

"It was Todd and Paul. You know how they are, they were making fun of me, teasing me about Luther, and they told me to prove I wasn't gay by doing it. I didn't even like it, but I had to."

"You're a fucking asshole, Jack. Why don't you go take a shower?"

*Shit, did she just buy that line? I'm not an asshole, I'm a fucking genius.*

I'm pretty sure Vickie would've preferred a monogamous, loving relationship, and I might've told her that that was what we had, but she took what she got and dealt with it. One of the benefits in finding pretty girls with low self-esteem is their willingness to see the best in you, and their ability to take a punch without calling the police.

You know, I was going to move on with the story, but I remembered something funny.

Vickie attempted to pay me back one night. I knew she'd been sleeping around because I'd talked to a few guys—it's hard to hide the fact that you're cheating when your part-time boyfriend knows everybody in town. I wasn't mad about it; it wasn't like we were exclusive, and the thought of her getting nasty kind of turned me on. But then Vickie came to one of my shows—all dolled up in a come-fuck-me outfit and positioned herself right in front of the stage. Then she started rubbing her ass against the poor guy behind her— I say poor because he didn't know she was mine. She was bumping and grinding against him, and he was bumping and grinding right back. I guess she thought I was going to jump off that stage and, in a fit of jealousy, claim her as mine and kiss her before the crowd, but I didn't. I just let that fucker behind her get as much of her ass as he could carry—and it was a lot. He was pawing all over that little outfit of hers, and she was getting real uncomfortable. I saw full tit grabs and drunken breath slobbering all over that little I'll-show-him neck of hers. It was hilarious.

I met Vickie at my house after the show. She was sorry that she tried to get me jealous. She said she'd never do it again, and she wanted to know how she could repay me. After we had sex she noticed a cut on my hand—more like a scrape really.

"What happened, baby?"

"I had a little trouble getting paid, Vick."

"I'm sorry."

She kissed my hand and cuddled up close.

I wondered if she could taste her little dance partner's blood on it. I'd popped him in the mouth a few times before I slammed his fucking head into his car door. I might have thought it was funny watching her get fucked with, but I sure as fuck wasn't going to let him get away with it.

## I I I

The Cathedral started playing local shows and, as TSOL did before, we had an almost instant following. However, as desired, I lost the shaved-head-swastika patrol, and picked up the push-up-bra and fishnet stocking contingent—I thought it was more than a fair trade.

My old friend Cuckoo's Nest Jerry had also stepped away from the land of parking lot lawsuits and punk police shootings. He'd opened himself a mid-size nightclub. It was called the Concert Factory, but it should have been called "An assembly line of bitches for Jack to sleep with." Sadly, Jerry didn't consult me on the name.

Cathedral was practically the house band. Every third Friday or so, four hundred little femdolls would line up outside Jerry's nightclub door and wait impatiently to get in. They'd look in their mirrors—checking their make-up and making sure that no white powder was drifting from their noses—and then they'd file in. These weren't punk kids anymore; these were young ladies that had no problem sucking down Jerry's sweetly overpriced well drinks. He was ecstatic. I never got to the club early. Jerry's idea of a backstage room was the men's toilet, so I'd get ready at home—primping my curls and lubing my vocal cords with a little vodka and a Valium or two—I sure as fuck wasn't going to be curling my hair and putting on make-up while some stomach-bloated concert goer was taking a dump.

The shows, well, the shows were exactly what you might think they'd be. The band came on—a five-piece outfit—and we gyrated and swayed to our newly minted versions of wannabe radio hits. There was no violent dancing in the crowd. Instead, they all swayed back and forth during our set—the liquid in their glasses maintaining a steady horizon as they listed from side to side. It was a bit boring. The only thing I really enjoyed was the spotlight dance.

We had a nice slow song—the kind of tune where you'd put your arms around your girl and rub all sexy up against her as you danced. The ladies loved it. They'd come out to the dance floor like a wandering gang of drunken bridesmaids, but instead of getting all grabby and snatchy trying to catch a bouquet, they'd stand starry-eyed and, I guess, just wait to get hit on. I had my pick.

One night, I looked down during the dance, and there was a different kind of girl—sadder, not hidden in make-up or a short skirt. She moved like the others, but her eyes were on the girls around her as much as they were on me. She was absorbed in the sound, and she looked familiar. I recognized her: she was Gina, a girl I'd met at a TSOL show. I remembered her telling me a spirit had sent her to meet me—fuckin' A, this was going to be more fun than fucking.

I came up to her after the show, and I told her that something had drawn me to her. "It was as if I'd been guided by a force outside my body, and the force said, 'Go. Go, Jack; go to her.'"

She stood staring at me, spellbound. I'd just fed her a line of shit a mile long and she was licking her lips and calling out for dessert. I gave it to her.

"You and I are to be friends, I promise, and we have a lifetime bond between us, sealed in blood." I didn't bother to tell her that it was going to be her blood, not mine.

I fucking love punching bags. Some people get tired of them, but I've got no problem consistently wailing on something that can't, or won't, hit back. It never gets old—like yanking a chair out from behind somebody as they're sitting down, it's always good.

My new friend was a masochistic little thing; so I guess you could call it a relationship made in heaven. I beat the fuck out of her.

The first night I made contact, I had her play a game with me. I told her the spirits wanted us to do it, but they needed us to do it in *her* car.

She was crazier than I was.

The game was called "Feel the Wheel." I'd invented it. The object of the game was to get in a car and drive—*where* didn't matter, it was *how*, that counted. Before you entered the vehicle you got as hammered as possible—I'm talking close-one-eye-but-the-world-still-won't-straighten-out fucked up. And then, when you got the vehicle up to speed, you just close your eyes and let go of the wheel—what happens, happens. It's kind of like a game of chicken, but with no other driver. You see how long you can let the car drift before you puss out and grab the wheel. We played one time and her driver's side mirror got ripped off by an oncoming car—we were *that* close to a head-on crash at sixty miles per hour. Her silver steel death trap took on a life of its own and swerved away at the last instant.

It was fun having a toy to play with, but I was worried that maybe another boy—or girl—might find her and make her their own. I needed to write my name on her, mark her as mine.

I'd taken her car keys and she wanted them back—fucking crybaby didn't want me driving drunk, and she wanted to go home.

I was standing in my mother's kitchen. I turned on the gas stove.

"Do you want your keys? Do you really want your keys?" I laid them on the burner. The flame was crawling up the sides of the metal. I grabbed an oven mitt that my mother kept close for hot pans. I grabbed the keys and pressed them to her arm. It blistered her skin.

"There are your fucking keys."

A locksmith could've duplicated the burn and started her car.

I remember when she finally moved on. I guess she broke up with me. It was okay, Vickie said she was afraid of her anyway.

Her last visit was on a Wednesday. I was in the garage, sawing the end off a shotgun—making myself a little freeway intimidator—when she arrived.

"I'm not coming back," she said.

"And you . . . came here to tell me that?"

"You don't care about me; you're evil."

"I'm sorry. I guess you're right. I get too wrapped up in my own life and I don't realize my friends have needs too."

I'd picked up my favorite rope. It'd been in that garage since I tied that little fucker Jim up with it—*Jesus, I didn't know rope had that kind of shelf life.* I was tying a noose as I talked, there wasn't gonna be any Houdini shit tonight though.

"You just don't listen, Jack."

"Yeah, you're right. Hey Gina, will you put this around your neck? I wanna try something?"

She grabbed the rope and put the noose over her head. It was like she was giving me a going-away fuck.

I threw the loose end of the rope over a beam, and then I told her to hop up on a small bench. She did it.

"You love me, Jack. I know you love me."

"Yeah, uh, you better try and . . . maybe grab that rope or . . . something."

I kicked the bench out from underneath her. She grabbed the rope above her head, struggling to hold on, shaking and kicking, holding her breath as she screamed silent tears. I just watched.

I let her hang for a moment, and then I put the bench close enough for her to touch. I guess I did care about her after all.

And all this caring about my little punching bag brings up an interesting point. I'd started to notice a few changes in the people around me. You might have heard the phrase "His shit don't stink" before, and mine didn't—at least it didn't used to. I told you 'bout those stretches of me doing whatever I wanted and no one complaining. And don't get me wrong, it was basically still like that, but I did notice a bit of resistance to my persuasive mouth and my threatening ways. Before, when I said something, I could make even the smartest fools swallow it like gospel, but now it took a bit more work to be believed—not a lot, but a bit. And stuff I wanted done, or stuff I needed to have, didn't quite come to me with the same easy grace it used to. And one other thing—that fuck who was rubbing all over Vickie at that show . . . well, there was a time that nobody like that would even think about fucking with what was mine, and yeah, he didn't know she was mine, but if a chick looked like that and was standing in front of me, he would've made sure she wasn't sexually related before he started pawing.

I used to leave my surfboard at the side of the house; it was open to the street, but who'd dare steal from me? I came out one day and it was gone. I felt violated and pissed. I put the word out, and shortly thereafter received a tip about the thief, and the location of my board.

The thief was a local troublemaker a few years younger than me—not a punk. He was one of a new breed of drugged-out losers who'd been hanging around—but drugged-out or not, he should have known better. I found out he'd sold my board to a surf shop in Huntington, so after retrieving my surf vehicle, I went to get him.

It was Easter Sunday and I had an old punk acquaintance with me. I stuck a pistol down my pants, just to liven things up a notch, and we took a drive. I got motherfucking radar when it comes to catching people, and I found my man standing on a street corner on the eastside.

"Hey Grisham, what's up, bro?"

*Bro* is surf-lingo for friend, but it can also be used in a very derogatory manner. I assumed he was working the latter. "Did you steal my board?"

"Fuck you, man, I didn't steal anything."

Do you see? Do you see what I'm talking about? *Last year, this motherfucker wouldn't have even walked by my house without a fucking shield on, and now he's "Fuck you"-ing me in broad daylight? What the fuck?*

I put the gun in his face and said, "Get in the car, *bro.*"

We drove to a field near the riverbed. It was secluded—a real nice place to dump somebody like him. I made him empty his pockets as we drove—I got a small bag of weed and six dollars and thirty-five cents. I stopped the car in the field, got him out, and then put a bag over his head and made him kneel down in the dirt.

I fucked with him.

"Probably shouldn't have ripped me off, huh?" I continued, "You don't even surf. Do you fucking surf, faggot? You think you're leaving here? Do you? You think you're gonna fucking walk?" I was punctuating the questions with slaps to his head and the barrel of the gun poking him at the base of his skull. I was pretty good at it; I remembered those Kansas troopers doing it to me, and you only had to show me once. I'm a quick learner.

"Jack, there's a car coming." My buddy was doing lookout and he'd seen someone—*probably a fucking dog walker. Oh well, not a good idea to be seen out here holding a gun to a bag with a head stuffed in it.*

I told him he was going to die for ripping me off, and then I stuffed him in the trunk and drove to my parents'. It was about five miles and we passed a cop or two along the way, but I always wave and smile at the police. *I should get one of those "Support Your Local Police" stickers on my window.*

I backed up into the garage, dumped my load, and then I pulled the car back out and shut the garage door. I had planned on bringing him back here, so I'd arranged a few things in anticipation of his arrival. I took the now-returned stolen surfboard and propped it up in a corner of the garage. I put a light on it, displaying it like a work of art, glowing in the garage, to remind him of what he'd done. I also laid out a sledgehammer, a two-by-four, and a surfboard bag. It was quite the arrangement.

I started out by making him lie spread-eagle on the floor as I stood on his wrist and dropped the sledgehammer as close as I could to his hand without hitting it. I'm pretty fucking steady—he should have been glad it was me torturing him and not somebody else. I

could see guys not doing this right and crushing his fucking . . .
sorry.

Anyway, when I got tired of that, I put him in a surfboard bag
and hung him upside down from the rafters. I picked up the two-
by-four and I hit him with it—not in the head, mainly in the
stomach and the legs, I think . . . although, it was hard to tell, him
being in a bag and all. I could hear kids playing outside so I was
trying to keep it down, but I probably should've gagged him before
I hung him up. *What the fuck were kids doing here anyway? Fuck, I
forgot it was Easter.* My aunt was over for dinner, and I hadn't seen
her for a while.

I set the two-by-four down, and I excused myself for a minute.
I wanted to give my aunt a little kiss on the cheek—she usually put
a little something in an Easter envelope for me, and it helped if I
buttered the wheels.

My mother was in the kitchen cooking up some green bean shit,
and the nephews and nieces were running through the house into
the yard—they'd been told to stay away from the garage. My
parents didn't know what I was doing out there, but they figured it
wasn't good.

My aunt was sitting comfortably in a recliner with a nice shawl
around her shoulders. I leaned down and gave her a hug.

"Are you coming in soon, sweetheart?" She's very nice.

"Yeah, I am, but I've got some business to finish in the garage
first."

I leaned down and gave her a kiss, grabbed a deviled egg, and
went back outside. I whacked my man with the board a few more
times and then I let him go. I wasn't really going to kill him—not
over a fucking surfboard—but I needed to protect the territory.

I was getting a bit concerned about some of my skills slipping, and
I wished the not-quite would show and get me straightened out.
Motherfucker needs a phone line or some shit. I was beginning to

feel like a girl that'd been dropped off on the wrong side of town, and who'd just been informed she was gonna have to hoof it home in the dark. I didn't feel like walking.

| | |

The Cathedral got an offer to make a record. It was with a label I'd never tried before—Enigma Records, out of Torrance. I was okay with cutting another disc, but I had no plans to tour. I just didn't bother telling them that.

I got up early a few days before the recording was supposed to take place, and I drove to the beach. It was cold—one of those mornings that refused to warm up, no matter how high the sun got. I parked my car in the beach lot, and I walked out onto the rocks. There wasn't any surf—hadn't been any for a few weeks—but it didn't matter; I wasn't surfing as much as I used to anymore.

I sat quietly.

Down the beach, I could see a man walking in my direction. I wasn't concerned; normally, there are quite a lot of people that walk this beach in the morning, he was just one dude—*I might even know him.*

As he got closer, I realized that I couldn't see his face. He was blurred, almost like the air around him was the only thing holding him together, and if that air stirred, he would disappear.

"I was wondering if I could sit by you." His voice was light like wind moving through the branches of a tree in the afternoon. It was He, the Man.

"I didn't know *I* was in a position to deny *you.*"

He sat beside me. If you were watching us from afar, He might have looked like sunlight reflected off the water and onto the rocks. And I hate to say this, but I was glad He joined me. He might have been on the opposite team, but at least He was playing in the same league. I had nobody even remotely close to my level down here and not having the not-quite to talk to was strange. I felt almost lonely . . . disconnected. I'd spent my whole existence being unconnected, and you might say there's no difference between unconnected and disconnected, but you'd be wrong. Disconnected means you had something flowing through you and now it's gone. Unconnected means nothing ever flowed out, or in—you were an observer or an actor without emotion.

"Do you know you're sick, Jack?"

"What? What the fuck are you talking about?"

He politely ignored my question and continued, "Why do you think he's staying away? Haven't you wondered?"

Actually, I had. He was talking about the not-quite, and I *didn't* know why he hadn't come to me. I was drifting, unguided, and I was weaker than I'd been.

The Man kept gently pushing: "Have you ever wondered what it's like to hurt?"

"No. I don't need to wonder, I've been hurt. I like it."

"I'm not talking about physical pain—although when a human is suffering an emotional disturbance it affects each body differently."

"Yeah, well, that's good for them then, huh?"

"I'm talking about a feeling of loss."

I wasn't sure He was even listening when I answered Him—*just plowing on with his line like I have nothing to do but sit here and . . .*

"Did you think lonely was going to feel like this?"

*Ugh, talking to God is like talking to stone.*

"I'm nothing. I'm telling you, I don't feel anything." I knew I was lying the minute I said it, and He knew it too. To tell you the truth, I didn't know why we even had to have the conversation. Why couldn't He just sit wherever the fuck He sat during the day and solve all this shit without getting everyone else in this universe involved? Involved? I was beginning to feel lonely.

"Do you remember Raziel?"

"Yes." *I remember him.* "Yes, I do."

Raziel was a demon. I knew him; at least, I shared a life with him before he fell. He got the sickness.

It's hard to explain the sickness to a human, and I'm not sure that anyone else has ever really tried, but I guess, if I had to liken it to something, I think it would be closest to the condition that you call schizophrenia. However, that mental disorder in you humans is so much more prevalent than the sickness is in demons—it's brought on by a combination of biological, psychological, and social factors—upbringing, trauma in childhood, stress. I've only heard of a few cases of demons getting sick, most notably Raziel.

Raziel had entered the body of a man—and not from birth. He had entered at the moment of the soul's transition to God. The human stepped out, and Raziel stepped in—risen from the dead, so to speak.

It's pretty rare, but the not-quite needed this fucking human to do something for him, and the fucker checked out before completion. Anyway, Raziel stepped in to do the work, and he got sick. The human had had children, and on the day that Raziel, disguised as the man, returned from the grave, one of his offspring—a daughter, a young girl, ran up to him and put her arms around his neck. She held him and put her face against his.

There's a very slight danger when a demon enters a host, and that's the possibility of transference on a cellular level. You see, contrary to popular belief, you are your body. Memories aren't just stored in your mind, but your body as well, passed down from mother to child, father to child, all the way back to the first two animals in the garden. It's a genetic line of connection that leads back to God.

When the child put her arms around Raziel's neck, the memory of the father's love for her rushed through Raziel and he fell. He became human. He was connected. The genetic predisposition to be human, coupled with the girl's love, caused a shift in the being of Raziel, and he became sick—he ceased being a demon.

Now, you might be thinking, why is that so bad? And if so, you've probably forgotten what I told you so long ago.

When God created humans, He instilled them with the need to seek Him.

Raziel felt nothing before that child touched him. He was without emotion. And now he felt love, and he felt sadness, and he had an incomplete taste of connection, and he realized that there was something more that he needed—he realized that he needed God to make him complete.

He was forced to seek Him, and he did.

When Raziel finally died—he went to God, absorbed in the energy of the Spirit, and we never saw him again.

It was a demon's horror story.

And now, the Man was suggesting that I was also becoming human. *Well, if that's the case, I'm gonna fight it. Or I'll just take myself out.* I said nothing but God heard me.

"He's not going to let you die."

"What do you mean?"

"He doesn't care about you, and he's going to enjoy watching you suffer. I can help you, but as you know, he controls the flesh; and I can't do a thing until you ask me." He stood up.

"Don't wait up, huh?" I started laughing. "I'm not sick. And I'm never going to turn to you."

He starting walking back from the way He came and, as a parting shot, He whispered a few words. I barely heard Him. But it was loud enough.

"I'm sorry about your loss."

"What? What did you say?"

"I said I'm sorry about your loss. He was a good man."

C'mon. See, this is what I've told you about—these Gods, they're not clear. You wanna throw a celestial sucker punch you might as well call the target by name. I didn't know any good men, and I sure as fuck hadn't lost anyone.

"Hey!"

He was gone—scattered to the breeze.

I got the call that afternoon. I was at home, watching cartoons and waiting for the sun to go down. I didn't go out much in the daylight anymore.

The phone rang and rang.

I wasn't going to answer, but whoever it was seemed insistent on reaching someone—the phone had already rung fifteen times and they were showing no signs of hanging up. I grabbed the phone. It was my mother. She was frantic.

"Your father's had a heart attack."

*Hmmmm.*

"He's at the Navy Hospital in San Diego."

I could hear Bugs Bunny having some sort of argument with Daffy Duck in the living room—*what the fuck are they fighting over?*

"It doesn't look good; he's resting now, but the doctor is concerned."

*He* was concerned? *I* was concerned. I was missing important plot development, and if my mother was in San Diego, the chance of getting dinner served on time was shit.

"Are you coming home?" I asked.

"No, I'm going to stay here with your father and when—"

I hung up.

My father had said to me, "I love you" just one time before. I was shocked. He was trying to hug me—which, in itself, was weird, being as he never touched me (at least not bare-handed). When my father desired contact, he usually transferred it through a Hot Wheels track or a leather belt—one time, he caressed me with an aluminum pool-cleaning tool. If he'd ever tried to hold me, it must have been when I was a child. But I don't remember. I think I'd recall something like that. I can remember getting washed, lying in a baby bassinette, and I can remember sitting in a bathroom sink pissing on myself. I can remember being small, but I can't remember being touched.

**Square**

Now, don't go getting all weepy and feeling sorry for me. This ain't that kind of story—I ain't a little bitch crying because his mommy and daddy didn't love him, or because he was put on a toilet seat backwards.

You know what I am—and I ain't crying.

My parents loved me the best they knew how. They weren't any good at it . . . but they tried. It's not their fault they were like a couple of retards trying to solve a calculus problem. They weren't dealing with a human child.

The first time my dad told me he loved me was after a real fucked mix-up I'd gotten into. I'd been beating on a kid who no one should have been beating on—a special kid. I didn't really hurt him, I just slapped him around a bit and took some stuff—lunch money, wallet, skateboard. Little fucker shouldn't have even had one—anyone who's got to walk around in a helmet shouldn't be skating.

Anyway, this special kid's dad came to our house. He wanted a man-to-man with my father—hoping to curtail the abuse of *his boy*. My dad shook hands like a gentleman and promised to square it up—he was genuine and concerned.

After the other father left my father acted strange. Pacing a bit, unsure of his actions, or what he was going to do, and then . . . he hugged me. I thought he was going to try and bear hug me unconscious, but then I felt a tear on me. He was fucking crying. And then he told me he loved me. Ha! That's what he was pacing for, he was trying to figure out if he should beat me for picking on the 'tard—maybe running over which punishment tool to use—when he realized that the beatings hadn't worked, and he might want to go another route. Idiot, *I* would have stuck with the beating.

He had his arms around me—I could smell the sweat on him—and he was telling me he loved me. So I told him . . . to get his fucking hands off me and said, "I fucking hate you." *How's that for your new strategy, Dad?*

And now there he was, lying all weak and scared in a hospital bed. He looked up at me, and, for the second time in my life, he mouthed, "I love you."

What the fuck did he think I was going to say?

"I love you too, Pops. Let's go out and get a couple of cold beers."

The only time I used the word love was when I needed something—if I needed you to stick around, I said I loved you. And what exactly did he love about me? I was a fuck; a vicious, self-seeking fuck, who had done nothing to earn his respect *or* his love.

And let's talk about my behavior. Did he love my ruthlessness—my callous indifference to pain? Did he love my ability to lie, to ensnare, and to take? Is that what he loved?

Love is weak. It's a setup to get hurt. It's vulnerability, and I didn't want it.

I wasn't fucking around when I said I was gonna take myself out if I started going human. I don't want to be weak. I can't believe the not-quite would let me go that way. I've served for years—I'm steady, and I'm strong.

So, yeah, I was looking down at a metal-sided bed, a cheap bed—something you wouldn't stick in your house if you didn't have to. I was looking at this man: a powerful man who'd inflicted pain on me countless times over. And he lay there, looking up at me, without defense, and he admitted he was weak. And I had nothing to say to him.

I don't want to admit it, but I could feel a small touch of that sickness creeping around inside of me—it was like a foul taint had just touched the edge of my being, and now it wanted to seep in.

I looked at him and I thought about what I could give him, what I could offer that would not show too much weakness on my part. I thought about lying—looking him in the eyes and saying, "I love you too, Pops," but I knew he'd see through my shit. That's one gift God gave the dying—He gave them the ability to see truth—and oh yes, my dad was going to die. I didn't tell my mother, but I saw it.

I'd never wanted to look at my parents' deaths before. I'm not sure why, but I'd never thought about it until then. I didn't have a reason to see it. But when I looked at my old man, it came clear.

I saw them pounding on his chest. His body looking like it fought, but it was doing nothing but reacting to the doctor's blows as it was hit. I've beaten on people when they're knocked out and their body jerks around as you kick it. It looks like they're conscious sometimes, but they're not. I saw the doctor call time of death—and then he asked a nurse about dinner. The skin that my father was clothed in lay silent in the bed. The majority of the energy was gone. The rest would leave as he decomposed.

*What can I offer him now that won't take from me? A token, a small token in appreciation of the two times he* loved *me. I've got it!*

I smiled at him and said, "I'll mow the lawn when I get home."

And then I turned my back and walked out.

The next morning I got a call from my sister's husband.

"Jack?"

"Yes?"

"Your father's dead."

"Okay."

That was it.

My mother was in San Diego; only my younger sister and I were home. I never spoke to her. I think the last time I said anything at all to her was a "How's that?" after kicking her in the stomach for taking my things.

She was probably close to my father—at least, closer than I was. I saw a few pictures of them together when she'd had a baby. She was vacuuming her room when I popped in the door. She was startled to see me. I greeted her.

"Hey."

"Yeah?" She was tentative, and yes, it *was* just one word. But it was a word that implied more than it said. Behind her "Yeah" there was fear. I wasn't going to hurt her. I was a messenger.

"Your dad's dead."

I turned and walked out.

I had two more things to do before I could move on. I went through the family's phone book, and I went down the list, name by name. I called every one.

"Hello. Mr. Abigail? Yes. This is Jack, Jack Grisham. Fine. Yes, sir, everyone's fine. I just wanted to let you know that my father's dead. I'm sure someone will contact you about the service. Thank you."

From Abigail to Young, and every name in between, they all got a polite, curt call from the evil son. I went through every name in the book, and then I walked upstairs. I brought some garbage bags with me, and I went into my mother and father's room. (Well, my mother's room now.) I got in her closets and her drawers and removed all my father's clothes and bagged them. I took them out to the back porch, and I was planning on dumping them on trash day.

It was the least I could do; after all, I'd never mowed the lawn.

## I I I

I had a record to finish.

The recording didn't exactly go smoothly. I blamed it on the stress of my father's death, but the bottom line is that I'd lied to the record company. That, in itself, isn't such a big deal—I lied constantly—but maybe I'd pushed it this time. There was a change of band personnel—a matter of mutiny and hurt feelings—and I'd neglected to inform the label that certain members were no longer with me. I knew Enigma wasn't going to be too concerned with that, being as how they had already told me that it was me they wanted, but in a nasty bit of spitefulness I refused to record songs that these "used to be" band members co-wrote. I was going to make sure that they benefitted as little as possible from their association with me. I wrote four new songs for a six-song disc.

This may not seem fucked up to you, but when a record company offers you a deal, it's usually because they've heard a demo of what songs you're going to give them, and that's what they expect. These fuckers were going to be surprised when they heard what I gave them—hopefully pleasantly. And if not, well, they already paid for it. What's that Latin phrase? *Caveat emptor?* Caveat-shouldn't-have-fucking-done-business-with-me is more like it. It's not my fault if they don't research their artists. Maybe they don't read the paper; in yesterday's edition there was a quote, from TSOL Mike, of all people: "Doing business with Jack is like going to the zoo."

I think that pretty much sums it up, don't you?

The record company was not happy when they got that disc— as a matter of fact, they were pissed. I think the company president's actual response was "What the fuck is this?"

I was hurt. If I woulda known he was going to be that way, I would have just taken his money and pissed it away on whores and candy. I didn't think the disc was that bad—there was a track on there that I thought had radio potential.

They disagreed and were in no hurry to release the record.

I've never been too concerned with what you want when I want something different. You're just a pain in my ass if you don't go along with the program, and if you think I'm going to listen to *you* when it's *my* life we're fucking talking about, well, then you're a fucking idiot.

I called the recording studio and told them the record company had authorized me to take a mixed copy of the recording in easy tape form for radio play. I needed it today.

I might have been slipping a bit, what with these bullshit cowards ripping me off and crybaby band guys not wanting to play with me and people not easily believing my "stories" anymore, but slipping a bit for a demon and slipping a bit for a human are two separate things. I was still persuasive.

I took the tape down to the local radio station and hand-delivered it to a DJ friend.

"Are you sure I can play this, Jack?"

"Oh fuck yeah. That's just one of sixteen killer tracks off this record. Consider it a gift for being so supportive."

As I was pulling out of the radio station parking lot, the DJ was jumping all over that song. It sounded great on the radio. Too bad there wasn't a record to go with it—or the fifteen other tracks I promised him.

The record label was livid. First, I gave them a sub-par disc of songs they'd never heard and didn't like, and then I went and fucked them over by giving it away.

I was tired of that band anyway.

I felt like going straight.

### III

When God told me I was sick that morning on the beach, it got me thinking. I've never had a progressive disease like cancer, or Parkinson's, and if I did, I'm not so sure I'd like to be diagnosed with it—especially by God. I mean, who you gonna go to for a second opinion?

"I'm sorry, Mister Omnipotent. I know you forecasted my dad's death, and you created the whole universe and all, but I think you're a bit off on this. Could you suggest someone else I could talk to?"

Knowing that you've contracted an illness and then watching as that illness slowly eats your body is fucking maddening. Every day you get worse, knowing what's in store for you. I knew people who had terrifying diseases, but they remained undiagnosed—completely unaware of their sickness until they died. They had problems—like everyone—but they didn't wake up every morning knowing that the lump in their throat got a touch bigger overnight.

I didn't like knowing I was sick, but now that I did, I could see the behavior associated with it.

I mean, take this whole wanting to go straight thing.

Working's for squares.

Yeah, I held jobs before, but I held them while waiting to step into the spotlight of leadership. Now I was thinking about getting a job just to pay the fucking bills. Instead of my hands getting shakier, or a lump in my throat getting bigger, I was filling out job applications and looking for work—I was becoming more and more human everyday.

Thank God for Valium.

I started dipping into my mom's pills after my father died, and she didn't say a thing. That's the good thing about Benzos—when you're stealing them from someone who's also taking them, you rarely get caught. You can't steal the bottle, because then they'd know you've been into 'em. But if you just pinch a few daily, they get confused over how much they've been taking. And if they ever confront you for stealing them, you come right back at 'em with, "You know, I'm glad you brought it up. I've been meaning to talk to you about *you* overdoing your prescription. Do you *really* know how many pills *you've* been taking?"

My mother would lie for hours in her room, crying. She wasn't going to confront me with anything. Her husband of thirty years was dead, and her home had been converted into a bodiless crypt.

The house took on a monochromatic appearance; the colors of the world waited on the doorstep as one entered. It didn't take a demon to catch the energy coming out of that place; anyone who walked by could feel it. It was pure pain—a middle-aged woman wrapped in dirty sheets, moaning and howling, demanding an answer to her loss. I could have given her one if she'd asked: God didn't care, and your husband was an overweight, two-pack-a-day smoking stress-case who couldn't calm down. There's your answer.

I was the only one of my mothers' kids who didn't attend the funeral.

I didn't see why I had to go. I made the phone calls. I packed up his shit. I was even blamed for his death. Why should I go?

There was a court case over my father's death. He'd had the heart attack at work, so it was possibly a job-related fatality.

Depositions were taken.

My mother said, "Yes, yes, he would come home under great stress."

His work added, "Yes, it was stress, all right. He was stressed from the strain his son put him through; he was stressed from the jailing and the trouble, from the drunkenness, and the insanity. Yes, the stress from that boy killed him."

My mom settled out of court.

I went surfing on the day of his burial. It was a great day—a nice little northwest swell was working, and it wasn't crowded. I ran into a few cats I knew. They offered their condolences, but they also knew what our relationship had been like. They didn't push any further than "I'm sorry."

I got a call from a department store. They wanted me to come in for an interview. I was bummed. I used to be a warrior, and now I was using my shield to see if I had my tie on straight.

The fuck who interviewed me was a joke. He was talking to me like he had something. *Yeah, you got something, guy. You got a fucking seven-dollar-an-hour shit-hole job, and you're getting off on a cardigan-sweater power trip.* I had to keep my eyes down so he wouldn't see the fire in them.

Luckily, I'd perfected the look-at-the-bridge-of-a-man's-nose trick—he thinks you're looking at him, when you really aren't. But I'll tell you, when he leaned back with his feet propped up on that desk and shook his head at my application while chewing his pencil, I almost killed him.

I thought about jumping on top of him and fucking him up: beating his fucking ass in that office, and then sitting on his chest as he sobbed—unzipping my pants, pulling my cock out, and then making him kiss the fucking tip of it before he apologized for being such a cunt. He was lucky.

I accepted his offer of six dollars an hour, plus commission.

Where the fuck was the not-quite?

I knew he'd help me—he had to.

Mr. "Lucky I'm Not Dead After Kissing Jack's Dick" assigned me to the University Department.

The University Department was where the supposedly hip college kids bought their clothes. That is, if they had no sense of style, and they shopped with their grandmothers. I had to dress just like 'em. No more leather pants and cowboy boots, no spurs, or super-sharp golf spikes—it was all nice slacks and polo shirts for me. If I could have, I would have kicked my own ass and thrown myself off a bridge.

The department store was down the freeway from my mother's. It wasn't a far drive, but anywhere on the freeway in southern California can be a drag if you happen to hit traffic.

I wasn't paying attention, and I cut off a car. It was no big deal; I didn't do it on purpose. Gone were the days when I cut quickly in front of someone and gave 'em the brakes—and my rear bumper.

I gave a wave after I did it, one of those "I'm sorry, but I'm aware" bullshit waves you see polite drivers do. The dudes I cut off, however, didn't dig it. They pulled up next to me, and then they got in front. Then they pulled behind and came up on my bumper, all the while gesturing at the side of the road, telling me to pull over so we could fight—three against one.

Now you gotta check me out: I was in my dad's old car—a little fucking Honda beige four-door sedan—and I had my hair slicked back like some junior-high cocksucker. I was wearing a sweater vest with a collared shirt poking through, and on my tit was a little square plastic name tag that said "Welcome to the Broadway." In other words, I had "Victim" spray painted on my rear window.

I gave up.

I pulled to the side of the freeway, and they pulled up behind me. I was out of my car before they were, and I reached under my seat and pulled out one other hidden piece of my attire . . . a sawed-off shotgun.

I turned around with that fucking blaster in my hand and I pointed it right at their fucking car. I was a skinny tie–wearing, sweater vest–sporting motherfucker, and I unloaded that sawed-off right at 'em.

Cars were honking and I heard people skidding. I'm pretty sure I dusted the front of their car, but the nozzle spray on those fuckers, when they're cut that short and filled with birdshot, gets pretty wide, pretty fast. And besides that, they were reversing at about sixty miles an hour up that fucking highway.

I jumped back in my car and got the fuck off—I was right by the Carson exit so it was a quick move—and then I shot into the residential section and doubled back towards my mom's. I was hoping some fucking citizen didn't grab my license plate. I was going home to call in sick.

I was almost at my mother's—maybe a mile away—just driving past the park, when I was red-lighted.

*Fuck, there goes my day job.*

I had a sawed-off shotgun under my seat—a federal crime and a supposed five-year minimum—and I'd just unloaded it on a carload of citizens. Worse, I was wearing stripes with plaid.

The officer got out and walked up to my car. I watched him advance in my driver's side mirror. He was alone, and his service revolver was holstered. I put my window down—I probably shouldn't have, you know, not keeping my hands in plain sight, but he didn't seem agitated. I probably crossed a line or something.

He came right up to the window and leaned towards the car.

"How does it feel to be such a fucking faggot?"

"What?"

"I was thinking I might like to contrast my bulletproof vest with a silk scarf. Do you got any shit like that at your store, or maybe you'd just like to blow a couple of holes right through me?"

It was the not-quite. I'd never been so happy to see the police in all my life. I started talking about getting sick and how I didn't want to go human. It was a traffic stop therapy session, and he just let me roll until I slowed down. He was uncharacteristically patient.

"You done?"

"Yeah, I'm done. Can you fix it? Make it stop?"

"No, I wish I could, but I can't. It's real complicated shit—I tried to get a straight answer out of the Man one time but He wouldn't give me anything—and only He knows what the fuck He's thinking."

"Well, do you know what's gonna happen to me?"

"Yeah, kind of; I know you're gonna hurt, and you're gonna hurt real bad, and no matter what that Motherfucker tells you, I ain't keeping you around to see you suffer, 'cause when you get like this, with the sickness, it's out of my hands. I'm not sure exactly what you go through, but if you get like them"—he gestured to the passing cars—"you're gonna have to submit to Him. He fucking set it up like that; I can't help you."

"Well, why don't you just take me out? Fucking shoot me, take me back."

"I can't, there are no more round trips for you. I told you, you're done. Let me tell you something, Jack—and by the way, I love the name tag—you wouldn't think I could, but I like you. I always have. You've put more thorns in that Motherfucker's side than any of my other men. I admire you for it, but there ain't a fucking thing I can do to stop it."

"So, I'm just gonna go human, and then what? What happens when I die?"

"Same thing that happens to all these other fucking animals, you go back into Him."

"I'm not gonna do it. I'll fucking deny Him."

"I'd love to see it, but I don't think you can hold. You're gonna have to submit one day. You can't win."

I sat in the car and stared at the road ahead and felt sorry for myself—it was just a trickle, but it made me sick.

"Isn't there anything I can do?" I asked.

"If I was you, I'd get fucked up, and I'd stay fucked up."

"What?"

"I'm gonna tell you something that I've only told one other, and then I'm gonna split. Because, frankly, you're starting to stink like them. When Raziel changed, it was quick—it wasn't all dragged out like you got going, and he didn't have your taste for the booze. You think I ain't been watching you stick that shit down your throat? You might be fooling your mother about those pills, but you don't fool me. I wouldn't be surprised if the booze did this too, opened you up to that fucker. Well, anyway, that's how you can hold him back."

"What? With what?"

"LISTEN TO ME! The alcohol, the pills, the weed—anything you can stick in that fucking brain of yours blocks Him from getting in. The only thing these fucking animals down here ever did that's worth a fuck is distilled booze. It's a synthetic God, Jack. Why the fuck do you think they call it spirits? Why the fuck do you think I told you to stay away from it? It imitates Him. When you start hurting or feeling sorry for yourself or feeling disconnected—

basically, feeling like a human fuck, just turn to the booze. It'll make it go away, it'll make it stop. Don't turn to Him, okay? You turn to that. I'd love to see you hold out."

"How long do you think I got?"

"I don't know. I can't see your end. With Raziel, it was quick; he was turned in an instant. He wasn't so lucky."

A car sped by doing at least eighty—the driver failed or chose to ignore the officer parked behind me. The not-quite smiled an evil fucking grin.

"I gotta go, Jack. You hold out, huh?"

He jumped in the patrol car and was gone. I felt sorry for that driver, he was gonna get one fucked-up speeding ticket.

Shit, I just said I was feeling sorry . . .

### I I I

Vickie decided it was time to take our relationship to the next level. She was going to move into my mother's house with me. My mother wasn't going to complain—she was still in mourning, and even if she wasn't, people didn't usually cross me. This was going to be a first; I never had a twenty-four-hour-a-day girlfriend.

She was coming that night, and she was excited. Vickie was proud of me for getting a "real" job, and she thought I was improving as a person. She called from the restaurant she worked at: "You got me space in the closet?"

"Yep."

"And you're hungry, right? I'm going to make dinner, and I don't want you spoiling it with shit."

"I won't."

*Wow, this is weird; it sounds like I just got a new mom.*

"This is going to be so fun."

"I know; I can't wait."

*Fuck.*

I heard somebody on the front porch so I peeped out the

window. It was a couple of cops. At least they dressed like cops—or used car salesmen. But used car salesmen didn't carry guns.

"Hey, I'm sorry, Vick, somebody's at the door. I'll call you back."

I walked over and opened the front door. I didn't go all the way out. There were two of them—a couple of Hispanic hard-ons from the Lakewood police department: big mustaches, little wee-wees.

"What's up?" I was calm.

"Are you Jack?" I knew the guy with the bigger mustache was in charge.

"Yeah, why?"

"We wanna ask you a couple of questions. Will you come outside?"

"No." I never heard of a cop who didn't like *Dragnet*, and these two seemed to appreciate the flow of the dialogue. You don't wanna go getting them all riled with a whole string of confusing verbiage—and you never go outside if you're asked. If you're in the house, the only way they can arrest you is with a warrant.

"Okay. Do you know Greg Talbot?"

Fuck, is that what this is about? Greg was the brother of a girl I slept with. He came into the store the other day, and he used a stolen credit card—at least I thought it was stolen. I knew that wasn't his name, and I laughed about it to another clerk—bad judgment on my part. The clerk, who I thought I shared a joke with, was really straight, and the fucking bitch must have fingered me to the cops. No reason to lie on this deal, they busted him in the store— I was innocent.

"I saw him in the store last week. Why?"

"That's it?"

"Yeah, I didn't even fucking ring him up."

"So, you knew he was buying something?"

"I knew he was standing at the register."

"And that's it then, you just saw him?"

"Yeah, I hadn't seen the guy for years before that."

"Okay, hey, we're sorry, Jack. You know how these things get.

Somebody sees somebody, and then it all gets blown out of whack. I hope we didn't disturb you on your day off. They told us you were doing really good over there—big difference from the punk thing, yeah?"

I laughed. *Fucking dodged a bullet.*

"Yeah, can't say I miss getting onstage."

"Hey, I hate to ask this, but could you sign a record for my kid?"

You got to love this, fucking hard-on cop who has a punk rock kid. Fucking scene out of a movie, huh?

"Yeah, sure, no problem." I opened the door.

"I got it in the car." They started walking out.

I walked out on the porch and down the stairs. I followed them over to the cruiser, and he opened up the trunk. I was wearing a pair of real short shorts and a ripped up tank top—kind of *Flashdance*. I wasn't wearing shoes. His partner, Mr. "Wish I Had a Mustache as Big as My Pal's," stood beside me.

The main dude was rummaging around in the trunk.

"Shit, I thought I had it in here. Oh well, I guess I'm just going to have to arrest you for armed robbery."

"What?"

Little mustache had me fucking cuffed and against the car before my egoed-out head knew what hit me. I thought I was having an autograph session, and now I was being stuffed into the back seat of a squad car. They didn't have a warrant and they needed me out of the house. What better way than to make the fool think they wanted a record signed? I *was* slipping.

I spent most of the night in jail.

Before I was bailed out—courtesy of Mr. Roberts—Vickie had moved into my room. She loaded up the closet and rearranged the furniture before she cooked what was going to be, for me, a very cold dinner.

It turns out the credit card that Greg used was acquired during an armed robbery. I was linked to Greg by admittedly knowing him, and since he tried to purchase items in the store that I worked in, the police deduced that I held the man at gunpoint while Greg beat him and stole his wallet. It was a brilliant theory—as police theories went. But there was a problem—well, actually, two problems. The first one was the police's issue: I wasn't even in the fucking area when it went down—that is, if I knew where it went down. The second problem was all mine; due to my stellar reputation as a liar, cheat, and vicious fuck-up, nobody believed I was innocent.

No one.

When I was arrested, my oldest sister went through my car and found the sawed-off shotgun underneath the seat—a federal felony for possession. She then took it upon herself to drive said illegal piece over to the bridge on Pacific Coast Highway—the large one that crosses the Huntington Harbor. And when she reached the top of the bridge, she let the gun fly—one hundred feet into the muddy depths of the channel.

She knew I did it.

My mother didn't even question my guilt.

Vickie was pissed at me for backsliding the moment she moved in.

And my closest acquaintances were hurt that I wouldn't give them the details.

When I said nobody believed me, I meant nobody.

I had an appointment to see Mr. Roberts.

Things hadn't changed with him—same shitty Santa Ana office, same low-ball address. My attorney was a man who looked better suited to fishing half-eaten sandwiches out of a dumpster than he did standing before the docket pleading a case. I walked into his office—actually kicking a couple of boxes out of the way to get in—and there he was, naked, slumped over his desk, recently dead.

I say recent because he wasn't too discolored—at least no more than usual. And he didn't stink—also, no more than usual. He had a porn clip running on the TV, and it looked like he'd been jerking off when he died—probably a heart attack. *Fuck, what was he gonna do if I got here early? Just zip up and shake hands hello?*

*Motherfucker.*

There was a cup of coffee sitting on his desk so I stuck my finger in it—it was hot—*Christ, this cat just died.* I was thinking maybe some mouth to mouth or something, but nah. I wasn't about do mouth to mouth on a naked guy that'd been jacking off—*you're out of luck, buddy.*

So, that was it, huh? Fucking attorney died naked before he could help me, and I'm still fucked. Was this why I couldn't see his death, because he was gonna die, and I was gonna go human? I don't know who blocked my vision of this shit, but I don't blame 'em. If I would've known how fucked things were gonna get, I probably would've just given up.

There was a bullshit attorney reference list on his desk. I grabbed it, picked up the phone, and randomly dialed. A pleasant female voice answered.

"Thank you for calling the law offices of Gervais, Hamill, and Ball. How may I assist you?"

"I need an attorney, and you guys came highly recommended."

"Okay, when would you like to come in?"

"Where are you located?"

"We're in the City of Garden Grove."

I did the traffic math in my head. I'm figuring ten miles at slow as fuck.

"I'll be there Monday."

"Great, could I have your name—"

I hung up.


"Okay, son, tell me how it went down?"

The attorney was as clean as his office—spotless; the secretary was all work and no play; and there was no porn or booze around. It was a we-mean-business establishment—very professional—but the counselor was hard of hearing.

"How what went down?"

"The robbery, how'd you do it?"

Motherfucker was sitting up on his chair like a fucking third grader at story time. I'd told him six times I was innocent.

"I DIDN'T DO IT!"

He sat back in his chair and breathed out hard. He grabbed a folder off his desk, opened it, and began flipping.

"Okay, Jack, you suit yourself. But you're looking at a solid five years on this one—they got you at the scene, they put you there. You can lie all you want, but I can't defend you if you don't tell the truth. Okay, here's what we're going to do: I'm going to need some letters of recommendation—quite a few of them—come sentencing. We'll put them before the judge. Who can you get to write a letter for you?"

The answer was nobody. This guy wasn't even talking about a trial—he was talking about sentencing—and there was not one person I knew who would stand up and vouch for me, let alone in print. I was fucked.

I left there one move closer to defeated.

I sat in my car before pulling out of the parking lot and popped a couple of my mother's Valium—two tens, just to take the edge off—and I washed 'em down with a mouthful of spit. I guess I'd just hang out like every other stiff waiting for an axe to drop. Not that I had much choice.

When I got back to my mother's, Vickie was waiting for me.

"Hey baby, can we talk?" *Yeah, and you can come visit too. Maybe I could get her to push her tits against the glass like in* Midnight Express.

"Yeah, what's up?"

"I'm pregnant."

"Great."

There I was, twenty-six years old, living at my mother's, out on bail for an armed robbery charge, no job, no money, a string of enemies twenty miles long, and I'm going to be a dad. Solid.

The next day, I got a call from the law offices. I was in luck. The charges had been dropped. It turns out the victim had been hanging around a public toilet in a city park, and he had never been robbed at gunpoint, he'd been rolled.

The victim was married with two children, but at the time of the "robbery" he was going by the name of "Cocksucker" and offering "real slutty" blowjobs to his fellow park patrons—one of whom took his wallet after ejaculating. The victim notified police and pumped up the story by adding a gun. He didn't know they were going to catch the perpetrator. When it came down, the victim didn't want his alter ego getting swabbed all over the courtroom, so in an effort to save his family future embarrassment, he conveniently told the truth to the detectives and then dropped the charges.

It was time to celebrate. I wasn't going to jail, and I was going to be a dad. I might have been on my way to being just another drone in the market, but I had a feeling it might be alright—a feeling that turned out to be a little too human. I fell victim to the belief that things were going to be okay, that everything was going to work out in the end.

Vickie had to work that night, so I was on my own.

I'd heard about a party being held close by, so I drove over and scoped it out. It was okay—a bunch of neighborhood kids getting loose. I walked into a few whisperings of "Do you know who that guy was?" It used to be "Do you know who that guy is?" I went to the kitchen looking for cocktails.

I grabbed a bottle of vodka that someone had chilling in the freezer, and after buttering the floor in front of the refrigerator, I went looking for a good time. (If you ever go to a party and you can get away with it—or not—try buttering the floor. Grab a stick of butter, and then just paint yourself an area, about four square feet in front of the fridge, and then sit back. If you like seeing people eat shit, you'll love this.) I grabbed a notepad by the phone and a pen. There were a couple of bills sitting on the counter—phone, gas, and electric—and after noting the name—I'm figuring the father of the house—I wrote a love note to him. I detailed every kiss, lick, and hug. I chronicled the first time he ever took me to completion, and I reminded him of how I laughed when he told me how good I tasted. I then signed the note "Love always, Richard," and I hid it in a book. Think about it, they might have just found that note today . . . Daddy has some explaining to do.

I was leaving the house. I'd had a few drinks, and I'd stirred up a little low-grade trouble—no more than any normal guy would do, just having fun—but now I was ready to go home. I was looking forward to seeing Vickie.

I was walking out the front door when she walked in—we collided on the doorstep—a tall, gorgeous blond with dark green eyes. She laughed at our, or rather my, unfortunate collision, and she steadied herself with a hand on my arm.

Her name was Casey, and she was fourteen years old.

I'd never been obsessed with anything or anyone in my life. Sure, I'd enjoyed things, and I got carried away at times, went on runs and maybe overdid it a bit, but true obsession is different. Obsession has a prerequisite of desire, and desire takes emotion, and emotion is human.

As a demon, I couldn't understand your **Father, Disfigured** art. I could acknowledge the picture; admire the time spent, the brush strokes, the work involved; but when you held a painting in front of me, say, of a woman holding a dead child in her arms, and you asked me for my thoughts, I'd answer, "Yes, it's a wonderful likeness." And then you'd say, "But look at the baby, see how she loved him." I'd acknowledge you with "Yes, I see. The slightly down-turned lines of her lips are well rendered."

Because, you see, I felt nothing. A picture never became more than a picture, and it was the same with movies and books. Because the actors were always just actors, and the printed words were always just words. I didn't have the emotion to bring these things to life. I couldn't even really appreciate music until the taint of humanness had started to slip in, and even so, look at the first music I liked—it was bold, powerful, and so full of energy and hate that a deaf man could hear every note. At the time, my underdeveloped sense of emotion wouldn't let me understand a subtler sound.

Now, funny as it may seem, God's need for adoration created obsession; it also created pride, greed, and lust, envy, gluttony, sloth, and wrath. These defects of human character were always blamed on my man. But he didn't create them, he only used them. God created your seven deadly sins.

If you ask me, I think He fucked up. Or else His plan was so convoluted and obscure that no one but Him could see what His desired outcome was. And if that was the case, well, I guess He's got it all figured out. But I don't think so; I think He fucked up.

He created a being with a desire to seek Him, but then He doesn't tell this being where He is. And not only that, He's peppered the world with decoys and dead-end streets. And when He sends a teacher—a Buddha, a Mohammed, a Christ—He sends them unprotected. God allows others to twist and warp the teacher's message. Why didn't God print a clear-cut message engraved in titanium so that none of the followers of these teachers could ever desecrate or change it—so the message would always remain pure and unaltered for all time to come? But God didn't. He sat back and He let these truths about His existence fall to shit. And He let you turn down those roads, knowing that you're going to fail, and He doesn't lift a hand to help you. He should be running a twenty-four-hour-a-day infomercial with a toll-free number: "When you get that itch, and the world won't satisfy, call me at 1-800-ALL-MYFAULT, and I'll be there in an instant. And, if you act now, I'll throw in two miracles and a burning bush experience."

I've spent lifetimes watching you fuckers. I've studied you—and I've laughed at your failed attempts at contact. Let me tell you what I've seen: I've seen you humans grow up standing on your own two feet, and you're raring to go. You jump into life, oblivious to what's about to take place. Everything's going well and then you get an itch of discomfort, so you buy something—maybe a new car or a tit job—and the itch gets scratched. And the discomfort goes away . . . for a while. But then the itch comes back—and you try something else, maybe a vacation, and it goes away again . . . but it comes back. You try property, power, prestige, and the itch gets scratched. But it always comes back, over and over again. And each time it returns, it's stronger and more resistant to satisfaction.

And so you humans say, "More, give me more," and you become obsessed. Because you've tried all those things and they felt good for a while, so those things must be the answer. Only, maybe you didn't get enough, or you didn't use them the right way, and if you tried one more time, the itch would surely get scratched for good. "More—that has to be the answer." But it fails, and you see people who look like they're getting true satisfaction with what they have, and you get envious, and you want his or hers. And then you might have something that you think is getting you connected and it gets stolen, and when you find who took it from you, you employ wrath. And then, when you mistakenly think what you have is *the* answer, you feel pride. And, as a final blow, when you tire from all your failed searching, you just give up—that's called sloth.

So, in reality, all these defects stem from an inability to get connected to The One who created you with a desire to be near Him. Fucking A, God might as well have dropped a crust of bread into the middle of a camp of starving men and watched them fight for it.

Well, I'll tell you what: I may be starting to feel things, but I got a leg up on you—I know how this shit works, and I know what you are, and I'm not going to do it. I'm gonna use the things in this world to stop whatever hurt may come, and then I'm gonna get old, and I'm gonna die—lights out, that's that. Besides, how bad could it really get anyway?

### I I I

Casey was a few months away from her fifteenth birthday, and I was twenty-five.

After bumping into her, and making my apologies, I walked out to the car. I had every intention of heading home, but instead I sat on the hood and looked back at the house—thinking of her. I was on my way to being a dad, trying to go straight. Vickie was probably at home waiting, dinner was surely made—and I had a thought that going home would be the right thing to do. But I also couldn't get the feel of that girl's hand on my arm out of my head. Do you know that when I was fully demon, I never had thoughts like this? These were human thoughts, thinking about people *after* they were out of your sight.

It wasn't long before she walked out—glancing side to side, hurriedly searching. She was trying to catch me, and she had no idea I was waiting. I called her over and we talked. She was a little girl trying to be big. It was endearing, especially the way she asked for a smoke and then hit on it like a virgin sucking on her first cock. Her lips were afraid of the cigarette.

For all my behavior, the one thing I wasn't was someone who preyed on children. Yes, I tortured kids my own age, because as a fledgling I knew no better. But no demon ever sets out to hurt a child—we leave that to you. You're much crueler than us. And if you want to beat on your own kids, you go right ahead.

This girl didn't look like a child to me—her eyes were older—but still, I was going to stay away. We could be friends. I'd never really had one of those.

I didn't even give her my phone number, or take hers. We talked about nothing, and we said our goodbyes.

That night, while I fucked Vickie, I made love to Casey. I thought of her smile and the way she looked for me when she ran from the house. I thought of her hands and how they might feel if I touched them, and I thought of the way her skin might taste if I was so bold as to put my lips to hers.

My relationship with Casey started innocently, I guess—seeing her at parties, the liquor store, and the beach. It was usually just a casual hello and then a smiling glance back as we parted. But from there it progressed; we'd stop and talk. It was talk about the beach and her friends at school; she asked me about music and what it was like to make records; she also talked about boys and how lame they were. She said she wished she had an older boy, one who wasn't so concerned with his buddies, and one who would be more into her. It was never more than talk. And surprisingly, I found her interesting—not intellectually of course, but as a person. I was interested in her life and what she felt. It was the first time that I was ever really concerned with anyone but me. It was fascinating to talk to a human.

Vickie didn't care for our friendship—she said it wasn't right, me hanging out with a fifteen-year-old girl. But I constantly reminded her that I never laid a hand on her, and my interest was of no harm to her.

A night came when my mother was visiting my oldest sister, and Vickie was away at her grandmother's. I was going to be alone, and on hearing this, Casey offered to come by and check on me. It didn't seem like such a bad idea.

She'd been drinking—wine that she'd stolen from her parent's liquor cabinet—and she was buzzed. I spent half the night holding her hair back as she puked. She was to be picked up by an older friend at eleven, and at ten forty-five, after rinsing her mouth out with gum and cola, she gave me a kiss as a thank you. It lasted longer than it should have.

I've heard humans describe kisses as electric—flashes of intense lustful light that spread through the body. But this wasn't one of them; it was the complete opposite. After I swam through the taste of regurgitated wine, her kiss was like nothing—like a plug had just been pulled, and all the power had been turned off. And the only thing shocking about it was its ability to take away the thought of being human—when she kissed me I felt nothing again.

When Casey's lips touched mine, I didn't care about being a dad. I didn't think about paying bills or my father's death. I didn't think about getting the sickness or leaving the band too soon. Casey's kiss brought me back to the feeling of unconnectedness I got by being a full-blooded demon, and in that kiss, I realized how much I'd changed for the worse.

It was over too soon.

I walked her to her friend's car and tucked her in—the power of her kiss still canceled out the human feelings. But as she drove off, heading further away from me, the feelings, or the sickness, which had begun to creep into my body, intensified and everything came back. I needed to see her again—as soon as possible.

There was only one other thing that stopped me from feeling, and that was getting loaded—it worked every time, but now I'd found another, and with these two, I could go through anything.

I met Casey at the movies one day.

I think we both knew what we wanted. I couldn't get her out of my mind—and if one kiss could make those feelings go away, then maybe this was the answer I was looking for: maybe she would heal me.

We didn't care what picture we saw. We bought tickets and then went looking for the emptiest theater—multiplexes may not have the class or charm of the old movie houses, but when you're looking for a discrete place to get it on or an afternoon of movie hopping, you could do much worse.

We found a theater with only one old man in it and we took seats in the back. We were all over each other—our hands diving and sweeping across each other's body. She'd been with boys before—fumbling attempts at intercourse in the backseats of cars—but she'd never been with a man. And I'll tell you, I'd never been with a woman.

I'd slept with hundreds of victims, and if I needed something long-term from them, I was an attentive lover; if I didn't, I'd just burn through them looking for release. This was different—the further I got inside her, the further I needed to go. If I could have ground her down and jammed her in my veins I would have, because the pain stopped when she was in my arms.

I didn't want to let her go, and I didn't want to go home.

When I arrived at my mother's, Vickie was waiting. She came up to get a hug but I blew her off. I lied, telling her I was about to get sick and as I lay in front of the toilet pretending to wretch, I thought of Casey and I got angry that I had to be away.

I stuffed my clothes deep into the hamper, and I hopped in the shower. I touched my groin and then held my hand to my face—I could smell her, and I was angry that I had to wash away and hide what I'd done.

When I came out of the bathroom, Vickie was concerned. "Are you alright?" she sweetly asked. "Do you need anything? Could I help make you comfortable?"

*Yes, you can get the fuck away from me.*

Her voice—while saying those kind words—sounded grating, annoying. Why couldn't she just go away? *She's always hassling me, wanting me to work and pay her bills.* I felt trapped.

I thought back to long ago when I watched Salome dance. And I now realized that the power she held was only electric when she turned away, when her attention had turned to another man. It was then that the jilted ex-partner was shocked into awakening; it was then that he wanted to kill. Salome was a sedative, not an amphetamine. When she was on you, you forgot your pain.

I kept my mouth shut, swallowed my annoyance with Vickie, and wondered when I could see Casey again.

At first, Casey's parents were okay with us being friends. I even dropped her off at home a few times. But I had some balls going over there. How could they believe that my interest in this pretty young thing was strictly platonic?

*It doesn't matter—fuck 'em.*

My need to have my feelings turned off overrode my discretion, and my blindness caused me to assume that no one saw through my intentions—that everyone was a fucking idiot who loved being duped.

Vickie knew better. She didn't dig my association with Casey one bit.

The first time I slept with Casey, I bathed and hid my clothes. I was like a teen hiding his first sips of whiskey with mouthwash and cologne. But now my relationship with Casey had matured and I'd become careless—I didn't bother showering after being with her and I sure as fuck didn't hide my clothes. I was drunk with my obsession, and I'd stagger into the house stinking of her perfume.

On the nights when I wasn't drunk with lust, I was just drunk.

Vickie and I had terrible arguments.

One night, during a particularly vicious fight, Vickie and I were pulling at each other's hair. We were locked together and no matter how bad it hurt, neither one of us would let go. I kicked her, and she fell to her knees, holding her stomach and screaming in pain. She was almost nine months pregnant at the time.

The next afternoon while Casey was in school and unavailable to me, I spent time with Vickie. We lay in our room watching a movie together. We ignored the pain of the night before, and we fell asleep.

I didn't realize how I looked to other people—kids who had thought me a hero had raised me above my fellows, but my image was tarnishing fast. And sometimes, you put your heroes on a pedestal, and you hang your hopes on the belief that you, like them, can be strong and defiant. But when you get the sad awakening that your heroes are just men—no longer gods, but weak, drunken men—then sometimes, you want your heroes beaten for what they just did to your dreams.

I woke to a loud crash and a large rock lying on the bed at my feet. The windows of my room faced the street, and where once a parade of girls had knocked on the glass looking for late night comfort, there was now only a broken reminder of those visits shattered on the bed. Vickie was scared and crying, but neither of us was hurt. The rock was huge, almost as big as the one I sent through that cop car window years earlier, and if our bamboo curtains weren't there to stop its progress it could have killed one of us.

In the moment, I was pissed—I would've shot the fuckers who did it. But afterwards, I just felt defeated. I was away from Casey, and I felt like a man who deserved to be attacked. And why wouldn't they strike—whoever they were? They probably thought I didn't have it in me to retaliate.

A couple of days later, someone ratted out one of the guys responsible. I knew him. He was a whack-job who lived down the street—a real fucking idiot who used to come by my house for a swim. Maybe he thought this was payback for all those times I held him under water until he stopped kicking.

I grabbed a shotgun and went to pick him up.

I figured there were only two places in my neighborhood that a whack-job would hang—the bowling alley or the liquor store. I scored at the lanes. He was sitting on his bicycle near the curb—it was about eleven a.m. on a Tuesday morning. I pulled up in my small sedan—a family man's car, a gift of my father's death—and I pointed the gun out the window.

"Drop the bike and get in the fucking car."

He did what I said like he was on autopilot.

"What are you gonna do, Jack?"

He was scared and wasn't entirely sure where I was going to go with this one. He'd ridden with me on another retaliation pick-up, and it didn't go well for the guys we found.

A quick aside: you might be wondering what kind of crew I had if a bicycle-riding whack-job was part of my team, but without going into a long explanation, I'd given whack-job a ride to get smokes—strictly out of the goodness of my heart. While at the liquor store, I came across three idiots who fit the description of these guys who robbed my neighbor. I asked whack-job to keep an eye on them while I called my sister to I.D. them. I was right. My sister gave me a positive nod and, at knife point, I fought these three fucks and put them in the car. Well, I put two of them in the car—the third one got away. Anyway, we stopped by my mom's, picked up a .38 that I'd stolen from a house party, and we drove the two thieves behind a market where I interrogated them one at a time until they talked. I was worried that the whack-job was gonna shoot one of them by accident—his hands were shaking so fucking bad that I'd emptied the gun before I handed it to him and had him watch the one who wasn't getting beaten at the time. It was no big deal, they quickly confessed—and they brought back the shit.

And now, two years later, this shaky-handed motherfucker was sitting in my car, wondering what I was going to do to him. I told him.

"We're just gonna talk, man. No big deal."

We drove back to my mother's, and I pulled into the driveway. I blocked the view from the street to the walkway underneath my bedroom window. I hadn't had time to fix the glass so there was a big hole where part of the window used to be. I laid him down in front of the window and I put the shotgun to his head. I made him talk . . .

You can punch or hit a man and it will do damage, but if you make that man think he's about to die, it'll ruin him. And if he's weak, he'll even rat out his own mother—if he thinks it will get him out of a beating.

Whack-job flipped instantly on his two buddies.

It turns out that he and a couple of friends got liquored up and then decided they'd go poke a stick in a bear's cage—late-afternoon drunk fun.

I loaded him back in the car, and we went to get his friends.

We could only find one of his co-conspirators, but he'd have to do. I brought them back to the house. This time, instead of staging them in front of the broken window, I took them into the living room, and I told them to make themselves comfortable. The three of us sat down. I turned the TV to the cartoon channel—and I pointed the gun at them.

I forced them to watch cartoons.

"Look at that little rabbit. If I was that wolf, I'd eat him."

I used the shotgun as a pointer.

"I sure wouldn't want to be him. That rabbit makes me mad."

The human brain is a strange thing, and the fear that resides in the mind will paint a picture darker than anything on the horizon. I offered them cartoons and their response was "What do you want from us, man? What are you gonna do?"

"I want you to shut up so I can watch my show. I love this crap and after this, maybe we could watch—"

"We got money, man; if ya want money, we got money."

"Okay, you owe me two hundred for the window, and I want it quick—today, I need it today. And if you're not gonna shut up, you gotta go because I'm trying to watch this and you're bugging me."

I pointed to the door with the gun and they were up and running.

I got a check later that afternoon.

### I I I

Casey was becoming jealous of the time I spent with Vickie. If it wasn't so painful, it would have been quite amusing to my old self. And yes, I did say pain—and it was increasing. When I was sober, I'd try to think about my old life, about how situations like this would be cause for laughter among my fellow demons.

"Yeah, and I'm fucking this chick, and she thinks I love her, but I'm also fucking this one on the side—who happens to be underage, and she's jealous of the one I'm cheating on with her. And oh yeah, get this, the first bitch is fucking pregnant. Ha!"

My life was losing its comic relief.

It was a few days before Vickie was to deliver the baby and Casey had turned up the heat. I called her house and after repeated unanswered rings, the message machine fielded my call—it was Diana Ross and the Supremes singing "Love Child" before the beep.

I tried to reason with her when she demanded I leave Vickie, but she wouldn't listen—what the fuck was I going to do anyway? It wasn't like her parents were going to be down with me fucking her, but she pushed it, and her new plan was "Well, since you're sleeping with another woman I might as well be getting some too—I'm gonna start fucking other guys."

I went nuts. She was my sedative—my release from emotion. If I could have lain in a dark room and just sucked on her body, I would have. But for some reason I couldn't cut Vickie loose. If she was to dump me, fine, but I couldn't be the one to do it. I was lost.

It was at this time when they showed up.

I woke one morning and walked into the bathroom. My first stop was the toilet—there were some mornings where I sat down to piss because I'd be so light headed, but this morning I stood and put one hand on the wall in front of me, bracing myself. My cock felt like it'd been stomped on by a bitch in stiletto heels—like I was pissing broken glass. I'd been using it way too much, but I just dumped all the liquor from the night before. Shit, I bet you could've lit my fucking stream on fire with a match—I was pissing one hundred proof.

When I pulled up my pajamas and turned around, I saw him. He was standing behind me—his cheek torn, blood drifting down his face. He had a hand on my shoulder. I tried shaking him off but there was nothing there to shake—he was only a shadow, a reflection of an old victim in the mirror. And there were others there also—they were standing around me—deep in the reflection. They were all waiting their turn. One by one, a parade of victims waiting to get their picture taken with a monster . . .

*Walk up quietly behind the animal, put your hand on his shoulder, pose, smile, and then step out of the frame.*

I called Casey, trying to make it stop, but she didn't answer.

Vickie started having labor pains that afternoon.

We got to the hospital and things were tense, uneasy. Vickie's friend had shown up to support her—both of them knowing they couldn't count on me—but I acted insulted that she was asked to come. I didn't need somebody doing my business. Vickie's mother and stepfather were also there, but I got no support from them either. I thought somebody should have maybe given me a bit a credit for sticking it up in there—after all, we wouldn't have been here if it wasn't for me.

Vickie's stepdad was a hard case Latin cat who didn't like me one bit. I could read the words *white trash* on his lips every time he saw me, and I could tell he would be happier with me out of the picture. *Fuck him anyway, rolling in here like he is someone, trying to run the fucking show—I'm hurting too, man—Vickie ain't the only one suffering.* I tried looking him in the eyes as much as possible, but every time I did I saw Casey's face echoed there.

Vickie was ready to go, so they wheeled her into the delivery room. She didn't want me to see her have the baby—she could tell I was already disgusted with her, and after hearing me constantly muttering about these "fucking human scumbags," she was embarrassed for me to see her as anything less than perfect. I went in anyway and she lay on the bed worried about how she looked as she gave birth.

Vickie was hurting. She went with no painkillers, and she was "motherfuckering" anyone who was within earshot—including the nurses and the doctors. I just sat there clueless, not sure what the fuck was going on. I hadn't attended any of the pre-birth classes or read any of the books so I was pretty much useless.

My daughter was born without my help.

I watched as they pulled her from Vickie's womb—the baby was gray and had not yet taken her first breath. In that moment I thought that God was going to punish me by letting my daughter come into this world without life, but as she gasped, sucking in the heavy air that filled the delivery room, I was punished a different way.

I was struck human.

The sickness swallowed me whole.

And I was suddenly overwhelmed with pain.

I hope you never know how it feels to have feelings where before there were none. I had never tasted regret, felt sadness, loss, or remorse, and now, they washed through me and over me. The weight of my past bore down upon me like the ocean—I knew what he felt now, the old homeless demon I'd drunk with in the Bowery. I knew why he was so beaten, and why he struggled with that weight.

I cried out in pain. "Oh God."

And I had no one to turn to.

I was trash, a failure, a beast that preyed on the weak. And this small child didn't deserve to have me as a father.

She looked at me when she heard my voice. She was beautiful— two small handfuls of child. And although a newborn's eyes are normally unfocused, hers were not. They were a deep green, and I recognized her—she was an infant that would grow into the young blond girl who had sat on the bed as I robbed that house, the same child that I drank away on the beach, her image sinking into the sand. I remember begging for death to remove the memory of her—and now, here she was. I couldn't stand it.

She knew everything I'd done—every punch I'd thrown, drink or drug I'd taken, and everything I'd ever destroyed or stolen.

I turned away and ran from the room.

There was a bathroom down the hall, and I sought refuge there.

I walked in and heard laughter. The bathroom mirror was full of all the people I'd hurt—hundreds of faces, ecstatic with glee. They'd all gathered to laugh at the once proud dark prince who was now nothing but weak human scum.

"Some fucking delivery, huh?"

I turned, and it was him, the not-quite—a businessman coming out of a stall with a broken door. His pants were around his ankles, and it looked like he'd just relieved himself.

"I thought you were gonna pass out when you saw her, fucking pussy."

I was going to answer him when . . .

"What do you expect? He wakes up to living like an asshole, and it hurts."

The stall door next to him opened, and another man walked out—a janitor in a perfectly pressed uniform. It was the Man—God. "You heard him call my name, right? At the end there, right after he saw her?"

"I heard him fucking squeal like a bitch, but I sure as fuck didn't see any genuflecting."

"Why don't you ask him? He'll tell you."

They both looked at me—an uninformed third party to their conversation—I was clueless. The not-quite spoke for me.

"Look at him; he still doesn't know what the fuck's going on. How can you say he broke? He didn't break—that's my man, my fucking man, through and through."

The janitor looked at me, walked to the sink, and washed His hands. He was thorough and a word wasn't spoken until He finished. He looked in the mirror, His gaze catching the not-quite. "I've got all the time in the world."

And then He looked at me, placed a fatherly hand on my shoulder, and said, "Drink up, Daddy."

And then He walked out.

I turned towards the not-quite but he was gone. He hadn't washed his hands.

Vickie and the baby were home for only a few weeks before they decided to split—I was oblivious, but at least I hadn't asked them to go. It was her fault, not mine, that she left. She could have stayed if she really wanted to.

I helped her load the baby's things into the car, and then I secured the car seat. I couldn't look at the child. I didn't say goodbye to Vickie, but I did close her door once she was in. As they drove off I thought about Casey. I was free now. I could be with her when I wanted. I pulled a joint from behind my ear, lit it, and took a big drag—the smoke expanded in my lungs.

As I exhaled, the sky turned a brilliant shade of blue-gray.

There are really only two things that bother me about this world: one is the phrase "You're going to have to wait," and the other is the word "No."

The first I can deal with. It's fucking uncomfortable, but at least I do know that I'll get my way in the end. With the proper bit of manipulation, I can probably weasel whatever I want out of just about anyone—so any bullshit attempt at controlling my desire is futile. The second, that fucking two-letter piss-off and slap to my face, is pure shit—the only one who's allowed to use "No" in this world is me.

## Disintegration

"No. You're not going to stop me from seeing her."

I needed Casey to remove my feelings, and I wasn't going to let anyone stand in the way of that. Vickie was gone; she took the baby and moved to a shit-hole apartment in the gay ghetto of Long Beach, and there was no reason why I shouldn't get my fill of Casey. *Unless of course, you're counting that she's underage, and that she's harbored by a mom connected with the police department and has a father who's an angry pistol-packing Vietnam vet.*

Casey's parents had started getting wise to the fact that I was sleeping with their daughter. They couldn't prove it, but you can tell when a girl's been getting loved on. They walk different, their voices get a bit deeper, and they leave fucking condom wrappers in their jacket pocket. I don't know what the fuck Casey was thinking leaving it in there; it was almost like she wanted to get me caught. And she probably did. Casey was still pissed that I had been sleeping with Vickie at the same time I was sleeping with her, and she made me pay for it whenever she could. Just like Salome, jealousy was one of her favorite strategies—Casey loved teasing me about other guys getting a hold of her.

I should have taken a better look at Casey's eyes when I met her. She might have been just turning fifteen, but with eyes like ancient dark green glass I should have known better. She'd been around.

I don't know why I couldn't see it at first, but there it was: that cool indifference to my pain, the way she handled her parents when they questioned her, and the way she loved to see me hurt.

Casey was a demon.

It made sense, I'm not sure exactly how, but that had to be the reason why I felt nothing when I was with her. When I was against her body, or even if her hand was just lying lightly in mine, the feelings went away.

Maybe she was a parting gift from the not-quite. He had almost shown kindness to me when I'd last seen him—fuck, he'd even come to the hospital to see the baby. Casey had to be a gift. But if so, why was she fucking with me so much?

Casey hooked up with an old pervert, and she'd told me about him—he had money and a nice car. There were always one or two of these cats in every neighborhood—guys with short money, but to the little girls it looked long. I didn't need him fucking with my hook-up—he was making me look cheap with his Corvette and his khaki slacks. I was pissed at her.

"Why the fuck are you with him?"

"He buys me things; you never buy me things."

"Are you fucking that creep? Is he giving you money to fuck him?"

"You're gross. You know what? You're just an asshole and you hate my friends."

"He's not your fucking friend; he's a creep."

I needed this to stop. If she cut me off because of this motherfucker I'd kill him. Besides, he wasn't giving *me* anything.

"I've gotta go. John's outside, he's taking me shopping."

"Hey Casey, you fucking—"

"Bye."

I might as well have been yelling at the wall—she was gone.

Now, I still had some skills. Just because I'd gone human didn't mean I'd lost all my faculties—they were weaker, that's for sure, but they weren't gone. I could still talk the wheels off a moving car, and I could still hunt—I was really solid at getting hold of who I needed. I just had to think of where he or she might be—I'd sit quietly for a minute and then I'd get a good picture in my mind of his or her location.

I thought of this old fuck, and I thought of his liver-spotted hand slipping off the gearshift and onto her bare leg, and then I saw him pulling into the gas station by my house. He was two minutes away.

I was on him.

I tore up to the gas station as good old "Uncle Fondle" was filling up. And look at that, Casey was with him. I figured I'd put a crimp in his gas hose before he put it in Casey.

He was checking himself out in a side mirror, so he didn't see me cruise up behind him; it wouldn't have done him much good if he did—it was probably better that he was getting beaten before he knew what hit him.

I walked up, grabbed what was left of his gray hair, and slammed his fucking face into the roof of the car.

"What's up, pops? You like fucking young girls, huh?"

Not that I was any better, but it was a good opening line. I slammed his face into the roof again.

That motherfucker must have been taking blood thinners because he was bleeding all over the place. *Shit, I got one pair of clean pants, and I don't want to get them dirty, I'll be careful.*

I gave old gramps a few more blows to the head, and then threw him to the ground. He slumped down with his back against the car, sitting up—he looked like he was just taking it easy on a hot day, that is, if you didn't notice the blood or the young girl.

*Fuckin' A.* Casey was just sitting there watching this old guy take a beating. She wasn't screaming, telling me to stop, or trying to get out—I wouldn't have been shocked if she pulled out a copy of *Tiger Beat* and started reading. She was completely unconnected.

I was jealous of her lack of emotion.

I kicked the old man a few times, and then I bent down and picked up the gas nozzle that had fallen from his tank.

I looked at it for a second, and then I beat him with it.

I drove off and left Casey with him.

You might think I would have taken her—the spoils of war after winning a battle—but as much as I needed her, I was furious. I was risking arrest to see that bitch—she was underage, I could have gone to jail any minute for it, and she should have cut me some slack.

I gave him that beating to warn her—I wasn't to be fucked with.

I drove around for a while, cruised the beach and a couple of old crew members' homes, but none of those guys were around anymore—they were either dead or in jail. I was okay with it; I didn't want to talk to anyone anyway. I was driving, looking for memories of happier times, but after a couple of hours, I realized there were no happy times.

All I could think about was my daughter and how much it hurt to be a father—the guilt of not being there, and when I *was* there, of not being able to stay.

I went home.

At the door I was met by my mother.

"Casey's been calling. I told her you were gone, but she thinks you're hiding. What'd you do?"

"I didn't do anything. She's fucking nuts."

The phone rang and my mother picked it up. She cocked her head with a smart-assed smirk and extended her arm to me. I knew who it was.

"Guess where I just got back from." It was Casey. "My mom and I just filed a restraining order against you. You really hurt him."

"Does your mom know he was trying to fuck you?"

"Why don't you come see me?"

She laughed and hung up.

"Motherfucker!"

I yanked the phone off the wall and threw it. *Fucking bitch—she's trying to get me to come see her, knowing I can't stay away, and then she'll probably rat me out to the cops. Fuck her.*

I went out.

I was hurting—and being apart from Casey wasn't helping. I was drowning in emotions—jealousy, anger, loneliness. *How can you fuckers stand this?* I needed it to shut off.

I needed it to stop.

You already know my emotion removal choices. Get with Casey, or get fucked up. Casey made herself temporarily unavailable, so . . .

I went with a little cocaine and lots of booze.

The booze was easy to come by, and I always knew what I was getting. My first stop was the liquor store.

I started to feel better before I even got there.

A human mind is easily desensitized to experience—so much so that when torturing a person, you really have to mix it up. You can punch and punch on your victim, but after while they will get used to it and the point of torture is lost—they know what's coming and develop a tolerance, or else just give up. That's why when I used to fuck with someone, I'd mix it up. A little knife play, then a couple of hard slaps, then a punch, then bring it back to the knife, and then maybe top it off with some suffocation. I kept 'em on their toes.

My brain knew what was coming when I had the thought to drink. Those little cells up there got all excited and they started doing what they do before the sauce even touched 'em—kind of like when somebody flinches before you hit him. Those cells said, "We're gonna feel good." And they did; they started feeling really good.

Before I got to the liquor store, I felt better. I was calmer, easy to please.

When I walked in, old Mr. Smiling Face Lee brought down my favorite and nodded "no charge"; I felt a whole lot better.

I walked outside, unscrewed the cap, and threw it—it was only a fifth and, as you all know, you don't need the cap once the bottle's open, that's for transportation purposes only. I was feeling much better.

And then . . .

I took that first big drink, and it was like a fucking janitor's push broom sweeping down my body and washing all those nasty old feelings right out into the parking lot. No more remorse, no guilt, and no shame.

I took another drink, and I didn't live at my mom's anymore. I had my own place—a penthouse with a pool. I took another drink, and I never quit that band, and I was still loved, and I was right back to being me. The only thing missing was a perfect girl and an eight ball of cocaine.

I knew just where to get it, and just who to take with me.

I called the Mole.

Coke ain't like booze. There ain't no fucking quality control on that shit—no government inspector slapping a label on cut-up blow. Sometimes the coke was shit—stepped on crap that you wouldn't give to a wannabe punk. I put back this yellow shit one evening that looked like somebody pissed in it. But then again, that's the problem with blow—when it gets late at night, and all the good blow's gone, well, let's just say the quality doesn't matter when you don't want to run out. I made the call.

"My friend, Charlie."

This was the Mole's real name—you had to know these things, you couldn't go calling people's houses asking for Lizard or Worm, could you? Most of my acquaintances lived with their mothers or their grandmas—that's the mark of all good fuck-ups.

The Mole lived at Grannie's.

"I was thinking you might wanna get some shit, Chuck."

"Fuck yeah, I'll pick you up."

Charlie and I used to get coke from this dude. We called him the Incredible Shrinking Man, because every time you went there, he got smaller.

He was sucking up right before your eyes.

We didn't have any money but Charlie had an old checkbook. A few years before, one of Charlie's girlfriends had left it at his house. He hadn't thrown it away. There's no real code of conduct when you're dealing with drug dealers—anything goes. They need your money as much as you need their product, so unless you do something real heinous, or continually fuck up, you're pretty well free to get loose on the odd occasion.

The shrinking man was afraid of us. He was chanting a mantra: "I've been robbed before; I've been robbed before."

Jesus, don't you think if we were going to rob him we would have just come in and done it? We were sitting on the couch, looking at porn.

Charlie assured him we were there to purchase.

"How much have you got?" I asked him.

"I've been robbed before, Jack."

"Fuckin' A, we're not gonna rob you. We want to buy some blow."

Charlie took a turn. "Come on, bro, how much you got?"

The guy finally realized that we meant business, and he told us. It was a large amount. Charlie said, "We'll take it all," and wrote him a bad check.

On the bottom of the check, in the space reserved for memos, Charlie scribbled *for cocaine.*

Charlie and I ended the evening early—at least, early in the morning. It was about three or four—the booze was gone, and so was the blow—and I was starting to come down.

Have you ever come down from blow?

The intensity of emotion when the crest of a cocaine high crashes is unlike anything I've ever felt—if you think you hurt now, just wait.

I'd play shows sometimes where I'd stuff my nose before the set, and it was great walking onstage pumped up on cocaine like a sexual champion, cocky as fuck. But then, mid-set, the blow would wear off, and the vulnerability would hit me, and then all I wanted was someone to put their arms around me and make it go away. The stand for the microphone is thin as a small rope, but I'd pull every inch of me behind it, and I'd try to hide—not an easy job for a big man.

I'd never felt more human in my life than when I was coming down off the shit.

## I I I

I decided I wanted to see the baby.

I wanted to touch her—hold her in my arms and try to remember what it might have been like before I was conscious.

I drove over to Vickie's.

*Jesus, they live in a fucking dump. I can't believe she stows my little girl in this fucking place.* I pounded on the door.

"Vickie. Vickie! Let me in."

The door opened to the face of a very displeased late-night two-job-working waitress who failed to get child support from her sperm donating piece-of-shit ex-boyfriend.

"What the fuck are you doing here?"

I put on a sad face, not hard—if you saw me, you'd probably think I was a candidate for suicide.

"I want to see the baby, Vick."

"She's sleeping; it's fucking four o'clock. Go away."

"I can't. I need to see her; she's mine."

I pushed the door in and walked right past her.

"I gotta take a shower first, okay?"

I walked into her bathroom and made myself at home. I didn't pay shit for this place—which, by the way, was at least clean—but I thought Vick could've shown me a little more courtesy. After all, I was hurting.

I took my clothes off and stepped in the shower. The water was warm and felt good on my body. I picked up the soap and I started to scrub—normally at first, but then harder, and yet harder still. I was dirty, and it wouldn't come off. It was what seemed to be an oil-based residue of disgust coating my skin. I could smell the stench; it was caught in my nose like the stench of jail—deep and rancid, unforgiving.

I finally gave up and got out. I didn't look in the mirror. I quit that a long time ago, but I could hear them whispering about the way I looked.

"I hope he dies."

"He's not well. Look at him; I told you, he's not right in the head."

I did my best to ignore them—buttoning up my pants and leaving my shirt and shoes on the floor. I walked into Vickie's room and stood over the crib.

Vickie was there—looking down on the baby with the most painful loving expression on her face. She held that love as she gave me a proud see-what-we've-made look, sharing the moment with me.

I reached in and grabbed the baby. Vickie tried to stop me.

"What the fuck are you doing? Give her to me."

The baby started crying, and I squeezed her tight to my chest. Vickie tried to pull her out of my arms but I held tight.

The baby smelled clean, pure—the scent I tried to get when I scrubbed myself in the shower. The baby didn't smell like violence and hate. The baby didn't smell like regret or fear. I started crying, wailing, with the baby in my arms. Vickie tried again to grab her but I turned away. I was going to take her to the car—drive off with her in my arms.

I was heading to the front door, but I felt light-headed, so I put my back against the wall and slid down to the floor. I hit hard on my ass, but I wouldn't let go.

The baby was still crying.

I leaned my head against the wall and that was it. . . .

I woke to the sounds of low tears—not the loud angry cries of a cranky child, the soft cries of a woman who'd given up.

I opened my eyes and Vickie was standing over me looking down.

I was bleeding.

When I'd passed out, blood started to flow from my nose in deep red trails down the left and right side of my face onto the floor—a steady stream of shame.

I got up and wiped my face with a towel.

I don't know what the fuck I wanted to be here for. Vickie was a real drag, and Casey was probably shitting herself wondering where the fuck I was. And for that matter, when I woke up here, *I* was wondering where the fuck I was.

### | | |

It's strange coming out of blackouts. I have pictures of me in places I've never been. I've got a great one—you should see it—where I'm standing in what I think is a run-down hotel room or a very unwell-to-do friend's house. The walls are bare and the lamp on the cheap bedside table has no shade on it. I'm leaning with my head thrown back and my elbow cocked—I'm pouring what looks to be a pint of something down my throat, and I have what looks to be a pair of cooked hamburger patties—with all the fixings—laying on my titties.

### | | |

If the goal was to turn off—get the stench of human off me—then I needed to shake the loneliness. I thought another trip to the stage would help—it didn't. It may have felt good for the moment— walking on as the lights went up, the crowd roaring its approval—but you've got to go home sometime, and at the end of the night, I'd wrap myself in a jacket of solitude as I walked out.

I'd started a new band—a post–punk rock outfit called Tender

Fury. I know the name blows, but it fit at the time. I was having what the normal man might call romance problems. I'd stolen the name from one of those shitty paperback romance novels, *Love's Tender Fury*.

I was sick of punk, and the gay lounge singer thing had played out, so I dipped into the rock pool. Don't be afraid though, I might have been associated with the "leather codpiece and womanly men singing in extremely high, ball-tightening wails" crowd, but, thank God, I can't screech like that—and I can't stand that fucking crap. I had long hair—very sexy blond curls—and I might have worn leather—although, I'm not sure a jacket made of cocker spaniel counts—but I was embarrassed to be associated with anyone who seriously wore a pair of spandex pants. And even then, if I got a chance, I gave 'em a beating.

Now, you know how I felt about Casey—I needed her with me, and I was risking jail being with her—but I also needed to make the feelings stop. And if a little extra booze helped, well, then maybe a little extra woman might help too. This might seem crazy, but like the cocaine, the quality of the woman didn't matter when you were alone and needed comfort.

I went out before a show one evening, and I saw a woman in a bar—I didn't usually have a type, but this lady definitely didn't fit any "not type" that I had either. For one, she was older, probably in her mid-thirties. She was also very well dressed—and I don't mean in fishnets and a short skirt. She was wearing business attire, a dark pantsuit and heels, like she'd just gotten off work. She was also huge, ten or fifteen feet tall. I was surprised no one else had taken notice of this, but they were all acting like it was normal—a giantess hanging around in a bar.

I didn't approach her right away; I was scared. Her shoulder-length curly brown hair had that Medusa thing going and when she threw her head back and laughed, the snakes danced and tossed angry glances in my direction. She was beautiful, what my detractors might say was "out of my league," and I was fascinated.

I had a drink.

A greyhound—vodka and grapefruit juice. It was a cocktail that said, "I'm not fucked up yet."

I was waiting for seventy-five cent "kamikaze night" to start. I had twenty bucks in my pocket, so that meant twenty drinks, and a five-dollar tip to maintain my suave factor with the cocktail waitress.

The bartender rang a bell signaling the drink special. I placed my order.

When my drinks came I handed the waitress my twenty, collected my change, and dropped the five as promised—a healthy gratuity. I winked. "There's a little something there for you, baby."

Yes, a five-dollar bill for the waitress I'd slept with before and probably would do again.

I nodded my head towards the giantess, but all I got in return from my server was a set of rolled-up eyeballs and a look of disgust—some people only see what they want to see.

I finished my greyhound and turned towards the tray, keeping my eye on the large woman. I needed to be prepared, in case she went on some sort of a rampage or a giantess hissy fit—I'd hate to be trampled. The heels on her shoes looked quite sharp.

I loved kamikazes—their little limey vodka bodies were perfect for one gulp. I put down six in succession—lift, swallow, slam, lift, swallow, slam—puckering my lips after each repetition. Then I put my eye back on point.

She didn't look as large as when I arrived. Maybe she was slumping—in my experience older large women could be sneaky.

I had another six drinks in succession.

She was talking to another woman now, and I'll be fucked if my giantess didn't look about right-sized, maybe a little large—big boned, plus size, but manageable, and pretty.

I put down six more.

My tabletop looked like one of those "pitch a dime in the goldfish bowl" games that you'd see in a carnival—the kamikaze glasses were waiting for dimes and little fish.

I looked over and the woman was smiling at me. The snakes in her hair were sleeping, lying silent on her shoulders—she had gotten even smaller.

I hit the waitress up for a pen and pencil. She was more than happy to give them, until she found out the number I wanted wasn't hers, and I got a very rude "Make sure the pen gets back to me" before she left. *I gave her a fucking five-dollar tip and she's gotta be a bitch.*

I pounded the last two shots and I went to make contact.

I walked directly to her table and laid down a piece of paper with my number and address on it.

"I've gotta go, but why don't you come see me tonight? Walk through the side door and make a right—my room is in the back. Wake me up."

I touched her hand and walked off.

Now, I hope you're not reading this as bullshit, because it ain't. When you run into as many women as I did, it becomes a numbers thing. It's like being a salesman. Sometimes you can just say whatever the fuck you want and they'll buy anyway. I've held a condom in my hand before and just waved it at a girl, and it worked—yeah, nine times out of ten you get flipped off, maybe slapped . . . but that one time makes up for it.

I went and played the show, then headed home.

I was tanked.

I don't remember driving home, but I woke up in bed and I was naked and jacking off. I was having what must have been a succession of quick pass outs and wake-ups because my consciousness was like photographs being placed down on my bed—I'm in this position, then that. Here, then there.

I'd pass out and come to, pass out and come to, over and over.

I came to once more, and I was lying on my back with a semierect cock spraying piss in the air like a child's Water Wiggle toy.

I pissed all over myself and the bed.

I was lying in the remains of twenty kamikazes, a greyhound, and half a case of beer, when the door to my bedroom opened and the woman from the bar walked in. She was back to her regular towering height and she had to bend down so as not to hit her head on the roof of my room.

I looked up at her from my bed, a little boy who'd pissed himself and had been bad.

She leaned down and pushed the bangs from my eyes and then she slid her hand to my crotch. The snakes in her hair entwined themselves around my body and held me down. She caressed my cock and then bent over and took me in her mouth—her right hand secured in my crotch, her left hand traveling up my body and coming to rest over my mouth. She squeezed my face hard. I couldn't scream or get a breath, and she dug her nails into my cheeks as she bit down on my cock. I thrashed in the bed, trying to get up, but I couldn't—she was huge, powerful, and then, even though I touched no part of her, I felt her cum, her body shaking violently in orgasm, and then she stood, straightened her clothes, and walked out.

I passed out again and didn't wake until late morning—still naked and lying in a bed soaked with cold urine and semen. I hurt where she bit me.

The phone was ringing. Normally my mother took it off the hook when I got home, but I guess it was later than I thought. I lifted the receiver and an angry questioning voice took a swing at my head.

"Where the fuck have you been?" It was Casey.

"Good morning."

"It's two o'clock, and I just got back from the police station."

"What?"

"My fucking mom told me we were gonna go shopping, but we went there instead. They took me in a room. They questioned me. They wanted me to tell them you fucked me."

"You didn't say anything did you?"

"I should have. You're a fucking asshole. Where have you been?"

"I was sick. I got hurt, baby."

"We can't see each other. They're going to arrest you."

"What are you talking about?"

"I gotta go. My dad says he's going to kill you. Bye."

*Why the fuck were people always hanging up on me?*

Casey's dad wanted me dead. I was fucking with his baby girl, and as he put it, he "wasn't gonna stand for another rooster in my barn-yard."

It was sure nice of Casey to warn me—as if I didn't already know.

Her dad had been cruising by my house pretty regularly. I'd see his light brown truck parked down the street, or I'd hear him drive by. The sound of his vehicle's engine had become so familiar—a low dark rumbling tucked underneath the repetitive ping of bad gasoline—that I could pick his car out of a thousand with my eyes closed. And I could hear him when he got out and shut his door. I could smell his cigarettes in the air.

It got to be routine, but it wasn't easy.

When I was devoid of emotion I stayed young—my face almost ageless, since there was no interior stress placed on the body. But when I started to feel, the emotions that flew from inside became so powerful that they started expressing themselves physically— blisters broke out on my fingertips, weeping yellow pockets of puss, and my hands were constantly shaking. Stress on this weak body of mine was doing strange things.

It got to be as if I was a hunted animal, and I'd developed a strong sense of predators and being preyed on—I was constantly looking over my shoulder for an attack.

I heard the truck pull up outside, only this time he wasn't alone. There were three or four men with him and they were moving fast—a commando-style raid.

They kicked the door in and entered.

Luckily, my mother wasn't at home. I don't know what she would've done. She might not even have noticed them, or she might have offered a snack while they were preparing to skin me—she was accommodating like that.

I ran upstairs and climbed out a window to the roof. I lay with my back against the gray stucco wall so they couldn't see me from below, and if they'd looked out, I would be hidden from window view.

I could hear them inside—yelling to each other—tearing apart the house.

"His car's in the driveway."

"Somebody made coffee. Look under the bed."

"I know he's here, the fucking TV's on."

I wished I had a book, or something to do while they ransacked my room. It wouldn't be long before they tired of their search.

Actually, it gave me time to think. I didn't tell you, but this wasn't the first time Casey's dad broke in. I woke one morning with the baby beside me. She was lying on the bed, dressed in her pajamas, and I was lying next to her dressed in my clothes from the night before—I must have passed out in them. I don't know how I got the baby—maybe Vickie had dropped her off.

Anyway, the room smelled different—I wouldn't go so far as to say like sulfur, but there was a scent of hate or anger filling the air. I thought nothing of it. I walked outside to dump the trash, and I found empty Corona bottles on the curb outside. There was nothing strange in that; some kids drank or wrote messages to me in the street in front of the house—my mother's was a punk rock Graceland of sorts. I was about to walk back in when a neighbor of Casey's pulled up—he was freaked.

"What's up, man?"

"Fucking Jack, I talked to Casey's dad this morning, and he was fucked up—he wanted to kill you."

"Yeah, he always wants to kill me. So?"

"No, man, I mean last night. I fucking talked to him this morning, and he broke down. He said he sat outside your pad drinking and then he broke in to shoot you while you slept. He said your baby was here. Is she here?"

"Yeah."

"Well, I guess she fucking rolled over or something right before he pulled the trigger, and she stared at him. She woke up and he ran out. Fuck, Jack, you gotta fucking stop this shit."

So, my daughter saved my human life. I don't know how I deserved it. I never did a fucking thing for her, and it probably wouldn't work a second time, but it did once, so I guess I owe her. I wonder if she would have done it for me when she was older, when she knew what I'd done. It actually made it even harder to see her, knowing that she looked out for me when I couldn't return her love . . .

I could still hear them inside.

They moved to the front of the house, and I wished they'd hurry up. My coffee was getting cold, and *Looney Tunes* was about to start. I didn't want to miss it.

Finally it became quiet inside.

Car doors slammed in the street, and that pinging low rumble headed away empty-handed. I figured it was safe to come in.

I was pissed. I'd missed about fifteen minutes of my fucking program.

I watched the rest of it and decided to take a drive.

I'd come into a bit of money—a surprise royalty check—and I'd bought a car. It was a 1969 Lincoln Continental Mark Three with green leather interior—a fifteen-hundred-dollar "maybe this will make me stop feeling" waste of money.

I was just pulling out of the driveway when I felt it—a prickling up my arms and across my shoulders. They were coming back, and I knew it. I stepped on the gas and took off. In the rearview was a car—an old sedan with two assassins riding in the front.

They were on me.

The stop sign at the end of my street was a blur as I blew through it. I narrowly missed an oncoming car. My assassins followed.

The Lincoln was powerful, but it was better on an open highway. It wasn't made for evading killers on tight neighborhood streets. I needed room to move.

I headed for the interstate.

I could hear screaming in the car behind me.

They were hunters chasing a wild beast, and they were intoxicated with the thought of my blood.

I got to the highway, but I was blocked by morning traffic. I needed to move so I closed my eyes and prepared to floor it—it was worth the risk, and if I got hit I might get lucky and die.

"Grisham!" I heard them furiously screaming my name.

"Grisham! Fucking stop!" I could see the guns pointing through their windows.

"Grisham! It's me! Human! Are you out of your fucking mind?"

It was Human, my old tour companion, and a friend. He'd just been released from detox, and he was visiting from Ohio with a friend.

My senses *were* sharp; I knew a car was coming for me. I wasn't paranoid. I was just slightly mistaken on the intent. You can't always take a chance on your visitors being friendlies—especially after that morning.

Human's buddy had a video camera; he'd been filming our chase scene, and he kept it rolling.

I started talking.

"Human, nice. It's real nice to see you. And your friend, what's your friend's name? It's good to meet you, man, it's real good to—what was I doing? I was just hanging out, and I thought you might be trying to kill me. I had some guys at the house earlier but I think they took off, and I might have some coffee still, if you want to come by and . . . oh, yeah . . . don't look at the side of the car; I crashed into a tree at Todd's, and I've been up all night and—do you guys want to go for a ride or something?"

They got in the Lincoln: Steve sat in front; the Ohio cameraman shot frantically from the rear. I thought I heard him say, "Oh man, this is great stuff," and I was proud that he appreciated getting a chance to meet me.

"What'd you say in the back? Steve's friend in the back. . . . Anyway, so I been up doing blow all night and they came to get me, but I'm sure I could have fucked 'em up but . . ."

I took them on a tour of the neighborhood—a rambling maniacal tour given by a psychotic guide who'd been dipping a little heavily into the blow.

"Here's where I hid out, boys, and over here, this is where I stole my first car. Why don't we go inside, and I'll show ya pictures of the baby."

I brought them into the house, and I shared baby photos with them. Some of the furniture had been flipped over, and the room had been heavily shaken down, but I couldn't see it. I was calm and collected—the guy from Ohio continued filming.

The phone rang.

I picked it up. My mood switched abruptly.

"What the fuck, Casey? Your dad came here to kill me. Did you know he was bringing friends? What are you fucking laughing for? You fucking bitch, did you send them here to kill me? You fucking bitch, I've got your purse and your pills. Do you want me telling your dad what a fucking whore you are?"

I was losing it.

Ohio kept the camera rolling.

As I was screaming and madly yelling into the phone, Steve stood near the camera and talked into the mic.

He and his partner were laughing at me.

I heard him say, "This is sad."

I hung up and drove them back to their car.

### III

There was a large mirror in my bedroom—it was left to me by my grandmother. I'd thrown a towel over it a few weeks before because

I couldn't walk by without seeing those ghosts and hearing their voices.

I shut the shades to my room and didn't turn on the light. The room wasn't dark; it was like being outside on an extremely cloudy day—right before it rains. I pulled the towel off the mirror, and stood before it. I had my reflection to myself for a moment. I looked sick. I hadn't been to the ocean in a while and my skin, although still olive, was pale. My eyes were swollen, ringed with dark circles, and I looked defeated.

"He's here. Come on, quick."

I'd been spotted, and the mirror ghosts were running to get a look at me. This was the first time I'd ever really stood there and faced them.

An old man moved forward—I didn't recognize him.

"How's it feel, scum bag? You like fucking that little girl?"

A woman appeared next. She was hideous, with a face ravaged by disease.

"I heard he pissed his pants. You need a diaper, little boy? You need a mommy?"

There were more of them crowding into the mirror—some sarcastic and mocking, but others were threatening and hostile.

"Why don't you fucking end it, you piece of shit? Where's the baby? When's the last time you saw your little girl?"

"He doesn't want to see her."

"Good, good for her. Why don't you do us all a favor and die."

"You know your father wanted you dead, don't you? How's it feel to kill him? How's it feel, huh, Jack?"

They were right, I was shit, and I didn't want to see my baby. I was a fucking coward who would rather run than feel; I'd rather black out than live. There was no reason for me to stay here. I failed as a demon, and I couldn't even make it as a fucking human. I wasn't a dad and didn't have the balls to be one. I killed my father, and now I was going to kill my daughter's father.

I left the mirror uncovered, and I walked outside to the garage.

I grabbed the rope—the one I tied Jim with, the one my father tied me with, and the one I used to hang Gina.

I walked back into my room and sat on the bed. The mirror was going crazy. It was like New Year's Eve. The crowd in the mirror was jumping and screaming, calling more spectators in to watch.

"He's gonna do it!'

"Come on, hurry! He's gonna do it!"

I fashioned a noose, and then I stood in front of the mirror, looked myself in the eyes. I held up the rope so they all could see it. I put it around my neck. It smelled like perfume—Gina's perfume—and the rope felt heavy and rough.

I walked over to a high built-in cabinet that was above the closet. I grabbed a chair, hopped up, and threw the rope over the open door, and then secured it to a door handle. They were screaming, "You're a piece shit. Do it! Do it!"

I leapt.

I fell forever.

Like Alice.

The floor, which should have been at most eight feet away, telescoped into the distance; I was waiting to hit, jerk my head back, and black out, but I didn't.

I woke up on my back. The rope around my neck, the cabinet door broken off at the hinges and lying at my feet.

There was no one in the mirror.

Not even my reflection appeared.

I didn't leave the house for the rest of the day.

My mother had driven down to visit my father's grave and, after a grueling questioning about what the fuck was going on in my room, I'd been left alone.

Robbie showed up around four that afternoon. He'd brought a bottle of vodka.

I had bandmates—at least as long as they could stand me—and Robbie was one of them. He'd put up with me for some time. He was probably the most astute musician friend I had, even going as far as to notice certain particular character "hiccups" I displayed—mainly, my problem associating feelings.

"I'm not sure if you're a sociopath, Jack, but there's definitely something wrong. Some days it seems like you only mimic the feelings of others—and you're very good at it, but you don't really seem to have any yourself."

*Cocksucker.*

At the time, I blew him off with a quick joke about my psyche.

"The good thing about being a sociopath, Robbie, is that I'm always having a good day."

But now I was feeling a little too much, and that vodka was just what I needed. I pulled the bottle out of his hand and poured us a couple of tumblers with a splash of Kool-Aid. Robbie wanted to talk.

"My chick is fucking with me."

I wonder how many two-man boozing parties have been started with this line. I think it only comes in second or third to "I hate my life" or "She's pregnant."

"What do you expect, Robbie? Look at the world, look at our lives. It's all shit, and all we can do is make other people's lives miserable so at least we don't suffer alone."

I knew how to cheer a man up.

"She doesn't hate you, Robbie. The world is cruel, and she's trying to share it with you. It's what love is."

We finished our drinks and I poured two more—the fifth of vodka Robbie brought was almost gone. I felt sad, like I was saying goodbye to a friend. *Fuck, it's almost gone. . . . We need to get more right now. . . . We need to go right now. . . . Oh, it's okay, as soon as the sun goes down, we'll just go to the liquor store—crisis averted.*

"I want to get a tattoo, Jack—a pair of dice, in honor of a bad roll."

I didn't know what the fuck he was talking about, but a tattoo did sound about right—a little something in honor of how much I hurt, a little something for the effort.

"You know, Robbie—we *are* on a bad roll. The world has never been kind to me. I myself was thinking about getting a tattoo—something right about here."

I pointed to my heart with my cocktail and spilt booze down the front of my shirt.

"I want a broken heart and a demon sobbing on my shoulder—that should pay testament to it."

"I don't know, Jack."

"You don't know what?" Robbie was getting sauced—he never could hold his booze. "Just drink up, Robbie. I'm buying."

The sun went down—the day was over, and we set out to get some ink. Of course, this was only after we stopped by Mr. Lee's, for another fifth of vodka.

We drove over to see the famous Mark Mahoney.

Mark was an old acquaintance and a brilliant tattooist; he was happy to see us, although he was surprised about me wanting a tattoo. Todd had been coming to Mark for years and when I was in company I professed to never wanting a mark on me that wasn't made by knife, gun, or broken glass.

Mark was immaculate in his word and his dress, a true East Coast gentleman, if you'd ever seen one.

"Jack, I saw a wicked video the other day. Human came by here, and you were funny, man. You sure were fucked up . . ." Ahhh, he might have been a gentleman, but these East Coasters should learn some tact.

*Fuck Human. I can't believe he's showing that shit to people.*

"Anyway, Mark," I chose to disregard his lack of manners—and I'd settle with Human later. "I wanna get something right here." I pointed to the wet spot on my shirt.

Mark grabbed the tattoo gun and after a quick pen sketch he outlined the heart. I started telling someone in the shop that I was gonna get a carrot peeler and start peeling them. It might have been Robbie.

The next thing I knew, Mark was politely showing us to the door. My tattoo was only half-completed—fuck that, it was only outlined.

Back in the car, Robbie slumped over in his seat. He could never hold as much booze as I could, and to me, he didn't look complete. I'd promised him a tattoo, and I was going to deliver.

We were no longer welcome at Mark's, so I drove down to the Pike. I didn't think Robbie's dice idea was a good one. He needed something more, something that would show his true nature.

I decided Robbie needed a cock on his forehead.

I walked into Bert Grimm's with a hundred dollar bill and an extension cord—it was the same shop where I'd met the old woman. I asked if they could do a tattoo at the car, because Robbie was too drunk to come in.

Now, even though this was the Pike, and it was where a fifteen-year-old Todd got a satanic heavy metal demon permanently etched on his back, some things are still not acceptable.

I was, again, politely asked to leave.

I came to at my mother's, and it was morning. There was a huge bandage on my chest, and I thought I'd been shot, I peeled it back, and there it was, an unfinished broken heart, outlined on my tit.

Casey thought my tattoo was funny.

I thought it was pathetic.

It would have been nice if it was finished, but now it was just the mark of a loser. It was supposed to be a stamp of pain—a representation of the cruelty of the world—but now it was like everything else in my life: a representation of failure.

I couldn't believe it, but I was actually starting to feel sorry for some of you. Not as much as I felt for myself—the depths of my sadness were rooted deeper than yours—but I wondered why we demons even bothered fucking with you at all. Can any of you even remember what it was like before you entered this world? Can you remember your connection with the energy of the universe? Is that what it is to be human—a being who forgets you're a part of a whole? No wonder you try to grab for anything you can—when you believe you're alone, you want something around you. A child maybe, someone to make you feel like you matter. Sometimes I wish I was naive enough to think that would work.

I was tired of them trying to keep Casey from me. I had to find a way to hold on to her forever; a couple of weeks, a month, even years weren't going to be enough for me. I needed something to secure her—I knew she was meant to be mine, a gift to make this world easier to tolerate.

I decided to marry her.

I knew the courts in California weren't going to go along with my plan, and I knew Casey's parents would rather see me dead than related, so I decided to take her to Mexico.

I was warned by my attorney that taking Casey to Mexico was a violation of the Mann Act—a statute against interstate travel with a minor for immoral purposes—but since I was taking her there to get married, a supposed moral act, I didn't think taking a minor across state lines for immoral purposes came into play. Besides, we weren't going to be gone long.

We drove to San Diego, where we grabbed the first train to the border.

I took her to one of those Tijuana lawyers' offices—the type with an overflowing ashtray and old Spanish-language *Playboys* lying around. I told the lawyer—who, incidentally, looked a bit like Mr. Roberts—that we wanted to be married. I could have said we were bank robbers or kidnappers for all the interest he showed. He didn't give a fuck. He made us recite a few vows, and then he gave us a very authentic looking license.

I don't know what I thought I was gonna accomplish with that marriage license; it wasn't like I could just march over to her parents' house and say, "Okay, you need to get off our fucking backs now, and by the way, I'm taking your daughter." It was just a mad attempt to hold her near me.

And maybe I was just trying to collect her—pull her close to me so I wouldn't feel so alone. It was a piece of paper proving that I wasn't by myself down here.

I celebrated our wedding without her.

As I figured, Casey had to return home, but I sent her with a promise that she wouldn't tell her parents what she'd done—I knew that after our next disagreement that she'd probably tell them just to fuck with me, but I took a shot.

I set out to get tanked.

There was a party in Seal Beach that night. It was invitation-only, but Robbie told me about it so I guessed that meant I was invited. . . . I wasn't. At the door, my reception was less than stellar. I was a drunk, a troublemaker, a thief, and a creep who dated—and was now married to—an underage girl. I think the only reason they let me in the house was because there wasn't anyone there that wanted to fuck with me.

I proved them right for not wanting me.

I headed straight to the keg, bullied my way in, and started throwing back large mugs of beer. I didn't like beer, it took too much to get fucked up, so I wandered into the kitchen and after rummaging about I found a fifth of booze—John Paul Jones, the cheapest whiskey you could get. *Motherfuckers, they're buying this shit but they don't want me in their house—c'mon, who's really the scumbag here?*

I took the bottle, dusted the cap, held the end in my mouth, and clenched hard with my teeth. I'd invented this trick.

"What the fuck are you doing? That's my dad's!"

*Great, fucking snob hostess doesn't wanna share daddy's booze.*

I tilted my head back, opened my throat, and just let the whiskey flow down like an office water cooler getting a refill.

Glug, glug, glug.

I spit the bottle out of my mouth and grabbed a knife from the counter. It was a large blade—perfect for cutting a pineapple or a hostess.

I flourished the blade and pulled down my pants.

"You fucking bitches are all alike. I can't stand you. You're not getting my cock anymore!"

I was fucking around but they didn't know it. I was about to show them the Knife Trick.

Some large knifes have a flat edge on one side of the blade. It can't cut you—one side sharp, one side dull.

I pulled on my cock stretching it as far as I could pull, and I put the knife underneath it—dull side against the flesh.

"I'm gonna cut my fucking dick off!"

I started sawing.

The hostess was screaming, yelling for Vince—an old friend and former V.C. member who happened to be there. He ran into the kitchen and begged me to stop.

"Come on, Jack. Come on, big man. Give me the knife."

I loved this.

"You want the knife, Vince? Here's the knife."

I stabbed at him—just fucking around of course, but he jumped back.

"Come on, Jack, put it down. Come on."

I kept poking at him, slashing and cutting, forcing him to move away.

Vince jumped towards me, maybe thinking he could grab the knife, but as he jumped, I stabbed, and the large blade went in and continued through Vince's arm. I released the handle amid screams and blood. The knife stayed where I'd stuck it.

"He stabbed him. He stabbed him!"

*Fucking hostess.*

I was surrounded now, tackled to the floor, kicked and punched.

I covered up the best I could, but I was taking a beating. I couldn't see who was hitting me. I saw nothing but bright black flashes as the blows rained down on me.

In the middle of all the violence, a crotch appeared in front of me. It was crystal clear in focus—I swung for the balls. I connected.

I'm not sure who I hit, but it was enough to get me some room to move. I got off my knees and ran for the door—the shouts followed me into the street.

Thank the not-quite that Vince had a spotty police record and he wanted no entanglement with the cops—he wasn't going to rat me out for the stabbing. Besides, he liked the story and he held no ill will for the accident.

It was getting pummeled by the crowd that really bothered me. I was a fucking hero. Kicking my ass was like beating up a veteran, for Christ's sake.

I can't believe they treated me like a common punk. I planned to retaliate, but I needed some backup.

I wondered who was still around.

I reached out to Paul.

Paul was a notorious Long Beach brawler and drinker. There's even a bit of a joke between Long Beach punks: "If you never fought Paul, you never drank in Long Beach." Paul was a drinking companion, and if we weren't together, or if we'd lost each other during the night while intoxicated, he'd drop by and see if I was okay. If it was early morning, I'd usually be up crying, solving world problems, writing rambling letters, and drunk-dialing strangers.

Paul and I used to beat on each other for fun.

I made the call.

"Hey, Big Jim." Paul was one of the last people alive who still called me Jim, an old Vicious Circle alias—it was heartwarming to hear him use the name.

"What's up, Paul? Hey, I'm sure you know why I'm calling; it's about that thing with Vince at—"

"You better be calling about Casey."

"What?"

"That waitress Alex, at Jonathan's, told Casey you pulled some woman out of there a few weeks ago. She told Casey you fucked her."

"What?"

I didn't know what he was talking about and then it fucking hit me—the giantess at that bar. Shit. I couldn't remember where I was, let alone the waitress's name—Alex, that's right, she knew Casey from high school. I went on the defensive.

"I didn't fuck her, Paul—she blew me. That's it, I swear."

"I don't give a fuck what you did; I'm just telling you Casey knows, so you better get your story straight. And by the way, you're a fucking asshole for stabbing Vince."

It wasn't long before I got the call.

"Hey, baby."

"Hey, Casey."

"Were you going to tell me?"

"Tell you what, baby?"

"Don't be stupid, you got one chance. If you tell the truth I might stay, but if you keep lying I'll never see you again."

I paused for a second

"She only sucked me off, and I didn't even want to do it but she forced herself on me—and I should really be calling the cops because she broke in when I was sleeping, and I woke up and she was doing it, and if you were there . . . You should have been there, you know, because you could have stopped it . . . And please forgive me, because she was nothing, and I love you and that's all . . ."

She didn't even need to bring out the duct tape. I broke before she had a chance to torture me—taking a rambling stab at covering all my bases.

"Is that it? That's all you did?"

"Yeah, baby, that's it, and I'm really sorry."

"Okay."

"Okay?"

"Yeah, it's okay. And I never want to see you again. Goodbye."

It was like somebody just drained the air from the sky—I was sucking and sucking but couldn't get a breath. She was my disconnection. She was the oblivion to my pain. She was my only link to what I was.

I was destroyed.

Casey wouldn't return my calls.

It had been a week since she'd confronted me, and since then we'd had no contact. My problems with Vince were a thing of the past—a fucking knife sticking through some punk's arm was nothing compared to this shit. I was fucked.

I stayed in the house.

I got a call from Paul one afternoon. He said that he'd like to come see me. I was hesitant, but as long as he didn't want me to go outside, it was okay.

The phone rang directly after I'd hung up from Paul. I figured he'd forgotten to tell me something, so I didn't answer. It kept ringing, finally stopping after twenty or so rings.

It rang again.

I was an idiot, maybe Paul wanted to know if I'd like a cocktail while we talked. This time I picked it up and placed my order.

"Vodka. No mixer, Paul."

"What?"

It was Casey.

"I'm sorry, baby. I thought you were Paul and I was kinda fucking around—"

"Are you having fun with me gone?"

"No, I'm not. I'm fucking miserable."

"I want to see you. I feel bad, and I think we should talk. I'm going out tonight, but would it be cool if I stopped there first?"

"Yeah, are you kidding? Of course, I'd love to see you."

I was stoked, and I felt instantly lighter. But I needed a little something to take the edge off—I didn't want to be too eager when she arrived, so I went upstairs and combed through my dad's old pill bottles. I found one with the international symbol for "You're going to get fucked up" on it—you know, the little drowsy man.

When Paul came over, I handed him a drink and a couple pills.

"Here, take these, Paul; the edge'll slide right off. They're wonderful."

I had no idea if they were wonderful or not, I didn't bother looking at the actual name of the substance, but I'm sure they were fine.

We sat around talking and drinking until Paul started to feel a bit unsteady. He didn't look well—kinda real sleepyish.

"What the fuck did you give me?" he slurred and not very nicely.

"I don't know," I said. "They were my dad's. My dad didn't take anything bad, did he? Are you saying my dad had a problem?"

My words didn't sound slurred. He was a pussy.

"Where's the bottle, Jim?"

"It doesn't matter where it is, Paul. I took 'em, and I feel fine. Why don't you just stop it?"

"Why don't *you* fuck off?"

He stormed from the house and left me alone.

Casey showed up a short time later, and she looked great. She was wearing one of those tight blue-jean dresses with no shoulder straps, and no panties.

I, myself, was pleasantly smooth and feeling very loving. "I'm glad you came over, baby. I feel bad about . . . you know . . . fucking up, and everything." My sweetest voice.

"It's okay," she told me, "I wanted to see you, and I also wanted you to see me."

"You're beautiful, baby. Always have been." Even sweeter voice.

"Yeah, I am. But I also wanted you to see what my date was gonna be fucking."

"What?"

"Yeah, my fucking date. I'm going out to get fucked. I just want you to see what he's gonna be pounding on."

This was her way of paying me back.

I went ballistic.

I started screaming and pushing her. I punched out the glass in the front door, and I slammed her against the wall. Blood was flying everywhere; my hand and arm were slashed wide.

I was completely unhinged.

I needed to go to the hospital.

Casey didn't want me in her car—she was willing to give me a ride, but I was bleeding profusely and sobbing. She threw an old beach towel on me so I wouldn't bleed on her seats, but I took it off—I wanted to mark her vehicle with my pain. She drove me to the house of a guy I surfed with—it was also a shelter that I used sometimes to hide from assassins. She dumped me off and continued on her date.

I was crying and pounding on their white front door with my bloody hand. When my surf buddy's mom, Susan, opened it, I staggered in. She took one look at me and grabbed her keys.

"You need to see a doctor."

"No, I don't," I sobbed. "I don't need a doctor. I need a bowl of sugar-sweetened cereal. No milk please."

"If I give you the cereal, will you let me take you to the hospital?"

I nodded my head yes, then I used my shredded hand to hold the spoon, and I bled all over my fruit loops.

Susan took me to the hospital.

As I was lying on a gurney waiting to get my hand and arm stitched, Susan drove to my mother's house to check the damage. When she got there, my little sister was outside, scared.

The front door was wide open, glass busted out, and the lights were left on. There was blood all over the porch.

Susan told my sister what happened, and they started cleaning up. They wiped up the blood and swept up the broken glass, and then Susan walked into my bedroom and cut down my noose.

After the cabinet incident, I'd hung the noose over my bed, just in case. I usually woke up with the first word out of my mouth being "Fuck," as in, "Fuck, I'm still alive." And then, I'd look up at the noose and say, "Should I hang myself? No? Okay, I'll go one more day."

My sister called my mother, and Mom had had enough. She decided I needed to be in some sort of mental ward, for my own good, and they sent my older brother to escort me there.

When Susan got back she told me I was going to a hospital for some rest; my brother was coming to take me.

"That sounds good," I said. "That sounds really good, I could sure use some rest."

I wasn't going anywhere—I just needed to buy myself some time to think. *If they lock me up I'll never get out.*

When my brother walked in, I instantly knew what to do. He doesn't really look like me; he's a bit wider with blue eyes, curly brown hair, and freckles—at the time, I had straight dyed-black hair and crazily sad green eyes, so I said, "Who's that guy?"

Neither Susan nor anyone at the hospital had ever seen my brother, but as they were stitching me up, the nurse answered, "That's your brother."

"No," I told her, "I'd love to go with my brother, but that's not him. Look at him."

Fuck, even lying on my back, getting stitches in my hand, my mouth was good—I was a beaten monster lying on a gurney but still hypnotizing and captivating with my words. The nurse looked at him and said, "Do you have I.D.?"

My brother was pissed and, of course, he'd left his wallet in the car. He slammed out of the emergency room door and headed to the parking lot.

The minute he was out of my sight, I got my half-stitched ass off the table and I ran.

"Stop! What are you doing? Stop!" They tried, but couldn't restrain me.

I jogged into the night.

I had to lie low for a few days until the whole "he needs to be locked up for his own good" bullshit stopped, then I quietly slipped back home.

My mother and my close relatives were treating my "outburst" as just another bad night for Jack, and the glass in the front door had been repaired. Paul had gotten over his anger at my improper pill dispensing, and a Tender Fury show had been booked for that night.

I hadn't heard from Casey.

Paul and a couple of the boys came by early to get primed for the show that evening. It was ten a.m. on a Saturday and we were going for cocktails.

There was a little biker bar in Sunset Beach. It's called Mother's. It's not the kind of place that I'd normally have a drink at, but I guess, since it was Saturday and the sun was out, a small beach bar serving alcohol was okay—the clientele and the shitty interior design could be dealt with.

I got in an argument with a biker.

It was about backing up.

I was pissed he didn't have reverse on his bike. Why should I have to work harder than him? Why should he get it easy?

"Fuck you," I told him, "you don't even have to back up."

He looked at me like I was crazy, but it seemed like a valid complaint to me. Then again, when you're fucked up, every complaint seems valid—the fact that this biker fuck didn't have to reverse became more important than who was buying my next drink. He walked off while I continued getting worked up—I didn't notice he'd left, but I wasn't going to stand for it.

"If I have to back up, I'm only doing it one time, one time only, and just right now."

I staggered out to the car and my friends hopped in.

I backed out of the parking space and backed down the street.

My friends were laughing but I wasn't done. I turned on to the Pacific Coast Highway and headed north. The PCH was the busiest street by the bar—it has four lanes, usually jam-packed with beach-tourist traffic.

It was now eleven thirty on a Saturday morning; I took it up to fifty-five miles an hour and backed into Seal Beach.

I stopped at every light and obeyed all the signs.

I backed into Long Beach.

It was a fifteen-minute drive to my mother's house, and I did the whole thing in reverse. I backed into my mother's driveway and I was facing forward.

I wouldn't need to back up again. I blacked out.

I heard laughing and my nose burned.

I thought I was in my mother's driveway, but I was in the back of my car. It was hours later and we were parked at the Scream Club—the venue for that night's show.

One of my companions had put coke in my nose and they held my mouth shut to wake me up—hence the laughing and the burn. I was lucky actually, I could have woken up being pissed or drawn on.

I went in for sound check.

Sound check usually occurs hours before stage call. It gives the band time to check their gear, and dial it in.

I knew I wasn't going to make it. I'd checked my gear and realized that I was about to piss myself or pass out again, so I told the band that if we didn't start playing now, we wouldn't play at all.

The club hadn't even opened the doors when we started our set.

As the crowd was filing in, I tried to take off my clothes, but I forgot to remove my shoes. So there I was, hopping around on one foot, pulling at my pants.

People were throwing things at me, and I was reciting the

warden's monologue from *Runaway Train*: "Look at you, animals, hiding in the dark . . ."

I was oblivious to the beer bottles bouncing off my chest.

I was being booed and pulled off the stage—a fool hooked from the wings and dragged off.

I drove home alone—weaving and drifting between lanes on the highway. Somewhere near downtown Long Beach, I ran out of gas and coasted to the curb. I slept in the car. In the morning when I woke, I found I'd pissed myself. I had no gas, no money, no one to call, and so I walked, wearing the same clothes I'd left home in the night before, only now they were full of piss and shame. I tried to forget how I got there—and the show the night before—but I couldn't.

I had about a ten-mile walk in front of me, but I didn't even bother to hitchhike. I couldn't face the look of disgust on the good Samaritan's face when I climbed in the car.

I was about three or four miles away from my mother's house when I walked in front of an outdoor restaurant. They had a patio surrounded with glass. I looked at myself in the window. My hair was a mess, matted down on one side. I was wearing black, but I had on my cocker spaniel jacket. If you could've looked inside my pants you would have seen yellow stained bikini briefs and red chapped legs from a piss infused walk. I was bruised and I was beaten, my hands freshly stitched. The mascara that I'd worn had run down my cheeks and my eyes were hollow with hurt. I was a monster, a Frankenstein creation—albeit more Warhol's than Shelley's—and I was a mess.

Just then the door opened and two people walked out. They were about twenty feet away from me, but I could see they were a very handsome couple—both blond and dressed well, upwardly mobile. They turned and saw me. I knew them. The young woman mouthed the words, "Oh my God, that's Jack Grisham." The young man laughed and, speaking loud enough for me to hear, said, "Fuck him, let's go."

It was Jim, the boy I used to torture. This time he was the one who happily walked away.

I got home and Vickie had dropped off the baby—she was wrapped in a blanket and sleeping on the couch. It hurt to look at her. I don't know what the fuck God was thinking letting me have a child—especially a little girl. He knew what I was, what I'd done. I thought of her getting abused by monsters like me—getting urinated on and dumped on the side of a road.

I never wanted to be connected to anyone, let alone a child. I've heard some people say that their children are their life, and yet mine was my death: everything else I had seemed able to drown with booze and women, but other than the time I removed her at the beach—sprinkling whiskey on her image—I had not been able to remove my thoughts of her. I couldn't stay there; I couldn't be next to her.

I told my mom I had to go, and I left the baby with her.

I'd reached the point where I struggled to leave the house. I got some sort of pneumonia, and my body began to shut down. I'd get up in the morning and walk into the living room, sit in my father's old recliner, and stare at cartoons all day. At night, my mom would tell me to go to bed, and I'd shuffle back to my room.

## The Basement

Day after day I'd repeat this.

I tried to figure out where it first went wrong, how I got the sickness, and how I could have failed so miserably on the road to greatness. But my mind wasn't clear. Sometimes it was impossible to even remember what I'd been—the demon I was, now buried under a suffocating blanket of disgrace.

I'd lie in my bed at night unable to sleep without the lights on. Each car that passed was, in my mind, loaded with assassins looking for retribution. The idea of standing up to my attackers was dead—obliterated by the beating I'd taken at that party. My true cowardly nature had been exposed, and I lay shaking and terrified in my bed.

And why couldn't I pull out when my life was nose-diving into the side of a mountain? Even if I was now human, I should have at least been able to eke out a bullshit existence—carry on a semi-happy life without having thoughts about God or the not-quite. Why couldn't I just be like those others—content with a bullshit job and a cold beer after work? Fuck, why couldn't I be normal? Have a family, get a job, struggle with bills, with health insurance, gas, and electric?

Why couldn't I die like everyone else? I'd be stuck in some shit job until the day when I'd be driving home from work in my champagne gray four-door family sedan and the crushing pain of a heart attack would bring me staggering to the side of the road; crawling out onto the shoulder, I'd lie in the broken glass and bits of old auto accidents that littered the sides of the highway. And then I'd clutch a photo of last year's family vacation to my chest, and I'd cough up my last—a bloated prole, wrapped in a pair of business slacks and a poly-blend shirt. My name tag would blow across the diamond lane and without purpose, wander into a field.

I wanted this to end. I wanted to wake up dead.

I wasn't useful to anyone. I was a waste of existence.

I was twenty-six years old.

Casey was fucking with me. I was an easy target, and she enjoyed it. She chastised me for being a shut-in, and if I gave her a ride to a store, she'd give me something in return.

If it wasn't for her, I never would have left the house.

I took her to a large department store, and I walked behind her as she shopped. She might as well have put a leash on me as I shuffled my feet behind her—I was a dying pet being taken for a last walk.

We went into the women's lingerie section.

There were other women there—and before I would have met their eyes and pictured them in their selection and transferred that thought to them. But not now. I looked at shoes. My eyes never left the floor unless I was spoken to by Casey.

"Do you like these? I bet you'd love pulling these off me, wouldn't you?"

I nodded.

"And what about this?" She held up a pair of sheer panties. "I bet you'd love lifting up my skirt and seeing these. Isn't that what you'd like?"

Again, I just nodded, and then I followed her to the cashier.

We got back in the car and pulled out of the parking lot and onto the freeway. I said nothing, I just drove.

"Thanks for taking me, baby. These are gonna look great on. He's gonna love them."

"Who's gonna love them?"

"John, you idiot. I've been making money by letting him go down on me. You didn't think these fucking panties were for you, did you? You're a fucking joke—a loser who's never going to be anything. You know what you're good for? You're good for a joke—my girlfriends and I talk about you and that pathetic little girl you have."

I lost it.

I started screaming and yelling—an unintelligible tirade exploded through the windows of the car. I was on the 405 Freeway heading into Long Beach unsedated, and now, as I reached into the center consol, armed with a razor blade. I cut my arm.

"Is this what you want; is this what you fucking want, my blood?"

"You're a fucking loser!"

I cut myself again and threw the blood at her.

"I'm fucking done, Casey! I'm fucking over!"

I pulled to the side of the road and kicked her out. She wasn't far from home—I guess I was screaming longer than I thought. Time was lost as I swirled in the unbearable depression of pain and feeling.

I was a big man, but I'd become so frail. My emotions were the frayed end of a noose.

There was a part of me that wanted her to fix it—make the hurt stop—but I knew she couldn't anymore.

People have asked me what it feels like to be admired, to be feared, to have anything you want, any woman you want—and I'd tell them it's wonderful, satisfying, and exciting. Until it stops working, and then it's hell. When the flavors of life cease to be bold and enticing, and everything you love has the taste of sand—bland, heartless, unsatisfying fare. When you get to that point where you finally realize that nothing in this world will ever fill you, it's the pinnacle of loneliness.

I abandoned my car down the street from Casey's house—I wanted it to stand as a tombstone on the end of her block.

Maybe one day she'd regret this; maybe one day she'd become human and find out what it means to hurt.

I climbed down into a sewer ditch that ran next to the park. The walls were straight cement, but I wandered until I found a small pipe to crawl into. The concrete was cool and damp, the noise of the street was held back by the stench. I lay inside, sobbing.

I used to come into these pipes to explore and now I was back to stay. My plan was to slit my wrists and die where they wouldn't find the body. I didn't want a funeral, because I knew no one would come. Except my daughter, the only true mourner, held by her mother—who thought happily of a life for a little girl without an embarrassment for a dad; my mother, finally able to rest, to have a night not spent wondering when I would die; and a host of enemies and victims that would raise a glass in celebration of the monster finally being put to rest—the black prince who would not live to star in a sequel.

I'd had enough, and I'd hurt enough.

I wanted it to stop.

I was finally going to get what I deserved: a burial in the tomb of my kind—the sewer.

I lay there for hours—the foul water slowly running in a shallow river underneath my body, sweeping the last remnants of my life out to the sea.

### I I I

I've never liked stories about redemption or continuing on after loss. Every time I watched *Goodfellas*, I stopped at the part where Henry lies to Paulie about selling drugs, and then I'd rewind. Why'd he have to fuck up? Why couldn't he just stay solid?

I like my boys to go out on top. I don't want to see them marching on into mediocrity, until one day they're standing in the market, and some fuck says, "Didn't you used to be somebody?"

I wanted the movie to end with the hero getting a blow job and laughing at you for paying ten bucks to eat shitty popcorn and sit on someone's spit out gum.

Fuck.

I wanted flare; I wanted flash.

I wanted headlines.

I wasn't holding fifty cops at bay with a grenade strapped to my chest.

I wasn't shacked up in a shitty little Bolivian hut, waiting to blast out—guns blazing into the vengeful arms of an angry army.

I was lying in a pipe, in a filthy little ditch, in Long Beach—Iowa by the Sea—and it was over.

I'd been a cross-dressing Alice and now I was lying in the black rabbit's hole. Only this time it wasn't fantasy, it was the reality of my existence.

I held the razor in my hand and I was ready to cut—a large stroke running vertically up my arm—but then I couldn't. I couldn't bring myself to do it. I didn't have it in me to die.

Fuck, this is what I'd been told, that I would stay here in pain forever, and that he, the not-quite, would not let me go.

I dropped the blade into the water where it flashed and turned its way down the channel.

I didn't know who to call for—the not-quite had abandoned me, and God wasn't mine to claim. I chose to speak to both. Whoever answered had me.

"Fuck you!" I started defiant.

"Fuck you for sticking me here in all this pain and not even giving me the balls or the dignity to take myself out!"

"Fuck you!"

"Why won't you help me? God, why won't you fucking help me?"

"Please! Please, fucking help me!"

I woke to a flash of nothingness.

"Motherfucker! You broke like a fucking bitch!"

It was the not-quite, and he was yelling at me.

We were standing in white. There's no better way to explain it. There were no walls, nothing. I was just standing in white with the not-quite and God. They were both clothed in my skin—three of us, triplets, standing in nowhere.

The not-quite turned to the Man.

"I don't think it was fair—the shit with him having a kid was cheating, you weren't supposed to bring in anything but feelings to break him."

"I make the rules," God said. "And I can change them if I feel like it. After all, my changing the rules is one of the rules."

The not-quite was furious.

"I had to follow the rules when we fucked over Job. I seem to remember you all high and fucking mighty laying down clear-cut instructions over what I could and could not do—where the fuck do you get off?"

"I get off right here, and so do you."

The not-quite vanished.

I looked at God—once again, I was clueless—a cloud drifting in a room.

"You're going to hate me for this, Jack. But it was a bet. Just like Job before you. I bet the not-quite that I could take you—his best man—and that I could get you to call for me, beg for my help."

"But he said you cheated. You used the baby against us."

"I didn't use anything against you—and he's a poor sport. It was always you, you broke yourself, I could never break you. There was no one in that world that could defeat you, except you. And now, you've come to me."

"But I didn't come to you; I just yelled out, it was an accident that I called your name."

"Was it, Jack? Was it an accident? Was anything working for you down there? There are no accidents: you can either choose to learn or walk away. The mere fact that you refused to end your existence shows me you choose to learn."

"But I couldn't do it, he stopped me."

"No, you stopped you. Do you really want to leave, Jack? Never see your daughter again? She's beautiful, by the way."

"I don't know." I paused, confused. "It hurts to be near her."

"It hurts because you love her. And even in your selfishness you want to protect her. But realizing that you can't, you would rather run than risk being hurt. You'd rather be afraid than live in love."

"I'm scared and I'm tired of hurting. I don't know what to do."

"Abandon self, Jack."

"I tried that. I tried to kill myself."

"No, you tried to remove your physical existence; you never surrendered to what you really are."

I was lost. I didn't know what he meant, and I didn't trust him.

"But you're a cheat and a liar, and you've rigged the game so we're nothing but marks taken in by your tricks. I won't surrender to you."

"You already have, Jack. And once you get to know me better, you'll know how to move even closer. I'll make it easy for you: remember Raziel."


I opened my eyes.

I was wet and covered with the green slime of the sewer, but I was not dead. I slid back down the pipe and crawled out into the channel. Nothing had changed, although I felt lighter. I didn't crave anything—no alcohol, no drugs. And above all, I didn't want to see Casey.

I wasn't numb, but I knew that what I had was futile. It was no existence. I'd spent my life hurting others and serving myself—at first, unconnected, and then fighting against being a part of the whole. I don't know if the Man had helped me, but I knew something had changed. I was still of this world, but I no longer looked at possession and dependence upon the material as an answer. I'd broken.

I walked back to my car.

The keys were in the ignition and the doors were unlocked.

There was blood on the steering wheel and the seats, but it no longer looked like mine—it was the blood of another man.

I started the engine, but then paused before driving off.

Where was I going to go? Maybe south—a drive down the coast to Mexico. I didn't have any money or food, but maybe I could find a shit job somewhere along the way.

I pulled out and headed to the freeway.

I was about fifty miles outside of Los Angeles when I saw him. He was pulled to the side of the road—a business man with what looked like a flat tire. I pulled over in front of him and walked back.

"How's it going?" I asked. "Do you want some help?"

He was tentative, a man about my father's age when he died. He looked stressed, and when I glanced at his left hand he had the indented skin mark of a wedding band on his finger; the band was no longer there—a recent vacancy.

"Yeah, it's a rental and there's no jack."

"Don't worry, I'll get it."

I walked back to my car and got my things and then I returned, jacked-up his car, and pulled off the flat. It was shredded, like he had tried to drive on it. I looked up at him and smiled—he knew what I was thinking.

"I just wanted to make it to an exit. I just wanted to get off and lay down."

"Yeah." I tried to smile at him, the recent sadness hanging in my eyes. "I know what that feels like. It's been hard, huh?"

I could see him holding onto the emotions—trying, like he did with the tire, to just get off the freeway, get away from the pain—but he broke.

"I just didn't know what to do. She'd been sick and I lost her last weekend and I left everything. I just wanted to be someone different, to have never been married, to have never known her at all; I just wanted it to stop. I wanted to go away. I didn't want to feel it anymore . . ."

I put my hand on his arm as he cried.

I didn't say anything for a while; I just let him go. When he became silent, I spoke.

"What are you going to do?"

"I don't know. I loved her; I've never been without her."

I thought about my little girl and how I was running away from her. I didn't want to hurt either; I didn't want to be close, connected to anyone. But I also didn't really want to be away. I was torn. I knew that nothing in this world would fix the pain and that, in the end, I'd run out of places to run to. Connection to something other than the material world was the only thing that might help me, but I wasn't ready for that. I was still angry, distrustful. Maybe by starting with my daughter I'd lose that fear. I'd be a father, and no matter how much it hurt, I wouldn't leave. If that little girl wanted me, I was willing to hurt.

I finished fixing the tire, and I put back my things. He wasn't driving off. I walked back to his window to say goodbye, wish him well, and then I did something that totally went against anything I'd ever done in my life. In my hand I held a piece of paper with my phone number on it. I leaned over and handed it to him.

"Here, take this. If you need anything or just want to talk, call me."

I don't know why I did it. I had no money to offer him, no place to shelter him. Fuck, I wasn't even great counsel—look what I'd done to my life—but maybe I could ease his pain in some way. I was willing to try.

He sat for a moment almost as if he was afraid to say something.

"Right before my wife died she handed me an envelope. It was sealed. I've never opened it. She told me that it belonged to a man on the road and that I was to keep it with me always. It's here in my pocket."

He reached into his pants and pulled out a crumpled envelope.

"I was going to leave it at home when I left, I mean, I left my ring, I left everything, but for some reason I couldn't leave this." He handed me the envelope. "It's yours; I know it's yours. And thank you."

He started his car and drove off.

I looked down at the envelope—there wasn't an address or anything written there—it was clean and white.

As I stood on the side of the freeway, completely stripped of everything I had thought would help me, I opened the envelope. Inside was a sheet of paper. I knew, instantly, who it was from. It was from Him: the Man.

On the paper, written in small, tight, neat script, there was just one sentence. It was a request.

"Find me."

That was it. No map, no fucking directions. No help of any kind. It was just like Him. I stared at it a moment and then I crumpled it and tossed it on the ground.

I got in my car and drove to the next off-ramp, where I exited and then parked. *What the fuck had God said about "abandoning self" and Raziel? He asked me to remember him. Why? What was it about Raziel that mattered?*

I thought about his change—how Raziel went human when the young girl, who wasn't his child by flesh, had hugged him. *Why? Why was that relationship, that connection, so important?*

I sat thinking about my destination, or lack of one.

*Am I really going to try and run again, and continue serving myself, after all that happened?*

No, I wasn't.

I drove back to the freeway and turned northbound—back to Long Beach.

I was going home to see my daughter.

If I had to start with a person to thank, it would have to be Bobby Sepulveda; he taunted me, practically shamed me, into doing something that I'd talked about for years—writing a book. He gave me the push, and then drifted to an arm's length so he wouldn't have to deal with my frustrated fits of anger as I slashed and burned my way through my first draft. I might have had a background in writing songs about fucking dead people and dismantling the government, but writing fifty-word songs is a long way away from writing a book—it doesn't even compare.

## Epilogue

I realized I needed help, so I turned to a friend and received a writing lesson from Stephen Uys—an underground genius who tried his best to tutor me in grammar and form. I was stubborn and at times uncooperative—an anarchist at heart—but Stephen succeeded in helping me clean up my rough draft and a year after its inception, I delivered it to a literary agent.

Rejected.

What the fuck?

Oh well, it was only a year of my life thrown down the drain, and I'd wasted far more time for far less, but I wasn't done. Some punks would throw in the beach towel after busting their ass for a year and then being rejected, but I thought nothing of it—after all, I'd had restraining orders placed on me before and I never took no for an answer. I decided to get another opinion, so I called my friend Jim. Jim was a high profile music manager with a head for business and talent—he'd see the value of my work.

"Jack, I don't like this. I'm only twenty pages into it, and I'd like to kill you. I'm sorry, but I know you in real life and you might be an asshole, but you're a funny and endearing asshole, this 'Jack'—the Jack in this book—isn't."

I decided to try another route: I stepped outside character and I asked Jim for help.

"Give me a couple weeks to look around," he said. "I don't know if I can do anything, but I'll give it a shot. Just wait."

Hmmm, just wait.

You've gotta be kidding me? One of the two things I hated most in this world—the first being the word no, the second, being the short phrase "just wait." People of my temperament struggle with concepts like these daily, they call us type-A personalities, or those that have no trouble taking a golf club to your fucking windshield. At least "just wait" wasn't "no," so I waited.

A few weeks went by and I got a call from Jim.

"I found someone who will represent you. He's a literary agent from New York—Ryan Fischer-Harbage."

"He liked my book?"

"No, but I gave him a CD of you giving a talk on being an ex-drunk, and he thinks we can do something. You've got the stories, Jack; you just need a producer to get them on paper." By producer, Jim meant a collaborator, or a co-writer, to help me be me.

I was cautiously thrilled—any time you get too pumped there's a distinct danger of deflation.

After a quick bi-coastal get to know you call, Ryan and I agreed to team up, and he set out to find me a writing companion and a publishing house that would handle my book.

In the meantime, I went bankrupt, got a divorce from my wife, became homeless, and suffered through the overdose death of a woman I'd married twenty years before—as I've said, waiting is not one of my favorite things.

The American economy collapsed as Ryan searched for a co-writer and a publisher. The business world had been shaken at its core. Huge advances for unknown authors went the way of vinyl records and right-wing presidents—right into the garbage bin. It took big money or a good reputation to secure a solid co-writer, and I had neither, so the task of writing the book fell back on me—another concept I disliked, having to do my own work.

Ryan thankfully landed me a deal at ECW, a publishing house in Toronto. It was actually a bit ironic, my ending up there; ECW once stood for Essays on Canadian Writing—I'd never written an essay in my life, and the fair country of Canada has deemed me unfit to enter its borders. Michael Holmes was our man in charge there, the senior editor, and now, my project's savior.

So, I had a book deal and a few bucks coming from a very humble advance, but I was still homeless and I barely knew the difference between a semi-colon and an asterisk.

Enter Elizabeth.

I was sitting in the front seat of my home—which, at the time, happened to be a 2005 Toyota Corolla parked behind the Starbucks on Pacific Coast Highway. I was trying to figure out how I was going to write a book while fucking around on the computer, when I sent out a call for help in the form of a status update on Facebook:

"I need a job. I need a good job. I need a job that pays. I need a job that satisfies my artistic sensibilities." I stole those lines from the film *Sid and Nancy*. I didn't know if they were right, but they did the trick.

Elizabeth was a headhunter—not the cool cannibal kind that eats their enemies, she was connected to an employment agency. She saw my post and offered her services. Elizabeth, like Jim, had also heard a few of my ex-drunk talks, so she had an idea of what I was about.

"I've been listening to you talk for years," she told me, "and there's a real problem when someone with your looks, intelligence, and charisma is sleeping in his car behind Starbucks, and I got a feeling that the problem is you."

She was precise—clear and to the point. I was the architect of my world and my inability to walk a straight line had landed me here.

Elizabeth continued, "Would you be willing to do whatever I ask of you?"

Now, I would normally meet this question with a very firm "No," but when your address is the small grey car parked next to the trash cans behind the coffee house, you get a bit more agreeable.

"I'll do whatever the fuck you say."

And I did.

Elizabeth came in as a partner—sort of an investor in the future of Jack Grisham Enterprises. She sent me to a school to learn Hypnosis and N.L.P. where, under the tutelage of Michael Stevenson, I began to learn how to harness and focus the power of the mind—to reel in that errant child of self-destruction and make him work for me. Elizabeth also helped me move into a small beachfront office that also became my new home—no kitchen and no shower, but at least it didn't have seatbelts and a gas tank.

One of my daily requirements—part of doing whatever Elizabeth asked—was for me to take a morning walk and do meditation. I was to use this time to train my thoughts and recreate the world as I wanted it. Every morning I'd walk through the wetlands. I'd do five or six miles along the edges of the marsh, stopping only to contemplate the beauty and the connection of everything involved—I was to do my best to sit quietly and listen for the solutions to my worldly problems.

After a few months of round-the-clock studies and calm morning prayers, I was becoming focused and ready to attack, but I still didn't know shit about writing. So I decided to see what other authors had done. Michael Holmes and ECW were expecting a non-fiction piece detailing the destruction of an underground punk rock icon—Jesus, did I just use the word icon to describe myself? Well, I've never listed humility as one of my qualities.

I went to a bookstore and asked directions to the section that stocked fucked-up, recovered-from-alcoholism memoirs and I then took a nap. I was wide awake when I got there, but reading those boring bullshitting tales of rockstars and actors who needed a spanking more than fucking rehab put me to sleep. I knew some of those fuckers, and I'd seen them loaded; not one of them was willing to take an axe to a church or slug it out with the police. It was the same sad tale told over and over—child of promise turns to drugs, pushes his way to the brink, and is later miraculously saved so he can continue being a boring self-indulgent fuck. I'd rather read a phone book.

Shit, I had what I thought was everything I needed: a great agent, a publisher, a business partner with a hardcore work ethic, and a lifetime of real stories about self-destruction and regret, but what I didn't have was a direction for the book, and I didn't have Kate.

She came before the idea—and my advance.

I'd known her for close to two years, but we were never more than friends until I asked her to dinner. She was the most beautiful woman I'd ever seen—loving and intelligent, playful, and not afraid to have a bit of good-hearted fun with an unsuspecting victim. During dessert I reached out and touched the back of her neck—it was like she'd always been mine. I hadn't expected to get into a relationship—being as I was newly divorced and semi-homeless, but the universe had other plans. Besides, the office was big enough for two.

One morning, as I walked through the mist bordering the wet-lands, an idea came: they called you a demon for years, so be a demon. They'll think it's a lie anyway, and you can always change the names.

I rushed home and kicked out eight thousand words before that evening—head down and swimming through the pain of remembrance. When Kate came home I handed a stack of papers to her and said, "Read this."

I wasn't aware that Kate knew how to edit, but that's what she did, she grabbed a red marker and leapt in. More than just correcting obvious grammatical mistakes, she challenged me on word choice and content. Line by line she followed me and in the early hours of the morning we'd finished the first chapter. Kate was crying.

"No girl should have to read these things about her boyfriend. I don't think I can do it, Jack."

I begged her to hang on. I'd never worked this close with someone I loved, I'd never had a partner who I was creatively involved with—I craved this relationship as much as I craved her body. She agreed to stay and that no matter what happened between us, she said she would finish the work.

It took us three months sometimes working eighteen or twenty hours a day—I'd write while Kate read or slept, and then we'd edit until she couldn't stand it anymore. Kate held me true to my voice. Sometimes she looked at me with fear in her eyes—she was, after all, editing the story of a reformed monster, a monster who lay next to her in bed.

One hundred and twenty thousand words later, we were finished.

The book was not what Michael or Ryan expected, but if I had ever done what was expected of me, I wouldn't have had the stories to write it. The expected is boring and commonplace; adventure and loose ends are the real fun in this world.

They loved it.

I owe a debt I can never fully repay to Kate and to Elizabeth, to Ryan, and to Jim, to Stephen and to Michael, and to Bobby for getting it started. But I also owe others: my two daughters, for putting up with a father that is a bit left of left; and my friends— friends who let me stay on their couches, loaned me money, and fed me meals—who supported me when I thought I had nothing left.

Thank you . . .

Anastasia, Georgia, Darleen, Kyle Hamill, Mark Hammer, Mel Shantz, Tuesday Miles, Danny Jones, Kevin Foster, Tom Callinan, Vern Gervais, the Ball family, the Wells family, the Cunninghams, Kent and Keith Zimmerman, Blaze James, Scott McSeveney, Chryss O'Raidy, Joe Porter, Sue Rutter, Steve Hall, Jim Kuch, Kevin Brickman, Greg Kuehn, Darron J. Hemann, Matei Tibacu, Bijan Oskouie, Louise Bialik, Kelly Murphy Pendley, Justine

# AN AMERICAN DEMON

Castro, Ray Suarez, Michael Tracy, Rob Yvonne and Jack, Matt McClain, Dave Sloan, Michael Shultz at Fender, Lester, Rod Verna, John Bishop, Derek S., Mike Ross, Anne Bauerlein, Kurt Soto at Vans, Jeff Hackert, Lisa Salamon, Dona, Stormy and Nicole at Leave Home, Robbie Allen, Paul McFayden, Mike McCready, Cindy Brewer-McKitrick, Jordan Weinstein, Tony Alvarez, Mike Butler, Ramona Medina, Robert Booth, Paul Cruikshank, Linda Sabo, Bill Miley, Rory Gollogly, Dr. Bob Chapman, Mark Smith, Bob Hurley, and Rob Kruse for the cover concept.

Now in heavy demand as a public speaker, **JACK GRISHAM** currently receives thousands of calls a month from individuals and organizations seeking his advice, expertise, wit, mentorship, and support, especially on drug and alcohol–related issues. Grisham is a master hypnotherapist and resides in Huntington Beach, California. He spends his time with his family, surfs, and voluntarily offers his services to his community.